VARIETIES OF STATE CRIME AND ITS CONTROL

Jeffrey Ian Ross
Editor

Foreword by Gregg Barak

D1570196

Criminal Justice Press
Monsey, New York U.S.A.
2000

Printed in the United States of America. No part of this book may be reproduced in any manner whatsoever without written permission, except for brief quotations embodied in critical articles and reviews. For information, contact Criminal Justice Press, Willow Tree Press Inc., P.O. Box 249, Monsey, NY 10952 U.S.A.

ISBN: 1-881798-20-8

CONTENTS

Contents

AUTHOR'S PREFACE

The idea for this project can be traced back to the fall of 1990, when I began both soliciting manuscripts for a series of books under the general theme of "Comparative Approaches to Controlling State Crime," and organizing a number of panels for the annual meetings of various academic organizations. The first book, *Controlling State Crime: An Introduction* (Garland, 1995), which was part of this effort, laid the definitional, conceptual, and theoretical groundwork for subsequent efforts. *Varieties of State Crime and Its Control*, is the second book in the series, and, like the first one, it includes the work of respected scholars, experts and activists in the field. In addition to the contributors to this book, invitations were sent out to other individuals of different ethnicities, genders, nationalities, racial and religious groups, and an effort was made to include chapters on almost every important advanced industrialized democracy.

This project was aided by a number of people. I would like to thank my contributors for their scholarship, diligence, and most of all their patience; Paul Bond and Tijuana Patty for research assistance; and both Paul Bond and Stephen Richards, who took time from their busy schedules to provide thoughtful reviews of the manuscripts. I also would like to thank Graeme Newman for adopting this book while he was running Harrow and Heston, and Rich Allinson and Ellen F. Chayet of Criminal Justice Press for shepherding the project to completion.

This book is dedicated to my brother, Barry Ross, whose struggles in life mirror my own despite the different paths we have taken. As usual, thanks to my wife Natasha J. Cabrera and my children, Keanu and Dakota, who tolerated my divided attention.

Jeffrey Ian Ross
Washington, D.C.

To my brother, Barry Ross

FOREWORD

STATE CRIMINALITY cannot be separated from non-state criminality. All types of crime — from political crime to transnational crime, from crimes against human and non-human species to crimes by corporate, white-collar, public, street and domestic offenders — are related to each other. This is true whether one's vantage point is within or between developed or developing nations. In the global village of scarcity and overproduction, state and non-state crimes are related to worldwide inequality, to competing national and international economies, and to interchangeable political elites who, regardless of mandate, seem inevitably destined to come up short in their "reformative" rather than "structural" efforts to make democratic governments accountable to the people. Hence, the promise of controlling state crime, like the promise of controlling non-state crime, seems always to reside somewhere beyond the "rule of law" and other formal arenas of conflict resolution.

If the history of controlling state crime is any indication of the future, then the control, let alone the eradication, of state crime does not seem very realistic. State crime has certainly existed in all its manifestations since the emergence of state regimes, totalitarian or democratic. As it has been argued, the creation of states did not arise without state crimes. The argument continues that state crime will wither when the state withers and not before. Unfortunately, neither is withering despite the fiscal cutbacks across the advanced industrialized countries.

As chapters in this book suggest, the inability to control state crime in post-industrial society is far from over. On the contrary, state criminality seems to be a permanent fixture of such democratic-representative republics as the United States, France, Italy, Canada, Japan, Israel and the United Kingdom. Nevertheless, in exploring the terrains of controlling state crimes in these seven Western democracies, this anthology provides the critically necessary data for a comparative analysis of state crime and its control. This book "succeeds" because of its case studies approach and because of each chapter's historically framed discussions. Broadly constructed, each essay addressing a different country, the anthology has captured the most frequent and salient expressions of state criminality and the various reactive attempts to control and regulate such behavior.

In a few words, the problem of controlling state crime has to do with the "reward and punishment" structures endemic to the political economy of development. Many of the policing activities of state and non-state crime by domestic law enforcement agencies as well as by the United Nations and its representative bodies are aimed at securing what T.R. Young calls a "false peace of transnational inequality." But, even less globally and more nationally speaking, the case studies included here reveal how both "internal" and "external" controls of state criminality are routinely coopted by a nexus of public and private power.

Mechanisms of internal control available to the state include, for example, special prosecutors, control bodies or legislative inquiries. These controls are vulnerable to collusion between the controllers and the controlled. As a result, the punishments of these crimes, if they come at all, are mild and without long-term consequences for the system as a whole. Mechanisms of external control that can pressure the state to confront these crimes include the mass media, public opinion and international organizations. These controls are vulnerable to burnout, especially since the benefits of regulating these kinds of crimes seem to be dwarfed by the costs of doing so.

In the final analysis, the problem of controlling state crime as revealed over and over again in this book is due, at least in part, to the inability to separate the state and the government. Such a relationship begs the proverbial question of who controls the controllers? The answer, so far, is not the controllers. At the same time, until some alternative comes along or the state withers, state crime in all its manifestations will continue to be, for all practical purposes, beyond incrimination. The challenges to controlling state crime, in other words, involve the need to transcend not only the existing laws and their reformed versions, but the very same people and institutions that are presently responsible for preserving democracy in the first place.

Such a political dilemma calls for nothing short of structural change. Instead of the prevailing notions of individual rights as epitomized in the formal legalities of rule of law, there needs to be an expansion of social rights emanating from various courts and tribunals across the globe, including the Economic, Social, and Cultural Rights of the International Bill of Rights. At the national level, there is a need for institutional reforms that establish other "popular" forums for controlling not only the powers of the executive, but of the legislative and judicial bodies. Securing this kind of a vision of social control goes hand-in-hand with securing a vision of social justice for all. Bringing to fruition such a vision of social justice would, of course, do away with the need for state crime in the first place. Such are the contradictions of the political economy of crime and crime control.

Gregg Barak
Ann Arbor, Michigan

ONE.
INTRODUCTION: PROTECTING DEMOCRACY BY CONTROLLING STATE CRIME IN ADVANCED INDUSTRIALIZED COUNTRIES

by

Jeffrey Ian Ross

SINCE THE 1960s, the power of the state to shape domestic and foreign policy has become a concern among a growing number of social scientists. Although the majority of analyses of this phenomenon has focused on economic affairs, legal, and, by extension, criminal matters, have recently been cast in this context too. Not only is the state (consisting of the elected and appointed officials and the bureaucracy) conceptualized as a victim, punisher, or mediator, but it is also identified as a perpetrator of crimes. This perspective has motivated a growing number of analysts to concentrate their efforts on describing and in some cases outlining the causes of state crime (Kauzlarich and Kramer, 1998; Friedrichs, 1998a; 1998b; Barak, 1991). Needless to say, the etiology of state crime is varied and its study fraught with difficulties and challenges (Ross et al., 1999), however, because of its immediate practical and policy nature, controlling state crime may prove to be a more pressing concern to invest intellectual, economic and political resources.

In the main, the greatest impediments to the study and control of state crime are definitional, conceptual, theoretical and methodological in nature, as well as the design of practical methods to combat this type of behavior, provision of adequate resources to accomplish this task, and the proper implementation and monitoring of mechanisms of control. Many of these problems were addressed in the author's previous edited book, *Controlling State Crime: An Introduction* (New York: Garland Publishing, 1995).

In an effort to continue to focus research and policy in this subject area, state crime, as defined here, is limited to coverups, corruption, disinformation, unaccountability, violations of a domestic and/or international law, "as well as those practices that, although they fall short of being officially declared illegal, are perceived by the majority of the population as illegal or socially harmful" (Ross, 1995b:6-7). Moreover, many of these actions are connected to violations of fundamental human rights, as defined by the multilateral agreements, international organizations and national constitutions in countries where the rule of law is a central feature of the political system. "This definition recognizes that legal systems are highly normative, slow to enact legislation, and often reflect elite, upper-class, or nonpluralistic interests" (Ross, 1995b:6).

The task of providing parameters within which to identify criminal actions by the state is most appropriately followed by an examination of the methods that citizens and public and private organizations have used to control domestic and international state crime caused by individual countries and their respective crime-producing agencies.[1] One of the best ways to achieve this objective is by providing rigorous case studies.

A systematic analysis of control efforts in individual states provides a contextual approach to the subject of state crime. By seeing how states compare with each other we can observe what deters, facilitates, or has no effect on state crime in particular settings. Research of this nature represents the basis of all informed hypothesis development and testing, theoretical analysis, and, perhaps more important, design, implementation and evaluation of public policies. These efforts provide the raw material for a sophisticated treatment of controlling state crime and possibly aiding those intent upon controlling, minimizing or reducing the frequency and intensity of state crime. In short, this type of inquiry is an important building block in the emerging study of state crime and in the broader area of political crime.

It must be acknowledged that state crime, whether we are talking about causation or control, is rarely treated in a comparative manner. Certainly, there have been comparative studies of political violence, human rights violations, and crime (e.g., Gurr, 1977). However, even academic journals traditionally known to publish articles on the subject matter of comparative criminology and criminal justice (e.g., *International Journal of Comparative and Applied Criminal Justice*) have inadequately examined state crime. Part of this shortcoming is connected to the growth of comparative criminology, which is underdeveloped (Evans et al., 1996). The other reason is the difficulties attendant with the subject of state crime (Ross et al., 1999).

WHY FOCUS ON ADVANCED INDUSTRIALIZED DEMOCRACIES?

Because data on state crime and measures to control it are variously unavailable, unreliable, expensive to collect and plagued with jurisdictional and mandate vagaries among different countries, those studying the control of state crime should select a sample of the total population of countries in the world. Although there are several possible systems and countries to analyze,[2] the study of similar systems offers many advantages (Lijphart, 1975; 1971). Moreover, even though communist, authoritarian, totalitarian and/or less developed states have been routinely identified as having a greater incidence of state crime than do the first world countries, data from these former types of states are most problematic. Adding to this problem, is the fact that state agencies in these countries differ substantially in mandates and organization within and between them.

For these reasons, this investigation focuses on "first world," advanced industrialized democracies. As compared with countries governed by other political systems, government bureaucracies of advanced industrialized democracies are relatively open to outside observers. Often state crimes are revealed to the public by the media when scandals (Markovitz and Silverstein, 1988a, 1988b) and/or crises of legitimation (Habermas, 1975) occur. Consequently, access to information on state crimes in advanced industrialized democracies is easier than in authoritarian or totalitarian states.[3]

On the other hand, democratic governments usually have a high degree of legitimacy and their coercive organizations usually are bounded (but not necessarily or always properly controlled) within the rule of law. It is recognized by scholars, politicians, policymakers, the bureaucracy and activists alike, that the state is accountable to the citizenry. This is accomplished through a variety of control mechanisms or processes.[4]

During the twentieth century, the number of democracies has increased throughout the world. However, in the 1970s, many of these countries have experienced so-called "crises of capitalism" (O'Conner, 1973). Governments in these jurisdictions have adopted a plethora of legal and parliamentary mechanisms to stay in power. It is interesting to discover how controls on state crime can fail when they are used to protect and hide those who are really responsible for such matters. Not only are some of the actions and omissions of politicians criminal, but they also violate the mandate of representation that the leaders have been granted.

With respect to the academic research, control is often discussed in research on public administration and policy. Experts have advanced lists of factors believed to be important in controlling particular government agencies or certain "deviant" actions perpetrated or engaged in by government departments or the individuals who work for them. Additionally, the notion of controlling government agencies is covered by studies that develop typologies, analyze reform, review discretion and study deviance (Ross, 1998b, 1995b).

In any organization, the principle of control arises from the need for members to perform their duties in accordance with some set of standards. Such control should be an ongoing process, not simply a response to some specific wrongdoing. Regardless of the organization, control mechanisms may be either internal or external. Internal controls include hiring policies, training, supervision, hierarchy, disciplinary codes, policy manuals, collective agreements, internal review boards and intra-agency competition. External controls include external review boards, legislation, and extra-agency competition. Both kinds of control mechanisms may include powers of review or sanction.

Control may also differ on an inclusivity/exclusivity dimension (Tifft, 1975). According to Bayley (1985), some organizational units, like civilian review boards, monitor the alleged misconduct of their local police force, while others, like legislatures, oversee law enforcement in the wider context of supervising other government functions.

Internal and external types of control may be further classified as "institutional/formal" (e.g., legislation, legislative oversight, congressional committees, courts, advisory boards, review boards, ombudsmen, ethics committees, commissions of inquiry, governmental regulation, monetary appropriations, prosecutors, inter-agency competition, etc.), and, "informal" (e.g., public opinion, media attention, public protest, educational activities, lobbying, critical international attention, etc.). The former are bureaucratic solutions, while the latter appear to be more unstructured and spontaneous. Informal controls are often the last resort for citizens, and usually have some influence on other forms of control. Conterminously, these control mechanisms (both formal and informal) can be ordered along a continuum from low intensity (e.g., letters to elected officials) to high intensity (e.g., riots, armed attacks, assassinations). In sum, institutional controls are primarily conventional and legislated, whereas informal controls are mostly unconventional and nonlegislated (Fyfe, 1988; Marx, 1988; Bayley, 1985, 1979; Sherman, 1978; Stark, 1972).

Most state agencies in advanced industrialized countries are subject to the previously mentioned types of control. The relative influence of these mechanisms, however, varies with the government agencies, units in the organization, government agents and the many different actions the government workers engage in. This process, a subject of recent scholarship, is often referred to as the power of state capabilities (e.g., Migdal et al., 1994; Migdal, 1988; Almond and Powell, 1966).

When intolerable levels of state crime come to public attention, there is often public and governmental indignation. Moreover, the nature of these political systems, unlike the non-democratic states, facilitates the expression of public discontent, which often leads to calls for, if not the implementation, of greater control.

Advanced industrialized countries are where much of this research is grounded. For example, Barak's *Crimes by the Capitalist State* (1991b) began with an introduction to state criminality in advanced capitalist states (nine of the 10 chapters focus on state crimes in advanced industrialized countries), and the present book is one of the natural follow-ups to this research agenda.

Understandably, there is considerable diversity (e.g., cultural, ethnic and developmental) among the plethora of states that are subsumed in the advanced industrialized democracies label.[5] Three groupings falling under this rubric can be identified: western states, non-western states, and Anglo-American democracies. States covered in this book range from the nonwestern Japan to the Anglo-American democracy of Great Britain, to Israel. Some are relatively new democracies such as Japan and Israel. Others have had a long philosophical tradition of democracy and accountability (e.g., Great Britain, France, the United States). This diversity, however, does not preclude generalization.

During the 1970s and 1980s, all of these countries were affected by "belt tightening" policies and practices situationally referred to as Reaganism, Thatcherism or Mulronyism. This has led to a decline in the provision of social services and, in many cases, an increase in public security functions. This situation has created the conditions for a variety of injustices, including state crimes.

Contributors review the most frequent types of state crime occurring in each state. State crimes take particularly unique forms in advanced industrialized democracies. Eight principle state crimes are covered in the countries analyzed. They are, from least to most frequent: military violence (2 countries); human rights violations (3); tax evasion by politicians (3); torture (3); illegal domestic surveillance (4); illegal police violence (5); corruption/bribery (6); and coverups (7). The chapters demonstrate historical depth, and cover events and processes that are connected to overt and covert causes that might otherwise be overlooked. The genesis of these state crimes as well as the success or failure, if any, of solutions implemented to control such crimes are an integral component of this book.

The original contributions to *Varieties of State Crime and Its Control* rely on empirical data, including the marshaling of historical examples, case studies, and statistics where appropriate. The bulk of the discussion covers the past 40 years, a period coterminous with what some researchers label the post-industrial phase of political development (Ingelhart, 1977), a time during which significant social, economic, and cultural changes have been made in advanced capitalist states.

OVERVIEW OF EACH CHAPTER

Including the introduction and conclusion, this book consists of nine chapters. The contributions are arranged in an order that takes into account the duration or longevity of the democratic nature of that country. One of the oldest democracies is that of the United Kingdom. In Chapter One, Jeffrey Ian Ross argues that the United Kingdom (encompassing England, Wales, Scotland and Northern Ireland) has been routinely accused of committing state crimes. These have been conducted by its police, national security and military person-nel. Although this country lacks a formal constitution, many individuals and organizations have sought to redress state crimes. This chapter identifies the major crimes committed by the three major crime producing agencies during the past four decades and focuses on the methods that organizations and individuals have used to combat this form of political crime.

Chapter Two, by Stephen C. Richards and Michael J. Avey, discusses the crimes of commission and omission by the United States and the results produced by agents or agencies of state power. They focus on controlling state political crime, state complicity with corporate crime and controlling crimes of the Federal Bureau of Investigation, local intelligence agencies and police. According to these authors, state crime is central to the repression of the non-elite classes, and is not a collection of isolated incidents but systematic subver-sion of democracy. The most important factor in controlling state crime is the empowerment of the actual and potential victims of state crime, the non-elite classes, by organizing and gaining political power. The thug state is defined as the direction by political and corporate elites of armed force (police, military, intelligence agencies) to "discipline and punish" (Foucault, 1977) the non-elite classes. The authors conclude with policy recommendations on political elec-tion reform, protection of union rights, control of police crime and ending the drug war.

Raymond R. Corrado and Garth Davies, in Chapter Three, examine the phenomena of state crime manifested in the Canadian context. The chapter starts by introducing readers to the variety of instances that conceptually constitute state crime in Canada. Examples include the 1919 Winnipeg General Strike, the 1970 October Crisis, governmental corruption and police use of deadly force. Then the chapter presents competing theoretical perspectives on causality in an attempt to provide a more comprehensive explanation and understanding of the nature of state crime in Canada. Finally, Corrado and Davies examine issues of response as they relate to controlling state crime. Relevant considerations include: whether control mechanisms exist, how existing mechanisms operate, how effective current control measures are and how existing means might be improved or created. Where relevant information is available, the chapter attempts to present comparative analysis of current and prospective measures.

The four most recently created democracies covered in this book include Israel and post-World War II France, Italy and Japan. In Chapter Five, R. Reuben Miller suggests that the founders of modern Israel had an idealistic and utopian view of the new state. The guiding principle was their vision that Israel would be a model for other countries. The establishment of a new state provided numerous challenges in creating political institutions, economic and social organizations and a military infrastructure. As in many other modern countries, the experience of building the Jewish state produced many difficulties and numerous crises and scandals. The military and security forces played an important role in the defense of Israeli sovereignty. However, transformation and deterioration in that role has taken place. Miller's chapter examines the transition in these agencies from defenders of the state to abusers of the privileges and powers they enjoyed. Attention is given to the perceptions that the various security forces have held over the years. The chapter also explores the Jewish underground, which has attacked Palestinians, and the legal system that has protected the assailants. Finally, the study identifies the various mechanisms available in Israel to check and control the coercive powers of the state. Among them are parliamentary commissions, independent investigative councils, human rights organizations, the state controller and a number of non-governmental agencies and watchdog organizations.

James Wolfreys, in Chapter Six, examines various instances of state crime in France: the October 1961 killing of Algerian demonstrators by police in Paris, the Ben Barka Affair, the tapping of journalists' phones by the French secret service, the Rainbow Warrior Affair, and the inquest into the transfusion of blood contaminated with the HIV virus. He then situates these elements within a theoretical context, particularly Poulantzas's (1978) theory of relative autonomy.

Chapter Seven, by Alberto Vannucci and Donna della Porta, reviews the widespread presence of corruption in Italian political life. Resources derived from illegal transactions, it is argued, have become increasingly important during the last two decades. Judicial data show how systematic corruption has changed the incentives in political careers, modified inter- and intra-party competition, tied together politicians of different parties through blackmail and generated hidden connections of top politicians with mafiosi. The issue of controlling state corruption in Italy has prompted an extended debate on institutional reform. Various proposals are examined in a micro-theoretical perspective, which highlights how different institutional settings could modify individual incentives and limit opportunities for corruption.

In Chapter Eight, David Potter suggests that state crime is rarely discussed in the academic literature on Japan. Potter reviews the most visible aspect of state crime in that country: political corruption. Political corruption is a major cause of the continuation of conservative rule in Japan and therefore of the constraints that rule places on the advancement of human rights and the achievement of a truly equal society. This chapter argues, moreover, that the widespread existence of political corruption in Asia's most powerful industrial democracy can be explained by the adaptations of large numbers of Diet politicians, predominantly members of the Liberal Democratic Party and its successors, to the contradictions between legal norms of political conduct and the perceived reality of creating and maintaining political careers. Finally, the chapter assesses the likelihood that political reform as currently debated will resolve those contradictions.

In the concluding chapter, Jeffrey Ian Ross reviews the controls outlined by the contributors, the need to conduct case studies in other advanced industrialized democracies, agendas for theoretical and policy work, and the importance of extending the discussion to include less developed and non-advanced industrialized countries. He argues that now that we have examined the control of state crime in advanced industrialized countries, we are in a better position to counsel the less developed countries in their efforts to create more democratic societies. This is not to suggest that we should impose some sort of government structure on them, or be insensitive to their own indigenous cultures or processes, only that the West has made many mistakes and perhaps can help the less developed countries to avoid similar errors.

The book provides readers with solid and accessible research that is conceptually informed to help them understand the phenomenon of controlling state crime within theoretical and empirical frameworks. Ideally, this effort should lead the reader to question what is the true meaning of the contemporary democratic system and the unjust and cruel essence of contemporary capitalism. If the book helps to reduce, minimize or control state crime in advanced industrialized countries, it has achieved its purpose. At the very least, this work offers some opportunity for understanding a complex problem that demands serious attention.

Acknowledgments: Special thanks to Natasha J. Cabrera, William McDonald, and Stephen C. Richards for comments on an earlier version of this chapter.

NOTES

1. Some of the chapters analyze how states can be both domestic and transnational criminals in their actions (Chambliss, 1989). Many of the advanced industrialized countries have supported and also exploited less developed countries. This phenomenon has led a number of development and dependency theorists to suggest that what the advanced industrialized countries are doing is a subtle form of state crime.

2. See Almond (1956) for an introduction to different types of political systems.

3. Although many newly industrialized countries (such as Taiwan, Singapore and Malaysia) have different historical and economic circumstances, most of them can hardly be called democracies. Consequently, the focus here is clearly on the advanced industrialized democracies. It is also recognized that the term "democracy" is difficult to define, and it consists of various dimensions and types (Lange and Meadwell, 1985; Lijphart, 1984).

4. For an excellent addition to the research on democracy, which explains the actors and instruments of this process, see, for example Diamond (1995).

5. For a review of different types of democracies see, for example, Lange and Meadwell (1985).

Two.
Controlling State Crime in the United Kingdom

by

Jeffrey Ian Ross

THE UNITED KINGDOM (encompassing England, Wales, Scotland and Northern Ireland), through the actions of its police, national security agencies and military branches, has often been accused of committing state crimes both at home and abroad. Consequently, a number of traditional and innovative controls have been advocated, some of which have been implemented to decrease, minimize, reduce, prevent, and hereafter control these types of illegalities from occurring. This chapter identifies the more salient crimes committed by these state agencies domestically[1] during the past three-and-a-half decades and focuses on the methods citizens and state organizations have used to combat this form of political crime.[2]

Identifying crimes by the state is not popular in Britain. Most Brits do not criticize the state because there is a strong belief in government legitimacy, loyalty, and patriotism and a high deference for authority. For example, "[o]pinion polls record widespread support for and confidence in the police.... The media and politicians regularly pronounce that UK criminal justice remains the envy of the world" (Scraton, 1985:9). Behind this popular image lies many incidents of state crime as well as selected public and governmental indignation when it occurs.[3] These sorts of crimes usually "led to the embarrassment of the British government" through "public opinion, Amnesty International, the European Court and the United Nations [which] have all denounced aspects of "various disdainful state actions" (Thurlow, 1994:357).

However, the police, national security, and military branches are not monoliths. The police are organized in a regional fashion, with Great Britain having 43 police forces, Scotland having eight, and Northern Ireland having one (i.e., the Royal Ulster Constabulary). Both the RUC and the London Metropolitan Police (hereafter Met) garner considerable attention for questionable practices. Each have a number of divisions. One of the more controversial developments has been the use of public-order policing units such as the Met's Special Patrol Group (disbanded in 1987) and Manchester's Tactical Aid Group. Ostensibly designed to deal with large scale protest or strikes, they have often been viewed as a political police (Bunyan, 1976). The national security services include Military Intelligence 5 (MI 5), the Secret Intelligence Branch (SIS) (or MI 6, as it is commonly referred to), the Special Branch, and the Anti-Terrorist Branch.[4] The military primarily includes the Royal Navy, Air Force, and army.[5] Finally, although Scotland has its own legal and civil code and mechanisms for control (e.g., judiciary), it has been slow to achieve its own parliament.

As a democratic country, the United Kingdom has a number of traditional mechanisms to keep state power in check and to monitor the abuses and crimes that government representatives and their agencies might commit against their citizens. However, in the last three-and-a-half decades, a period that corresponds to what some individuals (e.g., Ingelhart, 1977) call the post-industrial era, the legitimacy of state actions has increasingly been called into question (Thurlow, 1994), leading to the establishment of additional controls.

During the period covered by this analysis (1960-1997), state crime in the U.K. occurred in a variety of contexts, including, but not limited to, the ongoing conflict in Northern Ireland,[6] and the police role in responding to domestic and civil unrest and public disorder elsewhere in Great Britain. Among the acts of state crime that have received the greatest amount of attention are police and military use of deadly force, unwarranted surveillance, human rights violations and unfair criminal proceedings (e.g., burying of exculpatory evidence).[7]

CRIMES COMMITTED BY STATE ORGANIZATIONS

The liberal democratic state can be characterized by a range of agencies, organizations, departments and policies established to carry out the wishes, desires and preferences of a variety of constituencies.[8] Although state agencies in advanced industrialized democracies develop elaborate mechanisms to screen and monitor "undesirable" individuals from entering the civil service, and later from engaging in crimes, these processes sometimes fail either through neglect, poor design, supervision or implementation. Some organizations, by virtue of having the highest amount of contact with citizens (e.g., the military, national security agencies and police), are more prone to engage in acts of state crime than others; hence this analysis concentrates on these particular agencies.[9] It begins with a review of the military, the organization among the three that has committed the fewest state crimes.

CRIMES COMMITTED BY THE MILITARY

Britain has always prided itself on its military, particularly its naval fleet, which allowed it to expand and protect its growing need for raw materials and markets during its greatest time of capitalist growth. During the post-World War II era, Britain's military has been a pivotal player in the North Atlantic Treaty Organization (NATO). Despite this role, three prominent types of state crime have been committed by the British military: a variety of activities in Northern Ireland, some actions of the Special Air Service, and the sales of weaponry to particular states with questionable human rights records.

Perhaps the most important area of the military's state crimes has been in the context of policing the Northern Ireland conflict. The British army "is a controversial presence amidst the ebb and flow of violence between republican and unionist forces, and is subject to grim accusations that it has violated the human rights of detainees and been used as a partisan political instrument for the repression of Irish nationalism" (Kesselman et al., 1997:32). For example, in 1971 the army detained and interrogated 14 members of the Irish Republican Army Provisionals and exposed them to a variety of questionable interrogation techniques, including methods of sensory deprivation such as "prolonged wall standing, loud noises, hooding, and deprivation of food, water, and sleep" (Hurwitz, 1995:301; Roberts, 1976:16).

In February 1972, in Londonderry, British soldiers shot to death 13 people and wounded 16 unarmed civilians following a civil rights demonstration. This incident, generally referred to as "Bloody Sunday," was the subject of a highly publicized inquiry that culminated in the Widgery Report, which, in turn, was perceived as a whitewash of British army activities during this incident. Additionally, the army has been accused of being pro-Protestant because of its failure to act "during the Protestant workers' strike in Ulster in May 1974" (Roberts, 1976:16).

The Special Air Service (SAS), an elite strike force of the Royal Air Force, "tend to see all security in terms of force..... As early as 1969 some SAS soldiers were operating in Ulster, but it was not until 1976 that [former prime minister] Harold Wilson formally announced their presence.... The SAS soldiers were trained to shoot terrorists even if they were apparently surrendering, and they did so. When they appeared in court at the trial of the terrorists they were disguised and nameless" (Sampson, 1982:254-255).

The military has also been accused of selling weaponry and technology to countries with abysmal human rights records (e.g., Iraq) (Darwish and Alexander, 1991; Sampson, 1982). "The deals made with foreign governments in the

Third World are among the most carefully guarded secrets in the ministry, immune from parliamentary questioning..." (Sampson, 1982:251).

Nevertheless, the military is probably the most contained division of government as a result of its political culture, decreasing size, and continuing removal from formal political decisions and minimal public debate. As one commentator has suggested "[t]he place of the armed forces in the national psyche has always been uncertain. Britain has liked to regard herself as one of the least military of nations, able to put away the symbols of war as soon as peace is declared" (Sampson, 1982:246). However, "military values still play an unseen part in the country's thinking... The sense of military hierarchy and the ancient class division between officers and NCOs can still be perceived through the ranks of industrial corporations... In moments of national humiliation or bewilderment, the British can still summon up almost instantly the memories of the Second World War, which her former enemies had no difficulties in forgetting" (Sampson, 1982:246).

Since 1957, the number of members of the armed services has decreased. "The generals, admirals and air marshals had seen more rapid changes in their role and technology than almost any elite, as the territory they were defending had dwindled from a quarter of the world's population to the frontiers of Western Europe- including Ulster" (Sampson, 1982:247). Additionally, "[t]he army took the most obvious buffeting in the post-war decades, defending the indefensible positions in successive colonial enclaves, cutting down regiments, retreating from the Far East and Africa into Europe, and now moving between West Germany and Ulster" (Sampson, 1982:252-253).

The military has become less open to public inspection. "Since [former prime minister] Harold Macmillan ... abolished the political heads of the three services,... successive politicians have tried to integrate the three services into a more unified structure, but of all the many mergers of the sixties and seventies this has been the most resistant" (Sampson, 1982:248-249). Public debate on the armed services is less than in other countries. This was particularly evident during the discussion over the use of trident missiles. "Most cabinet ministers [are] kept in the dark, and... decision[s are] only debated after it had been made" (Sampson, 1982:251).

Not surprisingly, during the early 1970s, as a result of public statements by former high ranking officers and then current members of parliament, there was talk of a possible military coup d'état (Sampson, 1982; Roberts, 1976). This crisis, however, was dismissed in several quarters. According to Roberts (1976), "a direct military take-over seems most unlikely not only because it runs against military traditions, but also because it would arouse strong political opposition and would most probably be countered effectively by wide-spread civil resistance, including non-cooperation" (p.18).

CRIMES COMMITTED BY NATIONAL SECURITY AGENCIES

Although there have been security failures, British intelligence, collected through the country's national security agencies, has been credited with several successes, including but not limited to breaking the Nazi and Soviet codes during the second World War. In fact, "[a]fter the Soviet Union and the United States, Britain has the world's largest espionage, counter-intelligence and eavesdropping services" (Doherty, 1986:10). Unfortunately, security leaks, media exposés and the revelations of former national security personnel paint a picture of a national security establishment engaging in periodic state crime. The national security organizations have been accused of "mounting disinformation campaigns against elected governments (Dorril and Ramsay, 1991; Leigh, 1986:215-255) and summarily executing people believed to be engaged in violence against the state (Doherty, 1986; Kitchin, 1989; Stalker, 1988; Taylor, 1987)" (Gill, 1995:81).

It is difficult learning about these state crimes. "[F]or reasons of national security, and with the danger of compromising current operations, it is often very difficult for the authorities to comment on matters of alleged wrongdoing by the military, the police, or the security and intelligence services operating in Northern Ireland. Very often the political authorities are quite legitimately, on the need to know principle, not informed about the current operations. When such activities turn sour the media may pick up hints of alleged wrongdoing" (Thurlow, 1994:373). In particular, four major events can be classified as crimes committed by British national security organizations: the spy scandals of the 1960s, the Stalker Affair, the trials, conviction and incarceration of suspected IRA terrorists, and illegal surveillance of British citizens and interests.

First, the spy scandals inside British intelligence organizations, presents an interesting case of state crime. After World War II, a number of British citizens who were acting as spies for the Soviet government were detected. These individuals included, but were not limited to Michael Bettaney, George Blake, Anthony Blunt, Guy Burgess, Donald Maclean, Kim Philby, Anthony Price and John Vassall. Their presence "proved that internal security was still deficient, causing new problems between Britain and her allies" (Laqueur, 1985:208). In this case, the state was negligent in protecting its citizen's national security, causing a crime of omission, and thus committing a state crime.

Second, in the Stalker affair, John Stalker (Deputy Chief Constable of the Manchester Police) "was appointed to head an enquiry" to investigate the 1982 deaths of "six people by the security forces in Northern Ireland... In the first [incident] five known members of terrorist organizations... died [not carrying weapons] .... The circumstances of the deaths led to accusations that a 'shoot to kill' policy existed in Northern Ireland. This was, not expectedly denied strenuously by authorities whose position was reinforced by the subsequent acquittal for murder of four policemen who were involved..." (Jeffery, 1988:344). Stalker was instructed to "see if any criminal offence had been committed by the Royal Ulster Constabulary (RUC) and more generally, to consider the difficulties faced by police officers when acting on information which they cannot reveal in order to protect an informant... This ...enquiry turned into an 'affair' when Stalker was abruptly and unexpectedly suspended from duty in May 1986 pending an internal police investigation into allegations that he had associated socially with known criminals" (Jeffery, 1988:344). Although Stalker was exonerated and reinstated by his police authority, the jury is still out concerning the conspiratorial nature of the affair. Some suggest that the Stalker affair was a smear campaign at the hands of the RUC (Jeffery, 1988). Others have argued that the conspiracy was much higher up at the governmental level. Still some believe that there was no conspiracy at all (Thurlow, 1994).

Third, as a result of an October 5, 1974 IRA bombing of a pub in Guilford, four individuals were arrested, tried, and convicted of a variety of crimes, including the deaths of British citizens frequenting the pub. During the trial the prosecution concealed evidence that would have proved the innocence of those arrested. Only through the painstaking work of a lawyer working on their behalf was the state crime committed against them discovered. Between 1989 and 1990, the Guilford four, Birmingham six, and Maguire seven were released from prison after their convictions "had been declared unsafe"[10] (Thurlow, 1994:388).

Finally, The National Security Agency (NSA) and the General Command Headquarters (GCHQ) illegally undertook mass surveillance of activists, trade unionists and British business through the microwave network set up in the 1960s for such purposes. The extent of the activities of this network first came to light in the mid-1970s when Duncan Campbell revealed the level and sophistication of Signals Intelligence (SIGNIT) in the U.K., later referred to as the ABC affair (Thurlow, 1994).

CRIMES COMMITTED BY THE POLICE

Since the early 1960s, the United Kingdom has experienced many well publicized police-citizen confrontations that resulted in police use of excessive force.[11] In cases where questionable police violence has occurred, it was usually in the context of riots, strikes and deaths in custody. For example, the police were accused of using excessive force in: the 1980s race riots (e.g., Benyon, 1984; Harris et al., 1983; Cowell and Young, 1982; Kettle and Hodges, 1982; Fowler, 1979); the 1984 miners' strike (e.g., Fine and Millar, 1985; Coulter et al., 1984); other labor disputes (e.g., Geary, 1985; Dromey and Taylor, 1978); public protests (e.g., the 1985 visit by the Home Secretary to Manchester); and deaths in custody (e.g., Scraton and Chadwick, 1985; U.K. Home Affairs Committee, 1980).

The Met is often at the center of this type of controversy.[12] Some of the greatest threats to the legitimacy of the force occurred during the 1970s. Corruption, violence in handling political demonstrations, deaths in custody and insensitivity in dealing with visible minorities provoked great public concern. In terms of police violence, a number of well-publicized incidents by the Met have come to the public's attention. For example, the Met's Special Patrol Group has been accused of the death of Keven Gately at the Red Lion Square demonstration in 1974, the policing of the pickets at Grunwicks in 1977, the Lewisham case involving police brutality of those arrested in 1977, and the death of Blair Peach in the wake of a National Front election in Southhall in 1979.

In particular, "in their role as law enforcement agency the police have tended to come into specific conflict with the minority communities... These include what are felt to be examples of over-zealous policing, such as excessive stopping of young black people on the street, and excessive attention to use by black people of soft drugs. They also include perceptions of under-policing, as with the allegations from Asian communities of inadequate police response to racial violence and attacks" (Oakley, 1990:48).

Perhaps the most well-known episode of police violence took place in mid-April 1981, when the Brixton area of London experienced serious civil disturbances during which there were several allegations and documentary evidence of unnecessary police violence. Much of this violence was part of "SWAMP 81" where the Met, faced with increases in public and media concern over street crime in Brixton, increased the number of street stops, particularly of blacks (Jefferson and Grimshaw, 1984, 1982). To add insult to injury, during the mid and late 1980s a number of "mistaken" shootings or the use of deadly force against fleeing felons brought the Met under increased public criticism and demands for greater controls were made.

The majority of the police violence occurred in the black communities and in the pit (i.e., mining) villages. Civil disturbances in Toxeth, Liverpool, Moss-side, Manchester and Bristol have led to anti-police riots and deaths in police custody. Ironically, the Director of Public Prosecutions (DPP) refused to prosecute a single police officer in connection with deaths in custody and nearly thirty other cases referred to it since 1970. This official passivity was reflected in the coroner's court verdicts of misadventure, accidental death, suicide and unlawful killing (Brogden, 1982).

Perhaps the most controversial of the public order groups has been the Met's Special Patrol Group. It was regularly criticized for being overly aggressive and confrontational, particularly in the policing of public disorder. In the late 1980s, as a result of an internal inquiry, the SPG was disbanded. In 1978, Operation Countryman was established to clear up allegations that the Metropolitan Robbery Squad, the successor to the Flying Squad, was also corrupt (Brogden, 1982).

In sum each of the three principal state agencies has engaged in a handful of incidents which can be classified as state crimes. The following section addresses the controls that were implemented as a response to these crimes.

CONTROLS ON CRIMES BY STATE AGENCIES

Controls are exercised from a variety of institutions characteristic of democratic societies. Most of these organizations have typical constraints found in most bureaucracies. Regardless of the state agency, controls can be generally divided into two types: internal and external. Internal controls include such mechanisms as supervisors, chain of command, etc. External controls can be divided between governmental/legislative solutions and nongovernmental/citizens mechanism (Ross, 1995b). Among the governmental/legislative external controls are the parliament and its political parties,[13] the media and the European Convention on Human Rights. What distinguishes Britain from many of the western democracies, however, is the lack of a formal Constitution or Bill of Rights. No single written document serves as a constitution or a Bill of Rights. But a number of documents (e.g., Magna Carta, the Petition of Rights, and the Statute of Westminster) have constitutional status. Custom, precedent, and widespread familiarity with Constitutional precedents is perhaps more important in protecting human rights and civil liberties. Additionally, much written commentary exists on precedent and there is a willingness to play by the rules. Among the nongovernmental/citizens controls are the media, trade unions and interest groups such as the National Committee on Civil Liberties. The controls specific to each agency that exist will briefly be reviewed, those that were relied on or experimented with during the past three decades will be analyzed.

CONTROLLING CRIMES BY THE MILITARY

The detention of citizens and use of highly questionable interrogation methods by the army led to three official reports: two by Sir Edmund Compton in 1971 and another by Lord Parker in 1972. Lord Gardiner, who provided the minority (opposition) report to these documents, disagreed with the military's interrogation methods (Roberts, 1976). The Londonderry incident led to the Widgery report (1972) produced by Lord Chief Justice Widgery, which reviewed the events of Bloody Sunday.

In 1971, the questionable practice of detaining and interrogating actual or suspected members of the IRA motivated the Republic of Ireland to send a petition to the European Court of Human Rights. "Although the Irish petition contained a series of charges and demands, the most important and significant component of the Irish petition was the allegation that the British security forces in Northern Ireland 'tortured' suspected Irish Republican Army (IRA) internees" (Hurwitz, 1995:301). "These methods were termed 'sensory-deprivation'... and they were designed to elicit desired information from the internees... one of the major issues was not whether these occurred, but, rather, whether such behavior and additional actions by the British government constituted a violation of the European Convention" (Hurwitz, 1995:301).

Great Britain "admitted fault, stopped the practice of sensory deprivation, gave assurances that it would not be resumed, and made compensation of up to £25,000 to those subjected to the special interrogation techniques" (Hurwitz, 1995:302-303). Although Ireland appealed particulars of the case to the European Court, "the existence of the Commission and the European Court... [mainly helped to give] international publicity... to their experience, and Britain was chastised for its behavior" (Hurwitz, 1995:307).

Finally, in 1997 new material emerged in connection with Bloody Sunday to further implicate the British army in a planned act of murder. This included the Breglio report (with Raymond McClean's medical report), compiled by Don Mullan and published by the Bloody Sunday Justice Campaign. The Irish government, too, has just published its own review of Bloody Sunday to coincide with the 25th anniversary of the previously mentioned Widgery Report.[14]

CONTROLLING CRIMES BY THE POLICE

Although there is a difference between how the Met and other police forces are controlled, there are three dominant internal mechanisms: police orders by senior officers, chief constables and the commissioner of the police of the Metropolis (London). In addition to the internal mechanisms, the external ones include a variety of laws, including the Metropolitan Police Act of 1829 and the Police Act of 1964; Police Authorities and local councils;[15] the Home Secretary/Office and its Inspectorate of the Constabulary,[16] and the publication of annual reports and royal commissions (Alderson, 1984; Brogden, 1977; Banton, 1975; Marshall, 1965).

There are several nongovernmental organizations that exert a measure of external control over the police. These organizations include the National Council of Civil Liberties, the Association of Chiefs of Police Officers, other police associations (e.g., the Police Superintendents Association (PSDA) and Police Federation) and the mass media (Reiner, 1985).

Several individuals and organizations have criticized the police committees. For example, Simey (1988) presented a strong attack on police authorities, in particular their nonpolitical and non-accountable magistrate members. Additionally, the police committees have been accused of being "inundated with data of a largely insignificant nature which presented an image of the force as a painstaking body of experts. With financial matters minimized and the issues in question apparently covered in depth, the committee was more often than not presented with a fait accompli against which members were ill equipped to argue" (Brogden, 1977:x). Over the past decade, the balance of power in the committees has shifted once again with local councilor representation diminishing and the number of non-elected members increasing. This allowed the state to better manage dissent and deflect attention away from police abuses.

Moreover, some observers argue that the distribution of power within the tripartite structure has shifted considerably in recent years from the police authorities to the Home Office (Spencer, 1985). The power of the Home Secretary over forces outside the metropolis has grown since 1829, while discipline, which continues to be strict, remains primarily in the hands of professional officers (Critchley, 1967; U.K. Royal Commission, 1962; Reith, 1943; Fosdick, [1915]1975). In short, "Although the British tradition of local control by police authorities is still intact, the increased bypassing of Watch Committees through Home Office coordination with Chief Constables has led to several clashes between central and local government, particularly between Conservative administrations and labour controlled authorities. The ambiguity of the wording of the Police Act (1964), which made the Chief Officers of police responsible for operational matters, and gave the Home Secretary powers to veto decisions of appointment by the local Police Committees, ensured that the long-run trends toward greater centralization, more coordinated planning and protecting the independence of the constabulary would continue" (Thurlow, 1994:318).

In general, the most important controls on the police, in recent times, have been as a result of the recommendations of Royal Commissions,[17] the development of the Police Complaints Board/Authority, and Racial and Ethnic Sensitivity Training. First, throughout the history of the British police, a number of Royal Commissions (1855; 1908; 1929; 1959; 1962; 1977; 1981) have been conducted. On January 25, 1960, for example, a Royal Commission on the Police, under the chairmanship of Sir Henry Willink began. It was intended to clarify the constitutional position of the police, thus its legal accountability. As a result of its recommendations, tabled in November 1963, the government introduced a Police Bill that found its way into the statute books as the Police Act of 1964. Part of the act included the amalgamation of police forces that reduced roughly 126 police forces into 49. The Police Act also took the powers away from the former City Watch Committees who, together with the chief constable, had been responsible for promotions and discipline.

Because of mounting "...complaints against the police and their administration, a new Police Act (1976) established an independent Police Complaints Board and amended somewhat the procedure for handling complaints" (Jefferson and Grimshaw, 1982:82).

On June 23, 1977 the Royal Commission on Criminal Procedure examined the powers and duties of the police to investigate crime, and reviewed the rights and duties of suspected or accused people. That same year, despite considerable opposition from the Police Federation (an organization that represents the interests of police officers), the government established the Police Complaints Board, later called the Police Complaints Authority.

As a result of the massive public disturbances during the early 1980s, in particular the Brixton riots, Lord Scarman conducted a Royal Commission. The report examined the causes of the civil disorder and made a series of recommendations in five areas: recruitment, training, supervision and responsibility, dismissal from the force of racially discriminatory police officers and the implementation of community policing (Scarman, 1981). Unfortunately, implementation of the recommendations were "made at a snail's pace" (Thurlow, 1994:328).

Second, official and unofficial reports have been produced, including but not limited to, "the report by Bennet Hytner on the Moss Side disturbances, the report by Julius Silverman, commissioned by Birmingham City Council, on the Handworth disturbance; the Broadwater Farm Inquiry commissioned by the London Borough of Haringey" (Smith, 1991:2); the Bristol Trade Union Council's inquiry into the riot at St. Paul's in Bristol (Bristol, T.U.C., 1981); and at least two unofficial inquiries by the National Committee on Civil Liberties (1980; 1981).

There has also been increased attention by academics, including the launching of the scholarly journal *Policing and Society* and media coverage "in particular Robert Graef's six [television] programmes about policing in Thames Valley Force, shown in January and February 1982 [that] broke new ground by filming real police work" on a daily basis (Smith, 1991:2).

A number of reforms occurred both at the federal and municipal levels to increase control over the force, including the Home Office Police Complaints Board, the revised Met Complaints Board, and the London Greater Council Monitoring Unit. The Police Complaints Board (later renamed Police Complaints Authority) is an independent body whose chair (a layman) and members are appointed by the Prime Minister and Home Secretary, respectively. In 1979, on the occasion of its first triennial review, "the Board recommended that complaints of serious injury inflicted by police should be investigated by an independent body of police officers seconded for that purpose. Great pains have been taken to ensure that every complaint is properly investigated and, since 1976 an extra independent element has been introduced in the form of the Complaints Board" (Rhind, 1981:49). The main criticism of the complaint procedure is that it involves an internal investigation, the police investigating themselves.

During the 1980s, Police Monitoring Units were established by local governments in every district. For example, the Greater London Council (GLC) financed these units in each borough. In 1981, after the Labour Party came to power, a Police Committee Support Unit provided consultation services to the GLC. It also published a journal called *Policing London*. Other monitoring units included the Community Alliance for Police Accountability and the Newham Monitoring Project. The main emphasis of these bodies was their ability to provide personal contact to the cases for complainants.[18] These organizations, such as the London Police Monitoring Committee, had sizeable budgets and staffs. Nearly all of these outfits had publications that influenced both media and academic coverage of police-community relations. Another example of monitoring is the work of "Inquest," founded by families and friends of people who died in police or prison custody, or in circumstances in which police violence or neglect was alleged.

Finally, increased training in police race relations has occurred. Responsibility for this practice fell on "the National Police Training Council, which established a Working Party to review the current state of police community and race relations training and to make detailed recommendations" (Oakley, 1990:50). Conterminously, "[i]n these cases the public order aspects of the problem were of particular concern to the authorities. Although the Race Relations Acts have been used against instigators of racist behavior aimed at immigrant groups, it remains true that more arrests have been made against those who protest against racial violence than those who either foment it or who were directly responsible for it" (Thurlow, 1994:328).

CONTROLLING CRIMES BY THE NATIONAL SECURITY AGENCIES

A number of efforts have been made to reduce actual and probable state crimes by the national security agencies including, but not limited to: changes in the way individuals are recruited to these organizations, new lines of authority, the passage of the National Security Act, and a series of internal inquiries.

First, motivated by the scandals involving Soviet moles operating inside the British Intelligence agencies, the method by which individuals are recruited for MI 5 and MI 6 "was changed and the new directors were no longer military people but diplomats and civil servants or officials who had risen from the ranks of the secret services" (Laqueur, 1985:208).

Second, in 1970, increased control was achieved by the establishment of the Official Coordinator of Intelligence and Security in the Cabinet Office. The Official Committee of Security is "an in-house body,... which is an outside supervisory group usually headed by a very senior judge and made up of former career undersecretaries and military officers. The coordinator is directly responsible to the prime minister, acting as a two-way conduit, providing the prime minister with current information from MI 5 and MI 6 and Directorate General of Intelligence (DIS) and informing these agencies of the requirements of the prime minister" (Laqueur, 1985:209).

Third, although MI 5 is not established by "an act of Parliament, ... MI 6 is sanctioned by the Official Secret Service Vote. To whom are the agencies accountable? Clearly not to Parliament, which in a secret vote each year ratifies the MI 6 budget. According to a 1952 order by the home secretary, the director general of the Security Service (MI 5) is personally responsible to him, even though the organization is not part of the Home Office" (Laqueur, 1985:210).

"Some postwar prime ministers have asserted greater control than others over the secret services. Prime Minister James Callaghan reported meetings with the secret service chiefs and even the subjects discussed; Mrs. Thatcher told the House of Commons that MI 5 had been ordered to report directly to the home secretary (and to her) if any minister, ex-minister, or senior civil servant might be or might have been a security risk. Consequently, whether control is exercised and guidance given depends very much on the personality and forcefulness of the prime minister's coordinator of intelligence" (Lacquer, 1985:211).

Fourth, in November 1988, the Security Service Bill was introduced in Parliament. It "was...described as placing MI 5 'on a statutory basis,' but as Home Secretary Douglas Hurd made clear, the 'barrier of secrecy' which separated the operations of MI 5 from public accountability and political scrutiny was to remain intact. A new complaints procedure was unveiled, with a tribunal of lawyers to investigate complaints about operational matters, and a special commissioner to investigate questions of policy" (Hiley, 1993:378).

The Security Service "was placed on a statutory footing in 1989, but the inspiration for this was the threat of an adverse decision in the European Court on Human Rights... and therefore it was more a measure aimed at legalizing Security Service activities than the kind of rights-oriented proposal being advanced by Labour and Liberal Democrats" (Gill, 1995:88-89). The Security Service Act (1989), "requires ministers to sign warrants authorizing Security Service 'interference with property'"(s. 3). However, the prime determinant of the extent of ministerial interest in the Security Service is the amount, type and degree of public attention. "Therefore, it might be suggested that there is a direct relationship between the autonomy of the security intelligence agency and public ignorance or apathy. Of course, to the extent that security intelligence matters remain shrouded in unnecessary secrecy, being publicized normally only through state (dis)information policies, then this autonomy will be self-reinforcing" (Gill, 1995:93).

Unfortunately, the Act "permit[s] an expansion of its [MI 5] duties, for under section 1(2) MI 5 is charged with the investigation not only of 'threats from espionage, terrorism, and sabotage' but also of 'actions intended to overthrow or undermine parliamentary democracy by political, industrial or violent means'" (Hiley, 1993:379). Additionally, "[t]he autonomy of MI 5 had indeed been increasing since November 1987, when it was announced that, as part of the new 'grievance procedures,' a special staff counsellor had been appointed to hear complaints from disaffected officers" (Hiley, 1993:378).

Moreover, "[s]ignificant changes since the interwar period have included improved technology and more centralized administration, which have enabled the authorities to monitor and control unrest and the growth of extremism. This has meant not only more sophisticated methods of political surveillance, but also more international cooperation and pooling of sight knowledge between the signatories of the UK-USA agreement in 1947" (Thurlow, 1994:318).

Although a variety of suggestions have been made to improve accountability, such as "the possibility of Privy Councilors or other representatives...

being kept informed about the operations of the secret state," when scandals do in fact take place the "government always denies knowledge." This deniability is reinforced depending on the subcontractors, who often carry out the government's dirty work and who are difficult to link to official agencies (Thurlow, 1994:321).

Fifth, "the government... sought to limit the damage of... allegations by instituting a series of internal inquiries with narrow terms of reference. In 1992, however, the courtroom confessions of a former government minister that the government had misled the House of Commons regarding arms sales to Iraq led to the establishment of a judicial inquiry that started to shine some unaccustomed light into the murkier recesses of the British state, including its security intelligence agencies" (Gill, 1995:81). "Although it is quite clear that the forces of law and order and the secret state will not be subject to radical restructuring, piecemeal tinkering will no doubt continue to be the response to the failure of the authorities to defeat the PIRA (Provisional IRA) either in Ulster or on the mainland.... the Major administration is at least more sensible and less secretive about these matters than the governments dominated by his predecessor" (Thurlow, 1994:390).

Sixth, there is an apparent opening up of MI 5. Outwardly, and more recently (January 18, 1993), MI 5 has attempted to present an image of a more opened agency, a move termed "a charmed offensive by the state" (Thurlow, 1994:320; Hiley, 1993:371). For example, the Home Office announced that Stella Rimington was the current Director General. This public announcement "was said to be part of the Prime Minister's new commitment to open government" (Hiley, 1993:372). "The new prominence of the head of MI 5 naturally raised questions about her precise status within the government... In April... the Prime Minister revealed the existence of a standing cabinet committee, under his chairmanship, that existed to 'keep under review policy on the security and intelligence services" (Hiley, 1993:372).

Currently, "[t]he material gathered... [by MI 5] does not necessarily concern foreign espionage and subversion, for MI 5 has also developed an interest in economic and industrial affairs. Section 1(3) of the Security Service Act 1989 charged it 'to safeguard the economic well-being of the United Kingdom,' and it seems that MI 5 has expanded enthusiastically into this new era of operations. In June 1992, Robin Robinson, a former administrative officer in the Cabinet Office's Joint Intelligence Committee, thus revealed that the telephone and telex communications of British companies... were 'routinely' monitored by MI 5 and General Command Headquarters, along with those of their competitors such as General Motors, and that the results were circulated to government departments" (Hiley, 1993:379-389). "Yet other branches have certainly been expanding their areas of operation, for MI 5 has not only expressed an interest in assuming responsibility for the organization of security on state occasions, but has also been given a key role in the fight against terrorism" (Hiley, 1993:380).

In the spring of 1992, "the lead responsibility for intelligence work against Irish republican terrorism in Great Britain... pass[ed] from the Metropolitan Police Special Branch to MI 5 accountable to the Home Secretary" (Hiley, 1993:380). This "remove[d] a controversial area of domestic policing from any form of parliamentary scrutiny, but, remarkably, the government was not prepared to admit that this action had raised any question of accountability. In December 1992, when the Home Affairs Select Committee questioned the Home Secretary on this matter, its members were bluntly informed that there was an important difference between policy, which might be subject to parliamentary scrutiny, and operations, which could never be" (Hiley, 1993:380).

Many of the new controls were made or were a result of insistence by nongovernmental organizations. For example, in the use of new technologies and practices, including plastic bullets and sensory deprivation in Northern Ireland, a major counterbalance to the official line came from the British Society for Social Responsibility in Science, which produced a number of critical reports. Without this alternative interpretation, the techniques used on the prisoners would not have been identified as variations of sensory deprivation.

CONCLUSION

It is difficult to protect civil liberties and human rights in societies where there are periodic threats to civil order and the state is obligated to perform a policing role. In Britain, it appears that the state typically responds to crimes committed by its army, military and police by holding some sort of internal inquiry, and when this will not suffice, it may use a royal commission in the aftermath of particularly questionable event. These practices temporarily diffuse public and governmental criticism and often provide a series of recommendations. The implementation of the recommendations, however, is typically the responsibility of a different government (party) in power or a new set of administrators in the public bureaucracy, because of party turnover, attrition, or personnel transfers. Thus, there is ample room for interpretation, discretion or poor administration in carrying out the original recommendations.

Unfortunately, "[t]he British media is too well controlled by the establishment in London to allow a scandal of Watergate dimensions to be revealed. Even... Harold Wilson found this to be the case, too late, and to his cost.

Wilson's claim that MI 5 ran a smear campaign against him in an effort to destabilise his leadership (which proved to be successful) has never been probed in the establishment media in Britain" (Doherty, 1986:9). Periodically, however, the media has had some success in exposing government malfeasance. The *Guardian* newspaper, for example recently had legal victories in libel cases brought against them by Tory (conservative) politicians Neil Hamilton and Jonathan Aitken, whose careers have been ruined by media exposure of their corrupt actions. Former journalist Martin Bell's victory over Hamilton in the May 1997 general election was symbolic of the media's role in undermining the Major administration by relentlessly exposing corruption.[19]

Also formidable is "The network of interlocking club memberships, old school links, the honours system, the centralization of the upper levels of British society in a small area of London over which the royal family preside, all ensure that scandals are contained within proper boundaries. Individuals may be disgraced and hounded, but no whiff of impropriety will be allowed to affect the structures of the establishment, even years after the event" (Doherty, 1986:9).

Most commentators (e.g., Thurlow, 1994) agree that the coercive aspect of state power in Great Britain is increasing. But because of better resources, including the mobilization of the law, state agencies are increasingly insulated from external control. The occasional commission of state crimes simply buttresses this perception and argument. It is reassuring, however, that the public is not completely silent and that they have allies in parliament and foreign countries who will, on occasion, fight on their behalf to bring state crimes to the attention of British citizens and the world community so that pressure can be brought to bear on the British state.

Acknowledgments: Special thanks to Natasha J. Cabrera, Jim Wolfreys and Steve Wright for comments.

NOTES

1. Although other state agencies could be examined, the police, national security and military have received the lion's share of public attention. By focusing on the domestic context, readers should not infer that either domestic or international state crimes are more or less important. The focus on domestic state crimes is adopted to reduce the scope of the chapter.

2. In general, all material referred to in this chapter was collected from open source literature, including academic and "popular" books and articles, and newspaper stories written during this period.

3. In the 1965 "fight against crime" the Police Federation tried to mobilize public opinion. Subsequent interventions included Robert More's (Met Police Chief) 1973 televised critique of the criminal justice system and his much publicized resignation over the reforms to the police-complaints procedure three years later. Finally, in 1975, the Police Superintendents Association supported a law and order campaign launched by the Police Federation (Reiner, 1985).

4. The Ministry of Defense "established a Directorate General of Intelligence (DIS), which incorporated the intelligence sections for the armed services... Navy, air force, and army intelligence were still responsible for collection and internal security, but evaluation and dissemination was done by a combined unit, the Joint Intelligence Bureau (JIB). The body deals not only with military intelligence but also with political and economic affairs that impinge directly on overall strategy" (Lacquer, 1985:208). Several reviews of British Intelligence have been conducted (e.g., Lacquer, 1985).

5. Also included are the Guards, Special Air Service (SAS), and Special Boat Service (SBS).

6. The British government has had difficulty "to prevent intercommunity tensions, sectarian murders, terrorism and continuing violence in Northern Ireland since 1968. This failure has led to some highly illiberal features of government in the province: the ending of local self-government based in Stormont Castle, the termination of the jury system in criminal cases and the imposition of so-called Diplock courts, the internment without trial in 1971-2 of over 700, the use of uncoordinated evidence provided by 'supergrasses' and the permanent use of the military to aid the civil power since 1969" (Thurlow, 1994: 356). "The operations in the field in Northern Ireland have included MI 5, MI 6, Special Branch, Military Intelligence (14 Intelligence Company) and the Royal Ulster Constabulary. There has also been the shadowy role of the SAS units serving in Northern Ireland" (Thurlow, 1994:372).

7. This chapter will not explore in any detail the infringements of civil liberties as a result of the imposition of the "the Special Powers Act, Direct Rule; the Emergency Provisions Act, and the Prevention of Terrorism Act of 1978." For an extended discussion of this legislation see, for example, Thurlow (1994:356-357).

8. Including but not limited to the citizenry, ruling class and elites.

9. Although it is difficult to say that it is a state crime and who caused it, the Prevention of Terrorism Act (1974) "outlawed media coverage of some of the activities of terrorist groups. As with all such legislation, its provisions are subject to interpretation

and, as with all such legislation in a free society, it represents a tension between two legitimate concerns of any liberal democracy, freedom and order" (Miller, 1991:314). The legislation "sailed through the Parliament with incredible speed is all the more astounding. It presents us with an extraordinary picture of the reliance of liberal democracy on stability. Where stability is challenged, civil liberties do not find a conducive and hurting environment" (Miller, p.314). "Established as a 'temporal act,' the Act was renewed annually, and reviewed in 1976, 1979 and 1984. With renewal came new and harsher impositions on civil liberties" (Miller, p.314). "The BBC ignored Sir Micheal's threats to enforce Sections 10 and 11 against the corporation. Indeed they pursued a pattern quite commonly enunciated in American journalistic circles in similar circumstances: journalists are not policemen and cannot do their job and law enforcement simultaneously" (Miller, p.316).

10. In British jurisprudence, unsafe refers to that which is unsupported.

11. Police violence against citizens in Great Britain is not exactly a new phenomenon. Some of the earlier documented and well studied events include Tonypandy, South Wales, Clyside, the 1920's unemployment March, the weaver's strike, Birkenhead and the Northern Risings.

12. This may reflect a number of factors, in particular the fact that London is host to a variety of mass media outlets.

13. In general, the United Kingdom is governed by a parliamentary system. Members of parliament are elected and members of the House of Lords, the oversight organization on parliament, are appointed. Thus, police accountability has been the subject of intense party political controversy (Reiner, 1985). Advocates on the left (Labour and Social Democrats) favor radical constitutional reform to create a locally elected police authority for London and to grant all local police committees the power to determine aspects of police policy that have hitherto been held to be the prerogative of chief constables (Lustgarten, 1986). But the Conservative government is committed to retain the tripartite structure. However, the government is giving it initiatives designed to maintain or restore the partnership between police and community that, it is argued, has been the hallmark of British policing by consent.

14. Personal communication with Jim Wolfreys, July 1997.

15. The Police Act of 1964 gave all jurisdictions Police Authorities (sometimes called police committees), two-thirds of which are elected politicians from local councils and the remaining one-third are judicial magistrates. Thus the Police Authorities are both political and bureaucratic, just as the Joint-Standing Committees had been before (Banton, 1975). In Scotland, the role of the Police Authorities is essentially the same with two important exceptions. The Authorities are composed entirely of councilors drawn from the eight regional tiers of government. Secondly, the Secretary of State is

the responsible minister, but he is under no general duty to promote police efficacy (Mitchell, 1962).

16. Central government is Home Office for England and Wales and the Scottish Office for Scotland.

17. Most recommendations lead to changes in policies, procedures and/or legislation.

18. For legal reasons, these units could not take up cases unless they were representative of some broader underlying trend (Personal Correspondence with Steve Wright, July 1997).

19. Personal communication with Jim Wolfreys, July 1997.

THREE.
CONTROLLING STATE CRIME IN THE UNITED STATES OF AMERICA: WHAT CAN WE DO ABOUT THE THUG STATE?

by

Stephen C. Richards

and

Michael J. Avey

THIS CRIME STORY is about how the state is able to represent itself as a democracy, while it permits, perpetrates, and promotes systematic criminal actions against its own people. Democracy is a distant political rhetoric for many Americans, especially non-elites (e.g., the working class, poor), who are economically exploited, politically powerless, and harassed by a variety of governmental agencies. State crime is an integral part of the political processes that operates to deny oppressed segments of society basic democratic rights and opportunities.

State crime can be defined as the illegal and or immoral acts of agents of government. Ross (1995b:5-6) lists state crimes as "cover-ups, corruption, disinformation, unaccountability, and violations of domestic and/or international laws."[1] To this list may be added state activity that may not be officially illegal but can do violence to, violates the trust of, socially harms, or exploits individuals. This includes both crimes of commission or omission (Ross, 1995b; Henry, 1991).

Now that we have defined state crime, we need to delimit our discussion. In this chapter we define the thug state, discuss political state crime, state complicity with corporate crime, and crimes of the federal intelligence agencies, local police intelligence activities, and police and their control. By covering these diverse matters we argue that state crime is not a collection of anecdotal incidents. We conclude by suggesting that the most important factor in controlling state crime is the empowerment of the actual and potential victims of state crime, the non-elite classes, by organizing them to gain a share of political power.

DEFINING THE THUG STATE

Thug is a Hindi (India) word that refers to one of a group of professional hoodlums who rob and murder their victims. We define the thug state as government managed by elite interests that uses domestic surveillance and armed force to dominate the poor and working class. Agents of state power behave as thugs when they operate as rogues and scoundrels violating the law, exercise power illegally or exclusively represent elite interests. Government and corporate elites direct a thug state of armed forces (e.g., military, intelligence, police, correctional facilities) to "discipline and punish" (Foucault, 1977) the non-elite classes. Ferrell (1994:161) characterizes this situation as one of: "[t]he domination of social and cultural life by a consortium of privileged opportunists and reactionary thugs; the aggressive disenfranchisement of city kids, poor folks, and people of color...; and the careful and continuous centralization of legal, political, and economic authority."

Are state thugs building the maximum-security society as insurance against the social unrest produced by decreased government investment in public education and social welfare programs? Is the growth in thug state infrastructure — police, courts, jails, and prisons — the government response to disordered marginal populations? What can we do about state thugs that continue to ignore the criminal activities of elites? Is there anything we can suggest that might control the growing power of the thug state? This chapter begins to address these important questions.

The central feature of the thug state is the growing influence of intelligence and police power. Ross (1995b:15) wrote, "[a]t the core of each state are a number of powerful individuals and organizations capable of or actually engaging in a considerable and disproportionate amount of crime against their own citizens and external adversaries, sometimes as part of their policy and other times as a consequence of their mission." The monopoly of force is held by powerful organizations with police, military or intelligence functions; the police are heavily armed and skilled in the tactical use and deployment of deadly force, while intelligence agencies carry out covert activities. Military style police tactics are used to defend the elite by segregating and containing disorganized minority populations in felony or "deviant ghettos" (Irwin, 1985:10). From the perspective of domestic colonial communities, the "inside out" (Barak, 1994:9) or bottom-up view, the United States maintains its control of American urban ghettoes by overwhelming force of arms.

Controlling the thug state requires a critical perspective on state power. The thug state has developed sophisticated systems of surveillance, invading both public and private domains. State thugs have constructed an "electronic panopticon" (Gordon, 1991:50-91), including a "brave new world of electronics" (Young, 1996:110-112) to monitor citizens. The thug state is everywhere, pervasive and intrusive: the police at the door or the drug test at the factory, the police informer in the local bar or the computer dossier maintained by the Federal Bureau of Investigation.[2] Americans are now being video-recorded as they drive, shop, eat and walk on city streets.

Marx (1988:221) suggested, "[t]he trend in North America and perhaps in other industrialized democracies is toward rather than away from a maximum-security society." He described the state use of human and computer informers, mini-awacs, electronic leashes, telephone and computer wiretaps, video cameras, and personal truth technologies to scrutinize the American population. Might these sophisticated systems of surveillance be used against targeted groups? Marx (1988:229-230) describes the potential for abuse:

> Once the new surveillance systems become institutionalized and taken for granted in democratic society, they can be used for harmful ends. With a more repressive government and a more intolerant public — perhaps upset over severe economic downturns, large waves of immigration, social dislocations, or foreign policy setbacks — these same devices easily could be used against those with the "wrong" political beliefs, against racial, ethnic or religious minorities, and against those with lifestyles that offend the majority.

Or maybe, considering the astronomical increase in arrest, conviction and incarceration of immigrants, minorities and the "disorderly poor" (Irwin and Austin, 1997; Irwin, 1985) or "truly disadvantaged" (Wilson, 1987), the state has already selected specific populations for intense repression.

Additional evidence suggests that American intelligence agencies direct a "secret government" (Simon and Eitzen, 1993; Halperin et. al, 1977; Wise, 1976; Wise and Rose, 1968) of armed thugs, "off budget" and beyond community or congressional review. Simon and Eitzen (1993:317-318) wrote:

> Throughout the 1980s, it has become clear that the CIA [Central Intelligence Agency] and NSA [National Security Agency] are merely arms of the new secret government. Moreover, the so-called secret government is made up of a strange collection of players, including ex-CIA and ex-military mentors, international drug smugglers and

arms dealers, intelligence agents and public officials from a host of repressive nations and causes, and business and banking personnel.

These thugs are suspects in the assassinations of John F. Kennedy, Robert F. Kennedy, Martin Luther King, Malcolm X, and Fred Hampton in the 1960s, the Watergate conspiracy in the 1970s, Contragate and the Nugan-Hand Bank scandal in the 1980s (Simon, 1999), and Iran-Contra Conspiracy of the 1990s (Simon, 1999).

POLITICAL STATE CRIMES

Historically, elites developed creative ways to limit the potential efficacy of non-elite candidates voters, and specifically African Americans. These state political crimes were permitted by the U.S. Constitution and federal and state laws until the 1960s. In response, the labor, women's and civil rights movements fought to expand the American voting franchise, despite the resistance of elites.

Elites have also been instrumental in restricting the participation of non-elites as candidates for political office. It costs about one-half million dollars to run for congress; $30 million for the senate; over $60 million for the Democratic presidential nomination in 1992 (Alexander and Corrado, 1995); and more than $180 million for the 1996 Republican presidential nomination (Wayne, 1997; Federal Election Commission, 1996).

Politics is about money. Corporate money is the deciding factor in nearly all electoral contests and debates over public policy. Corporations commit state crime when they buy politicians to enact legislation or government policy that serves their interests. Currently, Americans primarily choose between two party candidates, both sponsored by corporations. Corporate/state crime also includes the purchase by large corporations of political influence between elections, (Reiter, 1993; Jackson, 1990). Corporate influence-buying makes the votes of working people practically meaningless (Greider, 1992).

Employing large campaign contributions, soft money, other legal contributions, and lobbying junkets to purchase political influence, the corporate elite has negated the political participation and power of the non-elite classes of political influence (Reiter, 1993; Ferguson and Rogers, 1986).

CONTROLLING POLITICAL STATE CRIMES

Like other advanced industrialized democracies, to reduce the effectiveness of corporate purchase of elections and legal bribery in the political system, free media time must be provided candidates during the election cycle. With free media time provided, campaign costs would be reduced by more than two-thirds (Alexander, 1992). Another reform needed to restore democracy and control the legal crime of buying political offices is limiting contributions to a level that encourages non-elites to donate small amounts of money to political parties. Contributions should be limited to a modest amount, for example $100, and volunteer activity emphasized. While this would seem to provide the election system with a middle-class bias, there is a compensating dynamic. Personal contact is about twice as effective with working-class persons as it is with middle-class persons; one worker talking campaign politics to co-workers could surpass the impact of a middle-class person's $100 dollar contribution (Zipp et al., 1983). Contributions to Political Action Committees (PACs) that give to candidates should be limited to $100, and a criminal penalty, rather than a civil penalty, should be assessed to protect democratic government from financial subversion. Freeing the system that selects politicians from dependence on corporate financing is essential to any potential effort to obtain assistance in fighting state and corporate crime, especially state crime that is complicitous with corporate crime (Reiter, 1992).

STATE COMPLICITY WITH CORPORATE CRIME

Although corporate crime can involve price-fixing, monopoly power, manufacturing unsafe products and environmental damage, perhaps the most egregious area where it has connections with state crime is in the area of labor-management relations. Tunnell (1995:210) reported:

> Although other types of state crime produce various harms, few are as far-reaching and consequential as state crimes against labor.... Understanding this type of crime and its potential for harming countless millions of individuals is imperative for both a broader understanding of state crime and various means of controlling such harmful activities.

U.S. labor history is the bloodiest in the industrialized world (Turk, 1982). Government has assisted corporations in their pursuit of what Chomsky (1985; 1988) called the "fifth freedom," the license to rob and exploit. Before the New Deal, massive violence was used against workers who tried to exercise their right to organize. Since the New Deal, secret police activity, usually by local police departments, has been used to gather information about unions (Tunnell, 1995; Davis, 1986; Clinard and Quinney, 1978). In some states, and not only "right-to-work" ones, illegal use of force by sheriffs and other local law enforcement agents has been employed to prevent unionism (Tunnell, 1995). The Federal Bureau of Investigation has used the Mafia to attack labor union leadership and to repress labor activity (Tunnell, 1995; Churchill and Wall, 1990).

The movement of industrial production by corporations from high wage to lower wage states and slave-wage countries has devastated the major industrial unions of the U.S. (Bowles et al., 1984; Bluestone and Harrison, 1982). American corporations used a "run-away shop" strategy to bust unions and force workers into wage concessions. Within the U.S., corporations have moved their low paid operations to places where a history of state crime and state-sanctioned crime provided a vulnerable workforce. The movement of factories "off shore" can be explained by the desire of corporations to take advantage of state crime; low wages, no benefits, few environmental restrictions and corporate friendly authoritarian governments, in Asia, the Caribbean, or Mexico (Hightower, 1993:97-100).

There are many examples of corporate employment of both private and public police to suppress labor unions. Employers hired private security troops, dressed for combat, with bulletproof vests and sidearms, to occupy high schools during a 1996 teachers strike in Cleveland, Ohio (Bacon, 1997). Private payment to local police departments occurred, making the police into company agents (Bacon, 1997). One of the largest hired-gun agencies employed by corporations is Vance International, grossing $90 million in 1995 for strike breaking activity. In the recent United Auto Worker strikes at the Peoria, Illinois Caterpillar plant (1991, 1994-1995), Vance supplied the local police with a list of "troublemakers," many of whom were active union members (Bacon, 1997). In a brazen act of state complicity, the federally chartered National Labor Relations Board (NLRB) allowed these hired guns to threaten and injure striking workers, who were then fired for organizing picket lines (Bacon, 1997).

The complicity of government, most centrally the NLRB, in corporate violations of union organizing has left workers politically helpless. The NLRB has been captured by pro-corporate interests, and now functions to obstruct the rights of workers to organize; NLRB's board members are accomplices to corporate crime (Greider, 1992). Corporations send spies to union meetings. "About 10,000 workers a year are illegally fired for their union organizing activities" (Parenti, 1995). Nationally, one in 10 workers participating in a union organizing campaign is fired (Bacon, 1997). Unfortunately, the NLRB generally fails to reinstate many people dismissed for organizing (Bacon, 1997). Consequently, the government is a full partner in violating the employee's right to organize. "The fact is, workers don't really have the right to organize unions," states Richard Bensinger, AFL-CIO Organizing Director (Bacon, 1997:35). The effective escape from legal enforcement of labor rights can be reversed. While all the accomplices cannot be prosecuted, the NLRB members and many people in the Department of Labor and in the Occupational Safety and Health Administration can be replaced.

CONTROLLING STATE COMPLICITY WITH CORPORATE CRIME

Low union membership in the U.S. is primarily caused by the failure to protect workers' right to organize. Throughout the Western world unions have grown (Greider, 1992). For example, since 1970, while U.S. union membership has declined precipitously, Canada's union membership went from 32% to 40%. According to a poll of the U.S. workforce by the University of Michigan, in addition to the 17% of American workers who currently belong to unions, 30% more of the workers would like to have a union contract (Greider, 1992). "By a margin of 60 per cent to 23 per cent Americans believe unions have been good for working people" (Parenti, 1995:216).

The idea is to limit corporate influence on unions and the political process. People who want to promote economic democracy should, following the European Union (EU), insist that trade communities require: (1) democratic government by members, (2) comparable per capita income, (3) aid from rich countries to poor ones, (4) discouragement from gaining advantage with poor working conditions and weak environmental standards, (5) community-wide parliament to supplement decreasing national authority, and (6) when private companies are accused of violating government regulations, the burden of proof should fall to corporations (Morris, 1993). For example, U.S. unions must act to unionize Mexican workers (Kelly, 1996) and other third world workers as a means of raising per capita income, improving working conditions, and supporting economic development while safeguarding the environment as a way of protecting the same for U.S. workers.

Our discussion of state complicity with corporate crime suggests that state remedies will not be enacted, enforced or effective unless the governing party is under pressure from inside its own coalition (Tunnell, 1995). By running candidates in electoral primaries, labor union organizations and low-income community organizations could transform the political process and take it back from the corporations (Tunnell, 1995; Piven and Cloward, 1985). Legislation and political action must be undertaken to separate the corporations from governmental power (Tunnell, 1995).

CRIMES OF FEDERAL INTELLIGENCE AGENCIES

Documentation of Federal Bureau of Investigation (FBI) state crimes is available from many sources (Kovel, 1994; Churchill and Wall, 1990, 1988; Criley, 1990; Domhoff, 1990; Donner, 1990; Linfield, 1990; Glick, 1989). Historically, the FBI has functioned as a domestic spy agency (Churchill and Wall, 1990). Since the Palmer Raids and Red Scare of 1919 its political victims have been groups who attempted to organize exploited segments of the American public (e.g., socialist parties, the Southern Christian Leadership Conference, the American Indian Movement, the Students for a Democratic Society, and labor unions) (Parenti, 1995; Glick, 1989).

Money, power and politics drive major state crimes in the U.S. (Barak, 1991). The FBI has employed illegal surveillance, burglary, mail tampering, propaganda and agent provocateurs to disrupt organizations the bureau considered opponents of the corporate, political and military elite. FBI violence forced these segments into physical and psychological submission, leaving these groups in a state of apathy and fear, minimizing their political representation (Avey, 1989). The Communist Party was targeted in the 1920s because they organized the non-elite classes against the corporate owners (Parenti, 1995). Civil rights organizations were investigated in the 1960s when they organized African Americans deprived of economic opportunity (Churchill and Wall, 1990). The anti-war movement was targeted for FBI attention in the 1960s and 1970s when it threatened the selective service draft and began to cooperate with the civil rights movement (Glick, 1989). Clandestine operations such as COINTELPRO were directed against the Black Panther Party, the anti-war movement and the American Indian Movement. Illegal and unconstitutional actions were used to delegitimize, victimize and criminalize organized dissidents (Churchill and Wall, 1988). Barak (1991:9) stated, "[a]ll these [episodes] reveal a domestic history of significant political repression and state criminality against citizens who have seriously challenged the status quo."

The FBI used "subversive" categorizations to deny organizations that represent oppressed groups constitutional protections (Barak, 1991). The FBI and local police intelligence agencies conducted illegal surveillance and intimidation of groups that attempted to exercise free speech and hold meetings to express concern with oppressive pubic and corporate policy (Caufield, 1991). For example, the FBI operation against the Committee in Solidarity with the People of El Salvador (CISPES) and activists opposed to U.S. policy in Central America and the imprisonment of illegal immigrants in the 1980s (Welch, 1997; Kahn, 1996; Hamm, 1995, 1991) illustrates the way in which clearly "protected" rights were brushed aside by state crime. The actions against these activists included break-ins, death threats, harassment and disruption (Berlet, 1992:89). Many of the FBI's "confidential reliable informants" were persons employed by right-wing organizations and corporations who engaged in agent-provocateur activity to justify their paychecks and ideology (Waltz, 1997a).

The COINTELPRO-type activities of the FBI are not over. The FBI "apology" for COINTELPRO operations and their promise not to continue violating human rights (Halperin et al., 1977) has proven to be insincere. More than 200 burglaries of the home and offices of Central American activists, in which political materials such as documents and computer disks were taken by the FBI, occurred from 1984 to 1988, after COINTELPRO was ended (Churchill and Wall, 1990). The FBI has not stopped violating human rights, it just changed the terms used to describe operations. The agency continues to infiltrate legal political organizations with provocateurs who promote illegal activities (Churchill and Wall, 1990). The bureau's current "Terrorist Information System" contains data on more than 200,000 individuals and 3,000 groups in the U.S. (Waltz, 1997a). The numbers themselves are prima facie evidence of political spying as there cannot really be "terrorists" in these numbers unless "terrorist" means political activists opposed to corporate and elite power.

Attacks on environmental activists by a number of federal government agencies, in cooperation with private corporate security firms, have included surveillance, harassment, retaliation at the workplace, agent provocateurs, anonymous letters, phony leaflets, and telephone threats (Bertlet, 1992). Moreover, even the Environmental Protection Agency has used secret police tactics against environmental activists (Berlet, 1992). A third federal agency, the Federal Management Agency (FEMA), known for its relief work during local disasters (floods, hurricanes, tornadoes), has also, since its inception in 1979, been involved in domestic counterinsurgency planning. FEMA held national exercises in 1984 to practice rounding up and detaining radicals and aliens in rural camps (Waltz, 1997a).

The federal intelligence apparatus also has a grip on cyberspace (Dillon, 1997; Frost, 1997; Madsen, 1997). Through the National Security Agency's (NSA) "ECHELON" program, large quantities of communications, including millions of e-mails and phone conversations, are electronically searched, categorized by keywords and sent directly to various intelligence agencies (Simon, 1999; Hager, 1997a). NSA has immediate access to almost all of the world's communication networks and takes action against those who expose this evasion of private electronic communication (Campbell, 1997). While the federal Privacy Act provides that a wiretap without a warrant by government agents is punishable by an automatic $10,000 fine, technology now allows the

NSA to tap any target all the time and send their communications to the FBI or any other spy agency they choose (Hager, 1997a).

The primary targets of this all-encompassing system of eavesdropping are not "terrorists," but political communications (Hager, 1997a). The list used to select who and what to study is very fluid, and can be altered quickly to monitor additional people and policy areas. Included on this inventory to be monitored are union activists and leaders, financial dealings, demonstrations and politically suspect groups and individuals (Frost, 1997).

Environmental organizations are seen by these intelligence agencies as "terrorists," while those who use violence against them are protected (Hager, 1997b). The electronic searching by the ECHALON process of the NSA is clearly a "general search;" the Fourth Amendment to the U.S. Constitution was designed specifically to prevent this kind of practice. The use of technology by the intelligence agencies continues the effort to make the Fourth Amendment meaningless.

CONTROLLING CRIMES OF FEDERAL INTELLIGENCE AGENCIES

The Freedom of Information (FOI) Act could help reduce state crimes by the FBI and other federal government agencies. However, federal administrations have made the FOI Act virtually worthless by assigning so few persons to the office that requests take years to process. We propose the Department of Justice assign more employees to process FOI Act requests. Ironically, the 1971 break-in at the FBI office in Media, PA by activists calling themselves the Citizen Commission to Investigate the FBI resulted in the release of 1,000 COINTELPRO documents, the most important "freedom of information" exposure to date (Gill, 1995).

Halperin et al. (1977) suggested over two decades ago that media revelations about the illegal activities of intelligence agents, President Ford's Executive Order 11905, which was meant to curb these abuses, and new FBI guidelines on domestic security investigations, would fail to stop civil rights violations by federal agencies. They recommended a series of reforms to: (1) reduce secrecy drastically; (2) repeal the Smith Act and the Voorhis Act; (3) pass legislation making wiretaps, paid informers, and FBI dissemination of non-criminal information illegal; (4) reform the grand jury system; (5) establish charters for the FBI, the NSA, military intelligence, the IRS, and the CIA; (6) legislate criminal penalties for violations of the charters, setting up a special prosecutor to enforce these laws; (7) make civil remedies exist for average citizens; and (8) set up "congressional oversight." Only the oversight suggestion was implemented, and it did not stop government agencies from continued violations of political and human rights.

Understandably, groups that try to act politically to control state crime by intelligence agencies have been made themselves targets for state crime. For example, the FBI initiated attempts to sabotage, censure, and discredit the leadership of the Committee Against Repressive Legislation (NCARL) (Berlet, 1992), and the ECHELON program intercepted the written (e-mail, fax, telex, postal) and phone communications of Amnesty International activists (Hagar, 1997). Churchill and Wall (1988) and Glick (1989) have suggested that activists learn the tactics used by federal agencies in violating political rights and develop countermeasures, including: (1) preventing informers and agents from provocateur activity; (2) countering state psychological warfare with group internal communication to control the influence of disinformation and rumor; (3) refusing to cooperate with legal machinery and having a sympathetic lawyer; (4) preparing for legal defense by keeping duplicates of important information; (5) developing plans for bringing media to life-threatening situations to restrain assassinations; and (6) using the media to expose state repression of law abiding groups.

CRIMES OF LOCAL INTELLIGENCE AGENCIES

FBI violations of constitutional and human rights are well covered in the popular and academic literature, while similar activities by the intelligence units of local police intelligence agencies, sometimes referred to as "red squads," are less known. The repression of the non-elite classes' leadership is a state crime predicated on the expectation that organizations that mobilize deprived neighborhoods will oppose the policies of those in power; these groups are then targeted to be victimized by secret police tactics. The use of secret police units against anti-establishment leaders of repressed communities has been going on for most of the twentieth century in many major cities.

In Los Angeles, from the mid-1970s to the mid-1980s, the police worked to compromise the activities of several community groups concerned with police crime (Donner, 1990). For example, an undercover agent of the intelligence unit of the Los Angeles Police Department (LAPD) infiltrated and became the salaried coordinator of the National Alliance against Racist and Political Repression. In the 1980s, the LAPD intelligence unit also penetrated the Citizen's Committee against Police Repression, one of the infiltrators becoming the secretary of that organization and reporting on, among other things, the planning of legal suits to stop political spying. The LAPD even placed at least four agents in the Coalition Against Police Abuse (Donner, 1990).

Occasionally, filing law suits against local police intelligence units has been effective in limiting human rights abuses. Civil action has been pursued against local police intelligence squads in many cities (Churchill and Wall, 1992). From the resulting cases it is apparent that court orders to prohibit political spying are effective only when monetary damages are paid. When the courts have awarded substantial damages and indicated they would continue to levy fines if the units did not desist, these local intelligence agencies were controlled. Where the courts did not award substantial damages, the police intelligence units tended to disobey court orders (Donner, 1990).

In Los Angeles (February, 1984), a settlement agreement provided $1.8 million, and provided that police investigations must be based on "reasonable and articulated suspicion" that individuals or organizations are "planning, threatening, attempting or performing a significant disruption of the public order." This settlement, approved by a federal court, permanently barred the LAPD from gathering any information concerning political activities, limited the deployment of informants and infiltrators to the investigation of criminal activities, and prohibited the compilation and dissemination of dossiers on political groups. Undercover investigations by officers "who assume a fictitious identity" were banned unless there is "good faith reason" to believe the subject of police surveillance is committing or seeking to commit "significant disruptions of the public order" (Donner, 1990).

The Alliance to End Repression (AER) organization was created in 1971 to stop human rights violations by the Chicago "Red Squad." Not only was the AER infiltrated successfully by the Chicago police, with two informants placed on the steering committee, but after the organization filed a suit to end political spying these informants provided the police with detailed reports on the evidence to be presented against the Red Squad in court. The Chicago police then destroyed the evidence in advance of each discovery request. Even after the court ordered the police to desist their spying, the Red Squad continued the infiltration of the AER. If the intelligence units use secret police tactics against groups developed to stop police crime, and will use those tactics to obtain litigation information beforehand, both the forming of such groups and litigation are compromised. The AER lawsuit, for example, initially resulted in only two court orders: one stopping the police from surveilling the AER's legal team and the second forbidding the destruction of evidence (Donner, 1990).

In 1981, the city of Chicago agreed to a settlement, including a consent decree to curtail the ability of the Chicago Police Department (CPD) to spy on political activity or to use agent provocateurs. By 1982, the city's auditor discovered that the police intelligence unit was violating the restrictions. From 1981-1983, the costs to the city for violating the agreement exceeded $2 million. Again in 1984, the unit violated the agreement twice, spying on numerous groups including the ACLU and received fines totaling $385,000. In 1985, they had to pay over $300,000 in fines. In 1996, the FBI counterterrorism task force provided the CPD with the opportunity to push for ending the decree; the FBI supported the effort by "claiming that Chicago's restrictions on political spying were cramping its ability to investigate terrorism" (Waltz, 1997b). During the 1996 Democratic Party Convention in Chicago, a multi-agency committee — including the CPD, Illinois State Police, FBI, Alcohol Tobacco and Firearms (ATF), Federal Aviation Administration and Secret Service — targeted political groups with surveillance, conducted searches without warrants in which documents, tapes, and other items were taken, infiltrated planning groups, and engaged in agent provocateur activities, which culminated in the destruction of the videotape and film documenting police activities (Waltz, 1997b).

In other cities, the consequences of suits has varied. In Memphis, a lawsuit against the city's police department led to both the destruction of files as a cover-up and then the abolition of the local police intelligence unit. In Seattle, civil court action encouraged a public campaign to control local political intelligence. In 1979, 50 Seattle civic groups proposed an ordinance, voted in to law, that not only banned political policing, but set up an independent civilian auditor to review police files as a means to monitor compliance. In the ordinance, the city agreed to be held civilly liable for damages resulting from willful violation of the ordinance. The presence of support among the governing coalition of Seattle provided this effective system of control during the 1980s (Donner, 1990).

CONTROLLING CRIMES OF LOCAL INTELLIGENCE AGENCIES

Churchill and Wall (1990) suggested that police intelligence units be abolished. As Donner (1990) reported, even the abolition of the units may not stop state crime. For example, in 1976, as a result of its own criminal activity, the Michigan State Police (MSP) intelligence unit was abolished. However, during the 1980s "state troopers, operating under the cover of another branch of the MSP, infiltrated peace groups protesting the construction of nuclear weapons at a plant in a Detroit suburb" (Donner, 1990:359). The abolition of all such units is a herculean task, as the Law Enforcement Intelligence Unit (a federally funded association of police intelligence units) documents list 230 such units, and the CIA has supplied at least 44 of these with sophisticated training and equipment (Donner, 1990).

Secret police units that violate people's rights can only be controlled by elected officials who have the power of appointments and budgets (American Friends Service Committee, 1979). This has occurred in several cities where such a strategy was undertaken (Donner, 1990). Local and state FOI Acts must be created and strengthened to permit the investigation of police intelligence violations. Even where this is the case, intelligence units will sometimes continue to violate political rights; for example, LA city councilman Zev Yaroslavsky, was spied on by Chief Gates's LAPD secret police while he wrote a local freedom of information act (Donner, 1990).

"Local police defined 'terrorism' much more broadly than the Feds, often applying it to environmentalists, animal rights activists, and union activities that affect large, powerful employers" (Waltz, 1997a:26). For example, during the 1990s in Portland, Oregon, groups like the Physicians for Social Responsibility were among those spied on, and persons advocating the establishment of a civilian review board were especially targeted (Waltz, 1997c). The "community policing" rubric has been used to form alliances with local companies without raising controversy (Waltz, 1997a). Local police enthusiastically responded to demands from large corporation's intelligence departments to share information on their political enemies (Waltz, 1997a).

Corporations contract with private intelligence companies that hired former CIA, FBI, and local police personnel to conduct activities that can be considered criminal, including burglary, illegal wiretaps and extensive infiltrations, in order to compromise environmental groups organized against nuclear utilities (American Friends Service Committee, 1979). These activities suggest that private companies and police agencies may cooperate in their surveillance of legal groups. Thus, the Los Angeles Police Department, when faced with disclosure in a local Freedom of Information act, stored most of its political files with the Western Goals Foundation (Donner, 1990). When these relationships were first developed there were suggestions that they perhaps should be licensed (American Friends Service Committee, 1979). Corporate intelligence investigators should be prohibited by law from access to official information collected on political activities (American Friends Service Committee, 1979).

The most recent strategy being used to continue state-crime spying by local police units is the multi-jurisdictional task force (Waltz, 1997a). The FBI uses its leadership of some of these organizations to pressure "local police to ditch limits on political spying" (Waltz, 1997a:22). Task force participation is explicitly promoted as a way to get around local laws restraining political intelligence work (Waltz, 1997a). Since these task forces use information gathered by local and state police departments — which includes the sharing of data on lawful political activity — off-site databases under private control are sometimes used to store such illegal data, voiding public efforts to check compliance with restrictions (Waltz, 1997a).

Funded in part by the 1996 federal Anti-terrorism Act, the FBI set up task forces in 14 major U.S. cities. This initiative met with resistance in several jurisdictions, especially when it was announced that the FBI was going to set up a task force in San Francisco that was publicly opposed by then Mayor Willie Brown (Waltz, 1997a). The task force approach removes restrictions against political spying in both directions. In the few places where the local police have been restricted by local ordinance or court order, the FBI, Bureau of Alcohol, Tobacco and Firearms and state police operatives can provide legal oversight, cover, and resources to "go around" the law. In most places, however, the task force approach worked in the other direction, with local and state police obtaining "information on a broad range of activities that did not conform to the current legal definition of 'terrorism' but were of political interest to the FBI" (Waltz, 1997a:22). Evading rules against partisan political spying became routine. If one agency is prohibited, it simply requests another agency to provide the personnel for the action. The multi-agency system has effectively voided effective control of political spying (Frost, 1997).

The multi-jurisdictional task force has provided the means for federal, state, and local police agencies to evade restrictions on political spying. To control these multi-agency consortiums, all units must be required to abide by federal FOI regulations, and all task force files reviewed by local regulatory boards.

CRIMES OF LOCAL POLICE

Criminal justice thugs continue to construct a "social reality of crime" (Quinney, 1977, 1970).[3] The legislature formed the laws, the police made the arrests, and the judicial branch brought in the indictments that hammer non-elite classes with millions of arrests per year (Irwin and Austin, 1997; Richards and Jones, 1997; Lynch, 1996; Miller, 1996; Gordon, 1991) while ignoring elite crime. Reiman (1997:77) wrote:

> Once we free our imagination from the irrational shackle of the one-on-one model of crime, can there be any doubt that the criminal justice system does not protect us from the gravest threats to life and limb? It seeks to protect us when danger comes from a young, lower-class male in the inner city. When a threat comes from an up-

per-class business executive in an office, the criminal justice system looks the other way.

Meanwhile, the police are employed to repress the modest aspirations of disadvantaged communities where the rate of arrest, conviction and incarceration escalates as gradual reconstruction of racial and class apartheid (Irwin and Austin, 1997).

The police are "increasingly losing legitimacy due to public and governmental concerns over the lingering memories of police corruption, as well as perceptions concerning inadequate response to crime, and excessive police violence" (Ross, 1995a:243). From a safe distance, the suburban white middle and upper classes perceive the police as heroes who use deadly force as they move in harm's way defending law and order. Up close, the inner city black, brown and white non-elite classes see the police as blue thugs, an occupying army of suburban "white boys," "white girls," or privileged token minorities with short tempers and drawn weapons.

Minority ghettoes are patrolled by police who control the streets with military tactics, armed to employ overpowering force, with precious little appreciation for the rights or welfare of the people they confront. Ross (1995a:250-251) wrote, "[t]here is also a deep feeling of distrust which varies with the ethnic, class, and racial composition of each neighborhood." Skolnick and Bayley (1986:141-142) describe the precarious situation:

> Policing in the United States is very much like going to war. Three times a day in countless locker rooms across the land, large men and a growing number of women carefully arm and armor themselves for the day's events.

> What is also striking and more than a little frightening is that the people going to this peculiar kind of war are very often hardly more than kids. They come out of police academies fresh-faced and naive. Many have never held a job. Most are unmarried. Yet they are sent out to deal with hard-core criminals, junkies, wife abusers, and psychopaths. We give a massive pistol to those tender-faced children and ask them to handle people whose life experiences they can't begin to understand. Dressing them to kill, we expect them to keep order so that we may live in security.

As the police arm for street war, the contempt of American minorities for the criminal justice system in general, and the police in particular, grows. This is blatantly evident in the police violence-inspired riots in Miami (1980s) and Los Angeles (1990s). The riots of 1991 that followed the court acquittal of the police officers responsible for the beating Rodney King, resulted from, among other causes, the frustration the people of south central Los Angeles experienced with attempting to control the police. Cullen and Wright (1996:198) wrote, "[t]he 1992 Los Angeles riots [rebellion], which followed the acquittal of police officers on trial for beating Rodney king, forced politicians to visit riot-torn neighborhoods and forced the nation to reconsider the plight of the inner cities." While the politicians talk, the thug state continues to direct the arrest and incarceration of millions of Americans disadvantaged by social class and race.

CONTROLLING CRIMES OF LOCAL POLICE

The control of state crime also depends on the ability of groups to defend themselves from police crime. If certain parts of the city, county, township, or state are governed, as if they were a "conquered province" (Goodman, 1967), no solutions to the problem of state crime will work; they will not be legislated, implemented, or effectively enforced. The victims of police crime require political structure and process to defend themselves.

The first crime of the police is that they protect and serve elite interests and protection of property at the expense of non-elites. Police serve the powerful and police the powerless. They generally ignore the crimes of the wealthy and vigorously pursue the culprits of street crime. Ross wrote, "modern-day policing has origins in private policing, which was established and continues to be the protection of upper-class or elite individuals and their property." Today, in the U.S., the local police continue this tradition by perceiving their mission as "controlling the lower and so called dangerous classes" (Ross, 1998:98). It is not surprising, considering the social class origins of police personnel, that they are intimidated by the wealthy who can afford expensive lawyers, while they focus their attention on the poor with little access to legal representation.

The police have committed a crime of omission (Henry, 1991) that includes restricting their responsibility to primarily combat street crime while they overlook the structural causes of crime. The police wage war against the poor, the young, and the rabble, "meaning the disorganized and disorderly, the lowest class of people" (Irwin, 1985:2). Guns pointed at the people below themselves on the social hierarchy, they enforce the laws legislated to suppress the petty street crimes, while the crimes of the elites continue with scarce attention (Friedrichs, 1996). The visibility of petty offenses on street corners distracts the police from the insulated but serious crimes of sophisticated persons; crooked judges, attorneys who steal from clients, embezzling bankers, dishonest stock brokers, corporate inside traders, slum landlords who refuse to correct building code violations, doctors engaged in medical fraud, corporate violators of employee safety regulations and environmental polluters. The "police of the future" (Bayley, 1994) must begin to look beyond the reach of their guns and handcuffs to begin to address the real life circumstances of non-elites, the "savage inequalities" (Kozol, 1991) and social chaos of racial segregation, relative deprivation, structural unemployment, "false needs and competitive individualism" (Young, 1996:119), that are the source of street crime, while they raise their sights to investigate the crimes above their own social level.

Controlling police crime requires a reordering of patrol priorities. If the police are to protect communities, they must improve and allocate more resources towards their surveillance above the street into the private suites where crime is perpetrated by corporate personnel who make decisions and profit from the social-economic conditions that guarantee the production of street crime. The state allows corporations to increase profits by externalizing certain production costs, like chemical and nuclear waste. The police should be protecting the community from corporate criminals who poison the environment, exploit and injure workers, or purchase public policy; for example, extorting economic concessions from taxpayers (property tax abatements, public financing of private infrastructure). Citizens should be able to go to the police to file complaints against private companies that pollute the community, operate unsafe factories, discriminate against employees, or use illegal means to obstruct union organizing. Corporations should not be allowed to use private property rights to protect themselves from criminal investigations resulting from citizen complaints.

The second state crime of the local police is that they are well trained in street combat, but poorly prepared to fight crime, because their formal education is inadequate. The law and its relationship to social-economic disparities is too complex to intellectually grasp without years of formal study (i.e., a university education). The standard requirement for applicants applying for police employment is a high school or general equivalency diploma, no arrest record and the passing of the medical, psychological, and physical fitness exams. As hired, they usually have no advanced education in social or behavioral sciences, including criminology. Nevertheless, "[t]here is a consensus among police executives that higher education for officers is a priority" (National Institute of Justice, 1997:12).[4] We suggest a four-year college degree be required for police recruits. The local police should be educated to deal with the powerful people and understand the social-economic problems that create the community disorder they patrol. Over time, university-educated police officers may develop the intellectual breath and social-economic insight to gather the courage to advocate reforms of the criminal code that begin to redirect their attention toward understanding elite deviance as real crime.

Kappeler et al. (1994:259) suggested that the police occupational subculture be reformed through the selection, training, and assignment of police personnel:

> First, police organizations can select employees who have demonstrated a commitment to cultural diversity and sensitivity... Second, police organizations can incorporate values and corporate models into their training academies...Third, police organizations can attempt to break the transmission of negative cultural influence from one generation of officers to the next by the careful assignment of new officers and the careful selection of training officers.

Alpert and Dunham (1992:89-90) advocated that "police need to develop social intelligence-the ability to enjoy and to interact effectively with people." Kappeler et al. (1994:259) proposed that police departments encourage their officers to develop outside interests, find opportunities for positive experiences to become integrated into neighborhoods, and "go beyond the 'us and them' dichotomy."

We suggest a more dramatic approach. The police need to be part of the community. They should be recruited and hired from the neighborhoods they are assigned to patrol. Ross (1994:16) wrote, "[i]f police forces do not recruit actively among minorities and newly arrived immigrant groups there will be even greater difficulties in mediating conflict among these communities." Cities need legal residency requirements for all city employees, including the police. City personnel should not be allowed to collect their salaries in the city and then spend it on suburban living.

We also advocate, for several reasons, that all off duty employment of officers be terminated. First, to avoid professional conflicts of interest, public police departments should prohibit its members from "moonlighting" as hired guns for private business. Second, police work is a demanding occupation that requires the alert attention of all officers. Police personnel who are exhausted from working second jobs may not be prepared to respond quickly to protect the public or back up their colleagues in emergencies. Third, with the high rate of unemployment in inner city neighborhoods, the very location where many police officers moonlight as security personnel, the restriction on police moonlighting would provide job opportunities for other persons. Finally, police officers should be adequately compensated so they do not have to resort to working second jobs.

In addition, police work should be demilitarized, formal rank ended and reorganized as a managerial profession "stratified according to function, performance indicators, auditors, and accountability" (Bayley, 1994:157-160). Police work is no longer a blue collar occupation, but has evolved into a profession, complete with endless paper work, computer entries and brief cases filled with reports. The military-style management is now archaic, a remnant of a prior era. For too long, the police have operated as an occupying army patrolling enemy territory. A "new police," better educated about cultural diversity and community needs, needs to focus on providing services, where performance is measured by police response to neighbor problems, and not just the number of arrests.

The police need to address their role in the community and develop creative ways to work with the community to improve the quality of daily life. Police officers who patrol blighted areas see the problems. Together they discuss the social-economic disadvantages of the neighborhoods, but have been given little opportunity, or official mandate, to do anything other than arrest and transport obvious violators of the law. It is time to empower the police to begin "community repair" as opposed to only crime patrol. For example, maybe the community is more concerned with industrial pollution, slum landlords who refuse to repair property, the lack of well-paid employment, boarded up houses, broken street lights and abandoned cars, than they are about the occasional drug deal. We suggest that police work could be gradually "civilianized," with the introduction of unarmed Public Service Officers (Skolnick and Bayley, 1986). These officers would bring a new civility to police work, that includes developing relationships with minority populations and community groups that have been intimidated by, or even hostile to, law enforcement.

The third crime of the police is corruption (Ross, 1995a, 1994, 1992; Kappeler et al., 1994; Skolnick, 1994; Skolnick and Bayley, 1986; Sherman, 1974). Media reports of police misconduct have alerted the public to a growing problem with police integrity. The "war on drugs" has created opportunities for crooked cops (Kappeler et al., 1994), including recreational off-duty drug use (Carter and Stephens, 1991), recreational on duty drug use (Kraska and Kappeler, 1988), violating the rights of defendants by conducting illegal searches, committing perjury and planting evidence (Carter, 1990), soliciting protection money from dealers, stealing drug and money evidence and outright sales of illegal drugs (Carter and Stephens, 1991) and police violence (Ross, 1992; Manning and Redlinger, 1978, 1977) such as threatening and torturing suspects, destroying personal property and terrorizing residents. Kappeler et al. (1994) reported, "[t]he immense profits in the illicit drug market, coupled with intensive drug enforcement efforts, have led to the corruption of police and other criminal justice personnel. It is safe to say that virtually every law enforcement agency in the country has been touched by some form of drug corruption."

The fourth crime of the police is the use of deadly force and violence (Bayley, 1994; Ross, 1994, 1992; Skolnick and Fyfe, 1993; Sherman, 1980). Ross (1994:2), defined police violence as "a physical action by police designed to affect an arrest, apprehend a suspect, or intimidate a member of the public." A recent National Institute of Justice report (1997:11) stated, "[t]he problem of police use of excessive force has received increased public attention in the past few years as a result of a number of highly publicized cases." For the first time, police violence against citizens is being captured on film by citizens with portable video recorders who have caught the police in the act. As a result of public pressure, the 1994 federal Crime Act instructed the Attorney General to "acquire data about the use of excessive force by law enforcement officers and publish an annual summary of the data" (National Institute of Justice, 1997:11). We suggest that community groups in inner city neighborhoods be provided federal crime control funds to purchase video cameras so they can monitor police violence on their streets.

There are many problems with civilian oversight of police crime (Bayley, 1994; Kappeler et al., 1994; Ross, 1994; Skolnick, 1994; Skolnick and Fyfe, 1993; Skolnick and Bayley, 1986; Sherman, 1980). Typically, investigations are referred to civilian blue ribbon commissions where they are hidden from public view until the press attention subsides and a sanitary report can be issued exonerating police personnel. We need to consider special police courts for the investigation and prosecution of crimes committed by law enforcement officers. Complaints against police should be referred to a special police prosecutor for investigation and possible criminal indictments. The court would then remove police-on-duty crime from the regular court system where police personnel enjoy professional advantages with prosecutors and judges. The police court should be staffed with its own investigators, prosecutors, and judges who are not dependent on the police bureaucracy for approval, cooperation, or promotion. The proceedings of the court would be open to review by the public and press.

CONCLUSION: END THE WAR ON DRUGS

Reining in the thug state requires an informed public with the courage to demand the administrative and professional constitutional control of powerful state agencies and corporate elites. We have suggested a number of recommendations for protecting democracy by controlling political state crime, state complicity with corporate crimes and the thuggery of intelligence and police agencies. Some of these ideas we have borrowed, a number are new, a few of these intended to provoke further study. We conclude our discussion with a call to end the "war on drugs." A carefully negotiated conclusion to the war on drugs is an important first step in controlling the growth of the thug state.

Critical observers attempting to describe the construction and operation of a thug state infrastructure have coined provocative terms to alert our attention, including: the "carceral archipelago" (Foucault, 1977:297); "American gulag" (Richards, 1990:18-28); "crime control as industry" and "western style gulags" (Christie, 1993), "corrections-commercial complex" and the "corrections-commercial triangle" (Lilly and Knepper, 1993:150-166); the "criminal justice industrial complex" (Donziger, 1996; Quinney, 1977:117-124); the "perpetual incarceration machine" (Richards and Jones, 1997), the "correctional industrial complex" (Irwin and Austin, 1997:1-18); the "American crimefare state" and the "law enforcement industrial complex" (Andreas, 1997:37-45); the "prison-industrial complex" (Davis, 1998:11-17; Schlosser, 1998:51-77), and the "drug-war industrial complex" (Veit, 1998:64-68).

Between 1980 and 1994, while the general U.S. population increased by 18%, and reported "index" (serious) crimes rose by only 4%, the percentage of Americans on probation went up by 165%, on parole by 213%, in jail by 199%, and in prison by 219% (Irwin and Austin, 1997). "The nation's prison population more than doubled in the 1980s and is expected to double again between 1994 and 2002, to roughly 2.4 million, the highest incarceration rate among advanced industrialized countries" (Andreas, 1997:38). Non-elites, particularly minorities, are subject to growing rates of arrest and incarceration (Irwin and Austin, 1997; Reiman, 1997; Miller, 1996). Irwin and Austin (1997:4) estimated that "1 of every 25 adults in America go to jail each year." This outrageous increase in arrests and incarceration is primarily the result of the drug war.

The U.S. government has lost the war on drugs. The grand plans of the federal drug czars have failed to significantly decrease the importation, manufacture, or consumption of illicit drugs. The state has squandered precious public resources on a misguided policy that was doomed to fail. The policy was designed by vested interests with scant attention to the social and cultural complexities of recreational drug use. This war on drugs was lost for four reasons. First, government bureaucrats have overreached their authority by attempting to legislate chemical morality and criminalize personal behavior. Second, the state has failed to consider the national requirements of drug exporting nations for foreign capital investment, a favorable balance of payments and the desperate need to raise their peoples' standard of living. Third, the drug-producing countries, for example, Colombia and Mexico, have converted their marijuana fields (1970s) into coca fields (1980s) and now into poppy fields (1990s).[5] Fourth, the prohibition of drugs has only increased the profit potential for smugglers, distributors and dealers. Currie (1993:4) wrote: "[t]he failure of American drug policy is depressingly apparent. Twenty years of the 'war' on drugs have overcrowded our jails and prisons with non-violent persons, immobilized the criminal justice system in many cities, swollen the ranks of the criminalized and unemployable minority poor, and diverted desperately needed resources from other social needs."

An end to the state "war on drugs" (see Richards, 1998) is required to control criminal justice corruption and crime. Drug enforcement has become the major preoccupation of both local and national police (Andreas, 1997; Reiman, 1997; Currie, 1996, 1993, 1985). Andreas (1997) estimated that the U.S. government has spent $65 billion since 1981 on drug enforcement, with some 40 federal agencies or programs in 7 of the 14 federal cabinet departments. The result has been millions of arrests per year, with the number of people incarcerated for drug offenses tripling between 1980 and 1990 (Andreas, 1997). The FBI reported nearly 1.5 million drug arrests for 1995 (U.S. Department of Justice, 1996).

The harsher sentencing of persons convicted of drug crimes has made the health crisis associated with illegal drug use impossible to manage (Johns and Borrero, 1991; Currie, 1993). The drug war hysteria has forced people who may use illegal drugs for recreation or self-medication without benefit of adequate health information or medical supervision to secretly consume powerful chemical intoxicants that are not approved or inspected by the Federal Drug Administration. People are afraid to discuss their covert use or abuse of drugs with medical personnel because of the possible harsh legal sanctions.

We suggest that illegal drug use should be demilitarized, removed from police responsibility and treated as a medical problem. Currie (1993:266) proposed, "[o]ne way to accomplish these goals would be through a network of public, community-based health clinics." The state could provide long term drug treatment programs upon request by converting vacant urban hospital space into inpatient and outpatient drug clinics.

Marijuana is a "controlled substance" that cannot be controlled since it is a easily cultivated indoors and out in nearly any climate. Reiman (1997:38) wrote:

The crackdown on importation of marijuana has given drug traffickers an incentive to shift to cocaine because much smaller amounts of it are needed for intoxication and thus much smaller amounts are needed to make big money. It remains the case that most drug arrests are for marijuana use or possession, and that marijuana is a relatively safe drug.

Scholars (Reiman, 1997; Nadelmann, 1993) and public figures (former Secretary of State George Shultz, William F. Buckley, former Surgeon General Joycelyn Elder, Milton Friedman, former Baltimore Mayor Kurt Schmoke, and former police chief of Washington, DC Jerry Wilson) have advocated considering the decriminalization of marijuana. Reiman (1997) reported there are no documented marijuana fatalities; in contrast aspirin causes hundreds of overdose deaths per year. We suggest that marijuana be legalized for Americans over age 21, taxed, regulated and subject to legal restrictions prohibiting use in public places. The police would be free to concentrate their efforts against laboratory-synthesized dangerous drugs, both legal and illegal, the powders and pills that create addiction and social chaos (Meier and Geis, 1997).

The future threat to the U.S., already developing in large cities, is the importation of inexpensive heroin that will become the new street drug of choice. "Drug seizures are insignificant in relation to this traffic, and the street price of drugs has declined rather than increased" (Johns and Borrero, 1991:73). The "reckoning"[6] (Currie, 1993), already apparent on the streets of New York, Miami, and Los Angeles, is the next wave of a South American commodity, a supply of cheap heroin. The Colombian cartel is now exporting high quality inexpensive black tar heroin to the U.S. The new fad among fashionable young people in East and West coast cities is smoking this potent narcotic. The cartel's market plan is to first hook these new consumers on high-percent black tar heroin selling at less than $100 a gram, and then lower the quality and raise the price; eventually converting recreational smokers of heroin into intravenous junkies (Richards, 1997).[7]

To avoid the "reckoning" (Currie, 1996, 1993), the U.S. must negotiate a peace settlement with major drug-exporting countries. For example, the U.S. government could consider a trade deal with Columbia, Mexico and other drug-exporting countries that provides an import quota of marijuana (like coffee or sugar cane) in exchange for the complete destruction of all coca and poppy fields. The result would be to provide these countries a means to develop their economies legally, while they cooperate in suppressing cocaine and heroin production. Imported marijuana would be subject to tariffs, taxes and age restrictions, then distributed by licensed vendors, much like alcohol and tobacco.

When a state loses a war it is subject to a war crimes tribunal, for example, Germany or Japan after World War II. The government of the United States has lost the war on drugs, requiring that the masters, merchants, and political architects of this war be investigated for war crimes. Johns and Borrero (1991:67-84) provided grounds for possible indictments:

(1) By pursuing a strategy of criminalization on the one hand and eradication on the other (of both drugs and people associated with them), the administration has guaranteed that the price society pays for the use of certain dangerous drugs is higher than it would have been had a policy of decriminalization, treatment, and education been pursued [p.67].

(2) The policing of complaint-less crimes such as drug use and trafficking deflects police time and resources away from other, more serious crimes, which are just as violent and arguably more destructive to the social fabric-white collar crimes, environmental crimes, and political crimes [p.69].

(3) Domestically, the war metaphor has whipped up a heightened perception of great external threat; consequently, it has led to increasing tolerance for the expansion of state power and erosion of democratic freedoms [p.84].

The war on drugs has wrecked havoc on the U.S., threatened civil liberties and turned neighborhoods into combat zones. Millions of Americans have been victimized by the drug war began by Nixon (1970), intensified by Reagan (1980), and continued by Clinton (1992). The drug war-victors are the champions of human and civil rights, attorneys and citizens, who have fought the drug-war thugs in the media and the courts. The victims of the drug war, the millions of American "prisoners of war" (Quinney, 1997:101) demand that a war crimes tribunal address the criminal harm done by the war on drugs.

A peaceful conclusion to the drug war suggests positive consequences, including freeing up federal and state court dockets to pursue corporate crime, providing an historic opportunity for police to reexamine their priorities, and the release of hundreds of thousands of drug prisoners from jails and prisons.

Acknowledgments: We would like to thank Rick Kissell, Crystal Litz, Angus McKenzie, David Potter, Jeffrey Ian Ross, Aron Tannenbaum and Mike Wood for their assistance with numerous revisions. An earlier version of this chapter was presented at the Annual Meeting of the American Society of Criminology, Washington, DC, in November 1998.

NOTES

1. The literature on state crime continues to struggle with definitions C. Wright Mills's power elite thesis (1956) — that an American upper class (Domhoff, 1983, 1967; Zeitlin, 1978) controls the dominant corporate, political and military institutions — suggests a "higher immorality" based on class privilege. Mills's analysis of the upper class and their shield of middle class managers has been examined as elite deviance and defined by Simon and Eitzen (1993) as economic domination, governmental control, and denial of basic human rights.

   White Collar Crime (Coleman, 1998, Friedrichs, 1996; Albanese, 1995; Weisburd et al., 1995; Shapiro, 1990; Geis, 1988; Hirschi and Gottfredson, 1987; Braithwaite, 1985; Benson, 1984; Geis and Stotland, 1980; Geis and Meier, 1977; Sutherland, 1949) is defined as violations of the law by persons for personal gain against businesses, corporations or government; for example, bribery, conspiracy, credit fraud, embezzlement, employee theft, extortion, false claims, fraud, income tax evasion, insider trading and mail fraud. *Corporate Crime* (Ermann and Lundman, 1996; Simpson and Koper, 1992; Mokhiber, 1988; Hochstedler, 1984; Clinard and Yeager, 1980) refers to an intentional act or omission of an act that violates civil or criminal statutes or regulations for the benefit of the corporation; for example, price fixing, monopolistic practices in restraint of trade, failure to comply with occupational safety law, industrial and chemical pollution, unnecessary surgery, unnecessary medication, padding medical bills, discrimination in hiring, firing, promotions and bank and insurance "redlining."

   Friedrichs (1996) suggests *governmental crime* (Ermann and Lundman, 1996; Friedrichs, 1995a) as a broad term referring to crime or immoral acts by government. He (1995:122) further distinguishes *state crime* (Ross, 1995; Barak, 1991a, 1991b, 1990; Chambliss, 1989, 1988; Quinney, 1977, 1970) as harmful acts carried out by the state on behalf of the state and political white collar crime as illegal activities by official or politicians for direct personal benefits.

2. Berger (1990:43) wrote: "Since my purpose is to comfort them, I will simply hope that the point has been sufficiently clear, that enough has been said to justify the suspicion that sociology is the dismal science par excellence of our time, an intrinsically debunking discipline that should be most congenial to nihilists, cynics, and other fit subjects for police surveillance."

3. The social reality of crime is constructed by the formulation and application of definitions of crime, the development of behavior patterns in relation to these definitions and the construction of an ideology of crime (Quinney, 1977, 1970).

4. "The Police Corps Act, Title XX, Subtitle A, of the Crime Act (see Appendix A, Statutory Authority Under the Crime Act for Criminal Justice Research and Evaluation) helps reimburse officers for tuition costs and provides scholarship assistance and training expenses with the aim of ensuring the infusion of a core of college-educated police officers in local and State police agencies" (National Institute of Justice, 1997:12). This program is in the process of being evaluated by NIJ.

5. This last observation is based on interviews conducted between 1993 and 2000 by author Richards with members of the Colombia Drug Cartel who were incarcerated in federal prison.

6. Currie (1993:280-281) wrote, "Just as unbreathable air and an endless flood of toxic wastes tell us that something is fundamentally awry in the way we organize our technologies of production, endemic drug abuse tells us that something is fundamentally amiss in our social organization...It is not accidental that the United States has both the developed world's worst drug problem and its worst violence, poverty, and social exclusion, together with its least adequate provision of health care, income support, and social services. Taking on the drug problem in an enduring way means tackling those deficits head-on."

7. See note 5.

FOUR.
CONTROLLING STATE CRIME IN CANADA

by

Raymond R. Corrado

and

Garth Davies

CANADA, LIKE THE other advanced industrial democracies examined in this book, has experienced and continues to encounter incidents that constitute "state crimes." The Canadian experience has not been as extensive or pervasive as that of the U.S., and Canada has avoided the worst excesses of its neighbors to the south (Laschinger and Stevens, 1992). Nevertheless, state criminality in this country has been frequent enough to be characterized as a significant problem. Moreover, Canada provides a unique context within which to examine illegalities perpetrated by, and in the name of, the state. Accordingly, analyzing the Canadian situation is important to the larger endeavor of presenting a comprehensive approach to controlling state crime.

State crime in Canada is normally identified with government at the national or provincial level. The Canadian context differs significantly from other advanced industrial countries with regard to state crimes perpetrated at the local or municipal level. Specifically, the constitutional division of responsibilities in Canada affords vastly superior powers to the federal and provincial governments. As a consequence, the range of opportunities for corruption and abuse of power at the municipal level is considerably more restricted. While there are certainly instances of state crime at this level, they tend to remain localized and are not treated with the same urgency by the media. The almost exclusive preoccupation with national and provincial authorities has served to concentrate Canadian concern about state crime in two areas: systematic political corruption, and abuses of power perpetrated by the various intelligence gathering organizations and institutions prominent in the evolution of counterterrorist strategy and response. The two other institutions identified by Ross (1995a:15) as "the principal state criminogenic actors who engage in state crime," the police (below the national level) and the military, have not been as prominent in Canadian concerns regarding governmental illegalities.

Until very recently, the role of the military in state crime had not been significant. This is likely to change in the wake of the investigation into the "Somalia Affair." In March 1993, while operating as peacekeepers in the war torn African country of Somalia, Canadian soldiers shot two Somali civilians trying to steal food from their compound, killing one of the Somalis. The subsequent inquiry concluded that Canada's military system was "rotten to the core," and that "the sorry sequence of events in Somalia was not the work of a few bad apples, but the inevitable result of systematic organization and leadership failures, many occurring over long periods of time and ignored by our military leaders for just as long" (Létourneau, cited in DeMont, 1997). Also telling is the federal government's attempt to effectively squelch its own commission: then Defense Minister Douglas Young closed the inquiry before several crucial witnesses could be heard and before some fundamental issues could be addressed. One cannot help but note the similarity between the current controversy and the one surrounding the McDonald Commission inquiry into Royal Canadian Mounted Police wrongdoing two decades earlier (RCMP; see discussion later in this chapter). While the Liberal government's angry reaction to the report would seem to stack the deck against real reform (DeMont, 1997), maintaining the status quo will almost certainly result in further debacles. At present, it is too early to tell whether steps will be taken to prevent such recurrences. If substantial changes are not forthcoming, Canada's military is likely to come under increasingly greater scrutiny and potentially become a leading perpetrator in context of state crime.

For a variety of reasons, the police similarly have not generally found themselves at the forefront of discussions concerning state crime in Canada. This is not to say that law enforcement agencies have not been guilty of misconduct. On the contrary, some forces, particularly the large urban forces in Vancouver, Toronto and Montreal, have been cited for significant improprieties (Ross, 1995e). But unlike many U.S. examples of police corruption, there is little evidence that police misconduct is systematic or politically directed. In Canada, there are few examples of using the state apparatus in a fundamentally destructive manner, as, for example, J. Edgar Hoover was able to do as the head of the Federal Bureau of Investigation. The increasing professionalization of the police and the advent of the Canadian Charter of Rights and Freedoms (1982) have further served to distance the police from the type of systematic misconduct that constitutes state crime. For all of the reasons cited above, this chapter focuses on political corruption and the illegal activities of state security and intelligence agencies, particularly the Royal Canadian Mounted Police Security Service.

This chapter is divided into four sections. The first presents examples of state crime in Canada, paying particular attention to two specific types of behavior: political corruption, and the abuse of power by intelligence agencies. In the second section, three theoretical perspectives are advanced as potential explanatory frameworks for governmental crime. In part three, a range of possible responses to state crime is examined. Finally, section four analyzes the future of controls on state crime.

POLITICAL CORRUPTION IN CANADA

The essence of political corruption is taking illegal advantage of a political or official position. Financial gain is the principal motive, and the most notorious cases have involved the exchange of money for political influence. Political corruption in Canada is made possible by the extreme interdependence of political and economic processes: business and professional interests have traditionally dominated the development of representative, democratic institutions. Starting with the first elections in Canada, wealth and access to resources have figured prominently in the ability to effectively contest elections. Since that time, business interests have remained crucial to the financing of political campaigns, resulting in an intimate relationship between economic and political elites. This symbiotic relationship almost guarantees that corruption in some form would become a consistent characteristic of the Canadian political process. Several examples help to illustrate the form and variation of corruption within the Canadian political system, ranging from individual-level, rather isolated acts such as the Rivard and Sky Shops Affairs, to more sophisticated abuses by provincial governments in the Maritimes, to the most systematic conduct perpetrated at both the provincial (Duplessis in Québec) and federal (under Prime Minister Mulroney) levels of government.

THE DUPLESSIS REGIME

The Duplessis regime in Québec is an example of systematic corruption throughout an entire provincial government. Maurice Duplessis dominated Québec politics by forming four consecutive governments, beginning in 1944 and ending in 1959. Through his conservative, rural-based Union Nationale Party, Duplessis managed to create a secretive and formidable government machine that intimidated the political opposition, the media and interest groups, including those representing businesses and corporations attempting to secure government contracts. For his part, Duplessis ruled his party machine in a manner not unlike that of a Latin American dictator, unsurpassed in his ruthlessness and contempt for established political rules and procedures (Roberts, 1963). As part of his tyrannical approach, he demanded total loyalty from his supporters, which included supporting and actively participating in corrupt electoral practices. Duplessis blatantly violated basic civil rights such as freedom of religion, political expression and economic association. Nonetheless, he was able to sustain his reign through the help of his rural, conservative Catholic supporters, who regarded him as a champion of French-Canadian autonomy and traditional values.

Although Duplessis was required to abide by certain constitutional and representative democratic processes, such as periodic elections, he and his Union Nationale party essentially developed their own political process in Québec. An important facet of this alternative process involved the "kickback" scheme, whereby businesses and key government-related institutions (such as hospitals) would add a specified percentage to their government contract costs. These additional sums would subsequently be distributed to particular designated officials or government friends (Roberts, 1963). This scheme became particularly lucrative when the developing industrial infrastructure and welfare state required contracts involving enormous capital and operational costs in areas such as highways, massive hydroelectric projects, schools, hospitals and universities. Transactions of this sort were institutionalized and commonplace during Duplessis's tenure.

Another notorious example of corrupt practices perpetrated for personal financial gains is the Hydro-Québec scandal. In 1958, nine cabinet ministers, ten other elected officials and a close personal friend of Duplessis engineered a "20-million-dollar market coup" in connection with the private sale of the gas-distribution assets of Hydro-Québec. The plan involved purchasing shares in the corporation at low "pre-issue" prices and later selling them for a significant profit once public trading in the new company began (Roberts, 1963). In retrospect, it appears that the entire Hydro-Québec affair really epitomized the arrogant level of corruption practiced under Duplessis. Trans-Canada, the private firm interested in purchasing Hydro-Québec, was virtually blackmailed into compliance with the scheme, even though the government was not in a legal position to sell public assets. Although both a commission of inquiry into the sale of Hydro-Québec assets and an investigation by the newspaper *Le Devoir* later detailed the conflict of interests of government officials and others involved in the conspiracy, Duplessis dismissed the allegations as "gutter journalism" and even defended the right of his ministers to make such investments and profits (Roberts, 1963). Despite the admittedly unique socio-

political context capitalized upon and fostered by Duplessis, the institutionalized corruption of his regime cannot be simply attributed to the parochial
politics of a rural and conservative Francophone society undergoing a fundamental transition to an urban, industrial and cosmopolitan society (Corrado et
al., 1992). Political corruption was not confined to Québec, but rather was also
evident in the federal political process.

THE RIVARD AND SKY SHOPS AFFAIRS

In 1963, purported underworld figure Lucien Rivard was being detained
in Canada at the request of the U.S. Department of Justice pending his extradi-
tion to that country to face charges relating to an alleged conspiracy to smuggle
heroin into the United States from Mexico. Lawyer Pierre Lamontagne, retained by the U.S. government to represent its case against releasing Rivard on
bail, claimed that an executive assistant of the immigration minister offered
him $20,000 if he would agree not to oppose bail for Rivard. Lamontagne
maintained that further pressure to accept the bribe was exerted by two aides
affiliated with the Canadian Department of Justice. As in the past, those implicated in the scandal denied involvement, and again the subsequent RCMP
investigation of the allegations was inept. Consequently, the Dorion Royal
Commission (1965) was created to investigate the Rivard affair. What emerged
from the hearings was an image of greedy political officials willing to accept
money from even notorious underworld figures in order to further political
ambitions. The illicit attempts to influence Rivard's bail proceedings revealed
the indebtedness of even senior politicians to their sources of funding. Although irrefutable proof was never obtained, the Rivard affair was a deeply
disturbing political scandal because there were serious suggestions that the
specter of organized crime had successfully infiltrated the federal cabinet.

The Sky Shops affair revealed a process of corruption in the sphere of the
federal government during the early 1970s. The scandal involved two prominent businessmen, Gordon Brown and Clarence Campbell, who offered
$95,000 to Liberal Senator Louis Giguère in exchange for his assistance in
reversing the federal transport ministry decision not to extend Sky Shop
Export Limited's lease to operate a duty-free shop at the government-owned
Dorval Airport in Montréal. Although Giguère's position as a senator was
largely ceremonial,[1] he was in fact very influential and had access to key government decision makers. Conspiracy charges were subsequently brought
against the two businessmen and Giguère for the arrangement, which allowed
the senator to purchase shares at a low cost and subsequently resell them at

enormous profit once the lease for Sky Shops Limited was extended and a new company bought Sky Shops at a substantially higher price per share.

Although Brown and Campbell were charged and convicted, Giguère was unexpectedly adjudicated not guilty of conspiring to accept a benefit. It was posited that Giguère had followed the normal political process of contacting the appropriate minister charged with rendering the final decisions of government contracts. Traditionally, decisions of this sort would depend on the political or financial payoffs for the party and/or the power of the particular politician advancing the request. Even though the original decision was unexpectedly reversed, all of the politicians involved denied accusations of corruption. The RCMP investigated whether any ministers were responsible for making recommendations on government contracts in Québec. Although the investigation brought no further charges, it was understood that the awarding of government contracts was linked to electoral finances: "The Sky Shops affair can be situated then in the days when electoral finances were traditionally secret. Contributions were paid to middlemen who then concerned themselves with refreshing the memory of the elected when it was time for granting contracts" (Pelletier, 1980:1). The opposition members of parliament and the media attacked the Liberal government for covering up the Sky Shops scandal and for not pursuing other conspirators, but the shroud of secrecy and official denial made uncovering the details of corruption very arduous. Indeed, this lack of access to incriminating evidence serves as a plausible explanation for the Giguère verdict.

"KICKBACK" ALLEGATIONS IN THE MARITIMES

Further examples of institutionalized corruption have been evidenced in the Maritime provinces. In Newfoundland, Frank Moores' Conservative government was accused by the Liberal opposition during the mid-1970s of egregious corruption within the public works department. There were even more grave accusations that evidence of the corruption was destroyed through arson (Plaskin, 1978). New Brunswick has similarly experienced highly controversial and unsatisfactorily resolved allegations of political corruption. "It has been an open secret for generations that patronage and other forms of questionable behavior are probably more dominant in New Brunswick than anywhere else in Canada" (Folster, 1977:23). In Nova Scotia in the 1980s, criminal prosecutions were successfully brought against Liberal party "bag men," individuals who's job it was to illegally extort money from interest groups and businesses.

– 64 –

As much as any single political figure, former New Brunswick premier Richard Hatfield epitomized corrupt government in the contemporary context. Hatfield originally rose to prominence in 1970, largely on a platform that emphasized honest government untainted by the corruption that had characterized previous administrations. In practice, however, Hatfield maintained the very same political "traditions" throughout the 1970s. He purportedly acquiesced to a kickback scheme under which companies attempting to secure government contracts had to pay a flat payment and/or four percent of their gross monthly income to the provincial Conservative Party finance committee. Hatfield denied the allegations, but he and some of his cabinet ministers apparently attended a meeting where the money collection scheme was devised.

It was additionally alleged that Hatfield received special considerations during a police investigation and his subsequent trial on a criminal drug charge relating to the possession of a small amount of marijuana. Hatfield was acquitted at the end of a very strange trial wherein the trial judge, a Hatfield appointee, accused a journalist of having planted the substantive evidence in Hatfield's luggage. When the journalist in question was immediately exonerated by the RCMP, Hatfield implied that the RCMP had conspired to damage his reputation by leaking to the media rumors surrounding the drug charge. In a later incident, Hatfield was publicly accused by two university students of providing them with drugs (including cocaine) and of paying their expenses to accompany him on an unofficial trip to Montréal. Prior to his trial, he personally approached both the federal Solicitor General (also a fellow Maritimer), who had the responsibility for the RCMP investigation, and the Justice Minister, who was ultimately responsible for final prosecutorial decisions. In this regard, Hatfield's actions clearly raised fundamental ethical and moral issues concerning special treatment before the law for a powerful political figure (Miller, 1985; Wood, 1985).

The tradition of political corruption in the Maritime provinces appears not to have abated. In 1990, accusations of misconduct were leveled against John Buchanan and the government of Nova Scotia. These included charges: that the Premier's cottage had been painted by government workers who were paid on government time; that friends and close associates of the Premier had been afforded preferential treatment in securing lucrative government contracts; and that he was occasionally the recipient of personal kickbacks. Buchanan vehemently denied all charges but was unable to offer evidence to the contrary. Following a sustained period of intense media scrutiny, the premier resigned his seat in the provincial legislature and was immediately appointed to the Senate by Prime Minister Brian Mulroney. It was revealed, after Buchanan's appointment, that the Conservative Party had paid him significant amounts of money to settle his debts and prevent his bankruptcy.

THE MULRONEY CONSERVATIVES

After sweeping to power in the fall of 1984, federal Prime Minister Brian Mulroney and his Progressive Conservative government firmly established themselves as one of the most corrupt and ethically bankrupt administrations in Canadian history. Instances of Tory indiscretion are as varied as they are numerous, including objectionable spending habits, blatant patronage and more widespread and insidious scandals (see Cameron, 1994). Lack of fiscal restraint characterized the entire Mulroney tenure. For example, it was revealed in 1985 that, over a five-month period, Defense Minister Robert Coates' personal expenses, primarily travel- and hospitality-related, were in excess of $70,000. For an excursion to Africa with his wife and one aide, Secretary of State Walter McLean spent well over $100,000. This outrageous misappropriation and abuse of public funds was not isolated but rather indicative of a recurrent pattern of irresponsibility. Mulroney's personal disregard for public funds was perhaps best exemplified by a $300,000 "loan" that he secured in 1987 from the PC Canada fund for custom renovations to his official residence.

Blatant patronage appointments to government positions were manifest throughout Mulroney's terms in office, despite the fact that he had originally been elected in part on the strength of a platform that pledged to reform a perverted patronage system. During his first four months in office, Mulroney approved some 150 "Order-in-Council" appointments, including patronage afforded to clearly unqualified individuals. In 1986, Tory organizer and fund-raiser William Hawkins was appointed to the Textile and Clothing Board, despite his confessed ignorance of textiles or clothing. That same year, Supply and Services Minister Stewart McInnes ordered the hiring of Conservative Party members as census commissioners, despite the fact that several had previously failed the routine examination administered to potential candidates (Corrado, 1992). Moreover, conspicuous evidence of patronage was by no means restricted to political positions and offices; the process of awarding governmental contracts was equally corrupt. During the length of stay in office, the vast majority of public works contracts in Québec (Mulroney's home province) and almost half of all contracts over $5,000 went untendered. Finally, Mulroney's government was characterized by grievous abuses of the public trust. In 1986, Member of Parliament Marcel Gravel was formally charged with 50 counts of bribery, influence peddling, and abuse of trust in connection to his attempt to elicit $100,000 from companies proposing to do business with the government.[2] The next year, Minister of State Roch LaSalle was forced to resign amidst almost identical circumstances.

While the preceding discussion does not represent a comprehensive examination of political corruption in Canada, it does provide a sample of the type and range of corrupt political practices in this country. Political corruption is not, however, the only manifestation of state crime in Canada. Primarily as a result of the McDonald and Keable Commissions, a substantial body of evidence indicates that the Security Service branch of the Royal Canadian Mounted Police (RCMP-SS) was at times guilty of systematic violations of the law.

ILLEGAL ACTIVITIES OF THE RCMP SECURITY SERVICE

Given the close military ties between Canada and the United States, including both the North Atlantic Treaty Organization (NATO) and the North American Air Defence System (NORAD), the Cold War between the U.S. and the Soviet Union involved Canada almost by default. Because of its close geographical proximity to the U.S., Canada provided a central strategic military location to combat the Communist threat. In this Cold War context, the security division of the RCMP increased its monitoring of citizens suspected of subversive activities. Unfortunately, the RCMP was deficient in the organizational resources required for this delicate work. Members of the Security Services were drawn from the ranks of regular police officers, few of whom possessed the university training necessary to gather and appropriately analyze information regarding the ideological dispositions of Canadians. Beyond this assessment, officers then were required to make determinations concerning proper response mechanisms (Sawatsky, 1980).

In retrospect it is clear that, in numerous cases, the RCMP proved unable to distinguish between legitimate and illegitimate forms of "subversive" expression. The McDonald Commission (the Royal Commission of Inquiry into Certain Activities of the Royal Canadian Mounted Police) was appointed in 1977 to investigate the RCMP's security division. This commission, along with the Keable Commission (convened by the Québec Minister of Justice in the same year) and subsequent criminal trials, confirmed a series of illegal and questionable activities. The picture that emerged was of a largely autonomous clandestine agency that was quite out of control.

They have burned a barn, stolen dynamite, engaged in surreptitious entries for investigative purposes, harassed suspected extremists, arranged questionable access to government records never intended for police purposes, falsified documents, engaged in prima facie illegal search and seizure, opened mail in direct contravention of postal legislation and copied the records of a legitimate political party [French and Belieau, 1979:1].

The illegal RCMP activities appear to have been precipitated by failure of the Security Service to prevent the terrorist actions of the Front de Libération du Québec (FLQ). In particular, the RCMP was widely criticized for and embarrassed by its ineffectual response to the October Crisis of 1970 (Pelletier, 1971).[3] Since it was generally conceded that the paucity of evidence surrounding the FLQ had made accurate assessments of their potential threat difficult, gathering detailed information about terrorist groups and potential terrorists, especially the FLQ, was adopted as the essential policy goal of the Security Service (SS). From this perspective, many of the subsequent crimes committed by the RCMP were perpetrated as part of an overly aggressive terrorism prevention strategy. Several incidents provide telling examples of the form and scope of repressive RCMP-SS activities perpetrated in the name of the federal government and national security.

FLQ COMMUNIQUÉS WRITTEN BY THE RMCP-SS

In December, 1971, the RCMP-SS itself incited Québec citizens to terrorism and sedition. In an attempt to discredit the FLQ and simultaneously alarm the population, the RCMP released a communiqué purportedly composed by the FLQ urging nationalists to take up arms and liberate Québec from oppression. It was revealed later that at least four such communiqués had been forged and attributed to non-existent cells of the FLQ. Ultimately, the fraudulent communiqués served only to justify the subsequent dirty-trick activities of the RCMP. In addition to being illegal, this behavior was morally and ethically bankrupt.

THEFT AND ARSON

The mysterious theft of a large quantity of dynamite from Richelieu Explosifs on 26 April was the first of two infamous events that occurred in the Spring of 1972. At the McDonald Commission hearings, three RCMP witnesses acknowledged the theft and provided contradictory evidence regarding the motives behind the thefts. One of the four stolen cases was recovered several months later by the Québec Police Force. The remaining 42 sticks of dynamite have never been accounted for. The second noteworthy incident occurred on May 8. Unable to properly monitor a pending meeting between Québec nationalists and the Black Panthers (an extremist group from the U.S.), the RCMP-SS chose instead to prevent the meeting by intentionally incinerating the scheduled meeting place — a barn at the P'tit Québec Libre farm.

OPERATIONS BRICOLE AND HAM

Operation Bricole involved the surreptitious entry by the RCMP-SS into the offices of three radical groups without a search warrant on 7 October 1972. Business records, financial statements, and membership rosters were removed. Following the operation, RCMP officials were instrumental in efforts to cover up "overzealousness" of their subordinates (Dion, 1982). Six years later, in front of the McDonald Commission, former RCMP commissioner Nadon admitted that Operation Bricole had been officially approved and had proceeded on nothing more substantial than mere suspicion.

Operation Ham, carried out on 8 January 1973, similarly involved illicitly entering the offices of the Parti Québécois, a completely legitimate political party. The operation was authorized by the Director General of the Security Service and supported by Prime Minister Pierre Trudeau and his ministers. The RCMP justified the operation as a strong preventive measure to protect national security. The Prime Minister argued that certain illegal steps may be necessary when national security is threatened, suggesting further that even broader powers might not be unreasonable.

MISCELLANEOUS CRIMES

In the course of his testimony for the McDonald Commission, Deputy RCMP Commissioner Stanley Chisholm confirmed that Operations Ham and Bricole were not isolated incidents and that break-ins and unauthorized wire taps were common practices. He revealed that between the years 1971 and 1978 alone, 47 surreptitious entries were conducted and 580 clandestine electronic devices were planted. Nor were the covert operations of the Security Service limited to businesses and offices. With the assistance of federal civil servants, the RCMP was able to garner access to the files of the Unemployment Insurance Commission. The RCMP similarly violated the Income Tax Act by receiving confidential information from tax returns under a secret, cabinet-approved agreement with the Minister of Revenue. The RCMP directly contravened the Post Office Act by routinely opening private mail as part of Operation CATHEDRAL between 1954 and 1976. The RCMP-SS also commonly applied physical force, blackmail, and intimidation to coerce informants and suspected "subversives" (Dion, 1982). Superintendent Donald Cobb vehemently denied all allegations of physical abuse, euphemistically suggesting instead that the officers merely persuaded informers with "offers they couldn't refuse."

These illustrations of illegal activities perpetrated by the RCMP security service, advanced in conjunction with the examples of political corruption provided earlier, serve to establish a conceptual framework of the types and ranges of behavior that define the phenomenon of state crime in Canada. It is readily apparent that government crime in Canada is not limited to any particular historical period, political party, geographic unit, or level or agency of government. Given its heterogeneous nature, it is highly unlikely that a single theoretical orientation would be able to adequately address the issue of state crime. Instead, a variety of theoretical perspectives are required for a full accounting of illicit government behavior.

THEORETICAL PERSPECTIVES ON STATE CRIME

Crime and criminality generally may be analyzed across three distinct levels: individual, organizational and societal (Corrado, 1991). Each of these levels corresponds to a particular explanation or perspective of how democracy and representation is achieved. They are the representative democratic, pluralist democratic and capitalist democratic perspectives. By extension each of these explanations for democracy provide cogent explanations for the cause of state crime and its attendant controls (Corrado, 1992).

In order to adequately understand state crime, it is necessary to approach it from a variety of theoretical perspectives. The representative democratic perspective is premised on the formal aspects of democracies and generally conceptualizes state crime in terms of individual offenders. On the other hand, the pluralist democratic approach emphasizes the processes of negotiation and accommodation that characterize politics in advanced industrial nations. According to this approach, state crime is the result of the inevitable competition between group interests. Finally, the capitalist democratic orientation is derived from Marxist theory and asserts that economic and social structures are the root causes of state crime.

CONTROLLING STATE CRIME IN CANADA

The theoretical perspectives provide more than analytic frameworks for particular instances of state crime. Each of the perspectives also carries with it strong implications concerning appropriate responses to the problem. The representative democratic orientation asserts that individual motivations and the lack of restraining laws are responsible for state crime. Consequently, it follows that state crime would best be controlled through criminal sanctions and legislative reforms. In contrast, the pluralist democratic approach, with its focus on organizations and interest groups, suggests that state crime should be addressed through measures to mediate the effects of organizational culture and the structure of interest group relations. Finally, the capitalist democratic perspective, emphasizing the structure of political and economic power, necessarily concludes that only a significant restructuring of the Canadian social order can result in the attenuation of state crime. These and other control-related issues are evaluated in the following section.

EXISTING STATUTORY FRAMEWORKS AND INDIVIDUALIZED CONTROLS

Attempts to control state crime in Canada have generally focused on criminal trials or legislative changes. Although it is underutilized, there is a statutory framework with strong prohibitions against many forms of political crime contained within the *Canadian Criminal Code*. It is worthwhile to note that frauds on the government (s.121), breach of trust by a public officer (s.122), municipal corruption (s.123), selling or purchasing of offices (s.124) and influencing or negotiating appointments or dealing in offices (s.125) are specifically mentioned among the types of behavior prohibited by the *Code*. All of the above-mentioned actions constitute indictable offenses and carry substantial penalties.

In addition to the criminal provisions of the *Code*, there are numerous other regulatory schemes directed towards conduct broadly conceived as "conflicts of interest." The *Parliament of Canada Act* contains a series of restrictions concerning Senators and Members of Parliament. Senators, for example, are prohibited from being party to any government contract or from receiving any form of compensation for service rendered in relation to any matter before Parliament (ss. 14-16). According to the *Rules of the Senate of Canada*, Senators are forbidden to vote on any matter in which they have a pecuniary interest not available to the general public (s. 49). Moreover, senators holding a pecuniary interest in any question before a select committee are barred from sitting on said committee (s. 75). The *Standing Orders of the House of Commons* contains similar provisions for members of Parliament (s. 21), and further prohibits bribery at elections and offering advantages to MPs for promoting a matter to be transacted in Parliament. Finally, the most explicit provisions regarding conflicts of interest are contained within two federal initiatives, the *Conflict of*

Interest and Post-Employment Code for Public Office Holders and a companion volume, the *Conflict of Interest and Post-Employment Code for the Public Service.*

A final set of laws worthy of mention in the context of state crime are the statutes pertaining to election finance laws in Canada. The *Canada Elections Act,* for example, sets out a registration procedure through which parties gain access to public funding in the form of income tax credits, partial reimbursement of election expenses and free broadcasting time. More specific regulations are contained within the *Election Expenses Act.*

For a variety of reasons, existing provisions of the type listed above have had a negligible impact on the prevalence and incidence of state crime. Rules and regulations are insufficient to cope with ever-widening spectrum of unethical and criminal behavior. Even supporters of individualized controls must concede their limitations.

> Certain problems, such as conflicts of interest or the leaking of government information, can be regulated to some extent by written rules, but even in these areas rules are often difficult to apply to concrete cases [Kernaghan, 1994:174].

Extensive modifications of electoral law, campaign financing rules and conflict of interest guidelines have failed to significantly diminish the prevalence of state criminal activity. Legislation is inherently limited in its ability to cope with what is essentially system-wide behavior, and overreliance on the legalistic response has contributed to the perpetuation of state crime by allowing the system to occasionally sacrifice individual perpetrators in order to protect the underlying power structure. Any public interest or consternation stirred by a sensationalized corruption scandal is quickly vitiated by a criminal trial that produces a scapegoat while simultaneously confirming the status quo among the power elite.

That state crime has continued unabated, demonstrates that criminal prosecutions have exhibited neither a specific deterrent effect on individual perpetrators nor a general deterrent effect on other elites. Given that corruption of some form is endemic to the majority of political administrations in Canada, the relative infrequency of trials for this sort of behavior clearly illustrates that the probability of any one person facing criminal justice sanctions is quite remote. Even when evidence of political misconduct is brought to light, successful prosecutions are not always forthcoming.

Despite the fact that his alleged co-conspirators were convicted, Senator Giguère was acquitted in the Sky Shops affair. Former New Brunswick Premier Hatfield was similarly able to elude conviction on a number of charges stemming from different incidents. In other cases, accused individuals avoided potential sanctions by resigning. Nova Scotia premier Buchanan gave up his legislative seat, only to receive immediate appointment to a lucrative Senate position. In cases where legal guilt is established and sanctions are forthcoming, the severity of the punishment imposed is often disproportionately low in relation to the social harm generated by state crimes. Those few RCMP officers ultimately convicted as a result of McDonald Commission disclosures received comparatively light sentences, and cases in which political figures have been subject to more than symbolic censure are exceedingly rare. Finally, even where a whole government has been held accountable for corrupt practices and has been voted out of office, nothing significant has been done to keep the new authority from acting in precisely the same self-interested manner. The transition from corrupt Liberal to corrupt Conservative practices in 1988 was immediate and entirely seamless.

The contention that individuals are largely irrelevant with respect to controlling state crime suggests by default that interest group dynamics and power structures are the more appropriate foci of attention. It does not, however, imply that the conduct of particular individuals should be condoned in any way. On the contrary, state criminals should be tried, convicted and sentenced in a manner more consistent with the gravity of the harm this conduct produces. Concentrating on organizational- and structural-level factors merely acknowledges that individualized responses to specific instances do nothing to inhibit the contextual conditions that facilitate state crime (de Leon, 1993). Prevention instead requires addressing the systemic organizational arrangements and power structures that provide both the motivation and opportunity for state crime to be perpetuated. Focusing on the individual is ineffective because individuals are only part of the larger problem. It is in the best interest of elites, however, that state crime controls remain limited to the individual offender level; criminal trials generally satiate an ill-informed public and obfuscate the central role of systems, processes, institutions and structures.

Occasionally, apparently significant legislative changes directed towards more fundamental structural considerations are introduced. In 1984, the *Canadian Security Intelligence Service Act* (Bill C-9) mandated sweeping transformations to the structure of intelligence operations in Canada. It established a new agency, the Canadian Security Intelligence Service (CSIS), as a civilian agency that inherited some of the security and intelligence functions formerly under the auspices of the RCMP. In addition, the *CSIS Act* also created a three-tiered system of oversight and review. Despite the best intentions of legislators, however, the RCMP was largely successful in corrupting the implementation of the *CSIS Act*. Although the RCMP had vehemently opposed civilian intrusion into its jurisdiction, the revelations from the McDonald Commission proceedings made further defense very difficult. Instead of conceding, however, the RCMP simply changed tactics. Given that it could not block the passage of the new legislation, the force chose instead to manipulate its implementation. Specifically, the RCMP was able to staff the new agency almost exclusively with former Security Service officers. The Security Intelligence Review Committee (SIRC) noted in 1984 that 95% of Security Service members had transferred to CSIS, prompting then SIRC chairman Ron Atkey to inquire as to whether CSIS was simply "old wine in a new bottle" (Malarek, 1985:3). While the "legal culture" response to state crimes committed by the RCMP initially appeared to be quite meaningful, in practice it was largely ineffective. Despite new laws, organizational structures and control mechanisms, matters changed very little (Farson, 1991).

ORGANIZATIONAL CULTURE

A synthesis of individual and group-based responses suggests that modifying organizational cultures is an essential first step in controlling state crime. The pluralist democratic perspective implies that group dynamics are more central to the issue of control than are individuals. But it is important to conceptualize group dynamics in an appropriate fashion. "Dynamics" includes: attitudes and patterns of behaviors, and is not restricted to structural considerations. Too often, proposed changes to organizations highlight methods of political and administrative control, clarifying lines of communication and chains of command and limiting individual discretion and autonomy. In the context of controlling state crime, the relationships between structures and attitudes manifest in these organizations are of much greater consequence (Farson, 1991). The "ethical culture" of any organization is contingent not upon rules, but on the values, beliefs and attitudes of the individuals comprising the organization (Langford, 1994). Addressing the group dynamics of state crime necessarily requires changing the nature of the organizations involved.

The earlier RCMP-SS example definitively showed that externally implemented mechanisms are unlikely to be very successful and that a balance between formal and informal methods of organizational control is a prerequisite to containing state crime. Despite the fact that CSIS is accountable to three distinct levels of oversight and review, charges of misconduct have continued. After the director of CSIS resigned and a number of senior staff "retired" in the midst of disclosures that CSIS had provided false information in a critical wiretap application, an Independent Advisory Team (IAT) was commissioned under Gordon Osbaldeston (a senior bureaucrat). Among other things, Osbaldeston recommended remodeling CSIS's corporate culture (Independent

Advisory Team, 1987). Despite legislative changes, CSIS's practical orientation remained largely unchanged; it was business as usual. As Farson argues, "attempting to deal with the scandals of the present without dealing with the fundamental cultural factors of the past is like blowing into the wind" (1991:205). While it remains to be seen if changes to the organizational culture of CSIS will be more effective than previous individualized or legislative responses to controlling state crime, at the very least the emphasis on group dynamics is a positive step in a new and potentially more significant direction. Unfortunately, it is more questionable whether cultural approaches can effect substantive change at the upper echelons of power.

HIGHER IMMORALITY AND THE POWER ELITE

Although the RCMP has established itself as a formidable institution, it is nonetheless a subordinate agency and is ultimately subject to the political will of its masters. The RCMP was able to forestall changes for many years, in effect by making political opposition not worth the effort; it was also in a position to manipulate the implementation of legislated changes it was unable to prevent. Still, it appears that, with the Osbaldeston report, the government may finally be making a concerted effort to reign in its watchdog. But while the government may be capable of controlling the illegalities of organizations under its auspices if it is so inclined, there is less reason to believe that political leaders will, collectively, ever be similarly motivated to seriously address their own criminal behavior. This realization, in turn, raises sobering questions about whether appropriate responses to state crime at the highest levels will ever be less elusive. The pluralist democratic perspective presents arguably useful alternatives to controlling some types of instrumental institutions, but it appears to be much less applicable to those in much stronger positions of resistance. In practical terms, this approach has a more difficult time answering the question of "who governs the governors." Who, in the individual or plural sense, is in a position to mandate change on the state itself?

In the 1950s, sociologist C. Wright Mills (1956) introduced the concept of a power elite, comprised of political, economic and military leaders in American society. With the exception of the military industrial complex, Wright's notion of the power elite is equally relevant to the Canadian context. The political and economic worlds are intimately related to one another, with power in these spheres of influence being concentrated and centralized in the hands of relatively few individuals. Mills's framework, which accords well with the pluralist democratic perspective, implies that state crime reflects institutionalized deviance within the ranks of the power elite. The construct that links the power elite to state crime and accounts for institutionalized criminality is referred to as "higher immorality," described by Mills as a *moral insensibility* among the most wealthy and powerful of the corporate and political elite (see Krisberg, 1975). Predicated on the desire to further monopolize power and capital, higher immorality is inevitably translated into a variety of unethical, corrupt and illegal practices that are systematic and institutionalized in the exercise of power.

The existence and functioning of a power elite further reaffirms that individuals are inappropriate foci in controlling state crime. Because political and corporate organizations are so goal-oriented, they are characteristically amoral, tending to justify and accept whatever means are necessary to accomplish specified objectives. Consequently, the deviance of these organizations cannot be explained adequately by the personalities of the individuals involved. Overemphasizing "character" is myopic insofar as it fails to recognize the potentially corrupting influence of circumstance and situation (Langford and Tupper, 1994). Given that a person may be "good," but act "badly" in pursuit of organizational objectives, it is more prudent to attend to contextual factors. Simon and Eitzen (1990) posit that there are three primary conditions that facilitate the "bad" acts of individuals. First, the potential benefits presented by state crime vastly outweigh the risks of apprehension and penalty. Second, in the process of perpetuating power and accumulating profit, members of the elite are, by virtue of their near monopoly of information, protected by a shield of invisibility. Finally, the structure and inner workings of the contemporary political economy contribute significantly to state crime. The limited possibilities of controlling state crime through individual sanctions has already been examined. However, controls logically derived to confront the "shield of invisibility" and "political economy" issues have not yet been articulated.

THE ROLE OF THE MASS MEDIA

In Canada, as in other advanced industrial societies, the mass media are central agents in the social construction of reality about all types of deviance, including state crime. In the process of shaping the boundaries of social order, the media inevitably legitimize the authority of certain control agencies and offices, offering these agencies preferential access to constituents and the ability to define important events and issues in their own terms. In doing so, the media necessarily contribute to the construction of social order.

> They are control agents themselves, using their power of imprinting reality in the public culture to police what is being done in the mi-

crocultures of bureaucratic life, including especially the activities of other control agencies [Ericson et al., 1987:356].

As the most common stock of knowledge about deviance, the news discourse is saturated with intra- and inter-organizational negotiations, differences and conflicts regarding meaning, power, and moral norms. These conflicts arise as bureaucracies struggle for control over problem definition and solution as a vehicle for asserting claims to authority.

Because they control (in the sense of selection, filtration and presentation) communications, journalists are powerfully located among the deviance-defining elite. A particularly important aspect of this power is the ability to systematically legitimize other members and practices of the deviance-defining elite; only certain organizations are allowed to routinely pass judgment on what is acceptable or unacceptable in the public forum. By the same token, the media also have the ability to undermine the legitimacy and authority of the deviance-defining elite. If the news media are institutions of social control, then journalists are the agents. As sources of knowledge, reporters can be catalysts of organizational change. As part of the political system, they contribute to the policing of organizational life. In less competitive markets, the corporate power of news agencies allows for selective forays into adversarial journalism, particularly exposes of government targets. Beyond these forays, institutional ties between the media and major bureaucratic sources can help to ensure a continued policing relationship. To the extent that journalists report on organizational deviance and state crime, they find themselves engaged in reform politics; news media institutions are significant contributors to the knowledge-power-control relations in society (Ericson et al., 1987). Regrettably, several political economic realities conspire to limit the practical effectiveness of the media as a mechanism for controlling state crime.

Although rational political dialogue requires knowledge of the type that only the media are capable of providing, the actual political discourse provided by the media is often very limited. Because they most often are denied direct access to the inner workings of the governing elite, the media are forced to rely heavily on particular elite members, spokespersons whose functions includes the dissemination of information. These persons may not have all of or even the best knowledge, but they are imbued with specific political authority. By constantly referring and deferring to the valued facts of authorized knowers, the media are able to offer the most common sense articulation of knowledge. In addition to securing access, the media profile the views of designated disseminators in order to bolster their own legitimacy. While the media are influential in establishing legitimacy for certain control agencies, these agencies in turn reciprocate and perform an analogous service for the media.

There is considerable evidence suggesting that members of the general public are skeptical and suspicious of the media. For example, survey research has indicated that a significant proportion of individuals perceive the news as serving certain corporate and special interests (Royal Commission on Newspapers, 1981). Although a greater proportion of people are becoming aware that the news is highly interpretive, speculative, selective, distorted and partial, they are nonetheless disposed to accept the legitimacy of media reports to the extent that they are construed by those with the most value in the social hierarchy of credibility (Ericson et al., 1987). Any legitimacy afforded the media is due to the fact that it reflects the views of the politically powerful; any claims to authority are really premised on the legitimacy of regularly cited sources. The media are rendered ineffectual in controlling state crime because of the necessity of maintaining institutional ties that are central to the journalistic enterprise.

The ability of the media to function as an effective agent for controlling state crime is further diminished by the fact that the mainstream media are themselves subject to market-force considerations of profit. The excessive concentration of ownership in the newspaper industry in Canada (as well as many other advanced industrial countries), is but one example of the financial imperatives evident in journalism. Simply stated, media institutions are businesses that inevitably respond to the fiscal environment like any other such organization. In the preceding discussion, this translated into the doctrinal practice of not alienating your sources. But business survival also requires compliance with the demands of the clientele, or in this case, the audience. For the present purpose, the most important facet of this compliance is the confluence between news and entertainment; as dictated by the consumer, the news largely focuses on personalities and characters, as opposed to substance. This is particularly evident in the phenomenal success of news magazine shows that appear to generally avoid "hard" news, unless it is of the very sensational variety. In short, trends requiring that news be simultaneously entertaining may have the unintentional consequence of ensuring that dry news concerning the machinations of the political and economic elite remains less "newsworthy" in comparison to more interesting but far less meaningful topics.

It would appear, then, that attempts to control state crime through public exposure, though logically defensible, are unlikely to result in substantive change. The improbability of individual or organizational solutions would seem to imply that only through drastic modifications to the political, social or economic structures is state crime likely to be contained.

THE POLITICAL SYSTEM

The decline of the representative capability of the Canadian Parliament due to its domination by an all-powerful cabinet and a burgeoning, unchecked bureaucracy has been the topic of great speculation for decades. At present, the system is a democratic charade that prevents members of all parties from properly representing their constituents. The system must be changed if it is ever to gain respect. To that end, Fife and Warren (1991) identify four means for reviving Parliament: less stringent party discipline, free votes, autonomous party committees and an elected Senate to represent the regions. The party discipline that is tighter than any other Parliament in the world and has served to neuter Parliament must be relaxed. The proceedings in the Commons have been characterized as farcical, culminating in votes that are predetermined (and very costly) wastes of time. Consequently, serious debate instead takes place "behind the curtains," among MPs from all parties. Ultimately, such clandestine negotiations jeopardize the legitimacy of the policy-making process in Canada. One manifestation of this new "openness" would surely be the existence of free votes. Whereas MPs currently vote without exception as directed by party whips, free voting would allow MPs to more accurately represent local interests, simultaneously demonstrating that Parliament has a *real* function and an interest in acting in accordance with the people's wishes. The costs of defeats on particular items would be more than offset by gains in honest reputation. Free votes have similarly been proposed by Laschinger and Stevens (1992).

Most committee meetings are make-work projects for members whose reports will gather dust. Fife and Warren (1991) argue that, in order for the Commons to act as a counter-weight to government bureaucracy, it is imperative to imbue committees with more power. In contrast to the Canadian system, which was devised without an independent system of checks and balances and wherein the cabinet and Parliament are controlled by a single small group, Fife and Warren cite the U.S. Congress and German Bundestag as examples of strong, working legislatures that conduct their work in vigorous, independent committees and come to act as effective watchdogs over the government. They maintain that an efficacious committee system could bring citizens back into the system (through the MPs), reduce partisanship and promote serious policy debate (Fife and Warren, 1991).

Finally, so long as the Senate exists as a final resting place for party hacks, meaningful political reform will remain frustrated. Fife and Warren (1991) suggest that the Senate must be transformed into an *elected* body representing Canada's diverse *regional* interests so that the regions may check the power of the Commons. The Senate is but one illustration of a badly abused system of patronage appointment. Simpson (1988) chronicles a history of blatant patronage in the federal system, as well as in all 10 provinces. While Simpson is unable to provide an adequate prescription for the problem of patronage, he nonetheless highlights a concern that has become an increasingly tangible electoral issue. Unfortunately, implementing the necessary reforms may be beyond the political will and ability of those who have created the present mess.

One of the major impediments to genuine, substantive reform is the reality of what Palango (1994:293) refers to as "controlling intersections of power." With the erosion of the RCMP's independence, and the politicization of the courts and judiciary through patronage, it has become exceedingly difficult for external agencies to monitor Parliamentary activities. In fact, the special all-party committee convened in 1989 to review the *Parliament of Canada Act* was primarily intended to further insulate parliamentarians from police search warrants (Palango, 1994). On the other hand, Parliament has demonstrated no inclination or desire to police itself. Pelletier charges that in consistently blocking due process and circumventing the rule of law, politicians have set themselves above the law (cited in Palango, 1994:296). In replacing the rule of law with the rule of politics (rule to please), politicians have created a two-tiered system of justice that threatens the integrity of the formal criminal justice system and raises more fundamental questions about the soundness of Canadian institutions generally. Disenchanted with the opportunism and cynicism prevalent in the political system, the Canadian public has become increasingly alienated from their elected representatives (Laschinger and Stevens, 1992). This crisis of confidence and loss of faith regarding the political process has inevitably affected all mainstream politicians and traditional parties and is alarming enough that it could act as a catalyst for significant changes to the political structure in Canada.

THE CAPITALIST ECONOMY

The intimate connections between political and economic considerations that seem to provide the context for a great deal of state crime suggest that modifications to the political structure should be accompanied by changes to the economic system. Indeed, approaches premised on changing the capitalist economy are explicitly advanced by the capitalist democratic perspective. The most widely advocated alternatives to capitalist democratic principles are, of course, those derived from the ideological "left" (see, for example, Alperovitz and Faux, 1984; Bowles et al., 1984; Harrington, 1984; Cohen and Rogers,

1983; Carnoy and Schearer, 1980; Hayden, 1980; Simon and Eitzen, 1990). Central to many of these positions is the supposition that the implementation of authentic socialism, in contrast to adulterated forms formerly practiced in Communist regimes, is both possible and desirable. Unfortunately, in comparison to other approaches, fundamental challenges to the capitalist economic system seem to be very limited in terms of their practicality and feasibility.

In addressing the policy implications of radical theory, Lynch and Groves (1989) assert a distinction exists between "desire to see" and "ability to do." Marx's prediction that mass social change would come whenever there was a fundamental change in the mode of production has not been born out historically. Absent a revolutionary class, revolution currently seems unlikely. The middle class is well enough off, while the lower class has no cohesiveness and less power than Marx's "proletariat." Lynch and Groves (1990) suggest that acknowledging the enormous problems inherent in implementing a socialist program is neither cynical or defeatist, but rather, is an accurate assessment of the limited extent to which superstructural institutions can inaugurate change in the economic/political sphere. To a considerable degree, this assessment is tempered by a distinction between long-term and short-term objectives; while fundamental systemic change may not be immediately forthcoming, there are middle-range policy alternatives and intermediate goals that do not compromise any overall design for fundamental social change (Cohen, 1979). Michalowski (1985), for example, maintains that crime should be defined according to amount of harm visited upon society so that the definition of crime and practice of crime control are no longer be organized along class lines. This would in turn equalize the treatment, prosecution, and policing of the crimes of both the powerless and powerful.

POLITICAL CULTURE

In light of the preceding discussion, it would appear that a compromise position, integrating the potential efficacy of structural change with the viability of middle-range initiatives, is theoretically the most promising strategy for addressing state crime. In the Canadian context, the most effective such compromise strategy might involve attempting to alter particular aspects of the Canadian political culture. As early as the mid-1970s, Gibbons (1976) asserted that the success of any program aimed at addressing a social ill such as corruption or abuse of authority, whether legislative or non-legislative, rests upon the foundation of a sympathetic political culture. Almond and Verba (1963) have employed the term "political culture" to refer to widely shared beliefs, attitudes, values and opinions about political authority, structures and processes.

The Canadian political culture is a mixture of liberalism, conservatism and socialism, interpreted by both the English and French cultures and marked by regional diversity. As importantly, Canadian political culture is characteristically "quasi-participative": as opposed to being active participants in the "political game," citizens are generally bystanders or spectators. The majority of the Canadian electorate perceives politics as more properly the purview of specialists and professionals (Kornberg et al., 1982).

The "quasi-participative" political value has resulted in a discernible trend toward "authoritarian democracy." Most liberal-democratic, capitalist societies have experienced structural changes that have led to "the increasing autonomy of the executive from the legislature, the increasing use of intersecretarial meetings by the government parties to decide policy in a way that bypasses the Cabinet as well as Parliament, the growth of the power of the bureaucracy over the political system and the development of new forms of representation based on the organization of a passive consensus" (Lumley and Schlesinger, 1982:605). Consequently, the tendency for many Canadians is to defer to the political elite and limit their personal involvement in politics to, at most, voting every four or five years. Reversing this tendency may be the most appropriate basis currently available for confronting state crime.

Changing the Canadian political culture, while certainly difficult, is more practical than fundamental structural modifications. Inglehart (1990) has argued convincingly that, although attributes of political culture are remarkably stable over time, they are nevertheless amenable to gradual change in specific circumstances. Of particular interest here, Inglehart posits that "as a result of three long-term processes linked with the evolution of advanced industrial society, mass publics are becoming more involved in politics." The three changes he cites as gradually increasing the potential for political participation of Western publics are: first, rising levels of education and political information; second, changing norms governing political participation by women; and third, changing value priorities (the rise of what Inglehart refers to as "postmaterial values"). While the effects of these changes have been masked by the countervailing decay of traditional political manifestations such as party machines, religious institutions and labor unions, the utility of addressing state crime through restructuring the modes of participation in the political process is clear. Increases in political discourse, unconventional forms of political participation and new social movements evident in advanced industrial societies suggest the potential for shifting from "elite-directed" to "elite-directing" political participation.

Appreciable progress in reducing state crime is unlikely until Canadians are willing to take greater interest in and responsibility for the conduct of elected officials and the political and economic elite. The notion of "elite-directing" politics implies exactly that; the public reclaiming some of the authority that it has abdicated. Without sounding trite, the Canadian electorate must reinvest in the precepts of genuine participatory democracy. Before state officials can be held liable for their conduct, the polity must first establish that it is sincerely interested in accountability and that criminal conduct in all of its manifestations will be punished in a manner commensurate with the harm inflicted by such behavior. Moreover, the concept of punishment must be tailored to the specific context; while it includes individual penalties in the traditional sense of criminal indictments and the like, it is broader than that. State crime is a group phenomena and should be punished as such. If entire governments were *consistently* voted out of office for infractions by even a few members, it is possible that the whole dynamic of group relations could be positively altered. The more cynical among us might contend that politics and government are about money. But without power, the opportunities for profit are summarily denied. Officials currently operate with relative impunity, secure in the knowledge that their actions will almost certainly not have significant repercussions. Furthermore, any sanctions that are brought forward against a particular individual almost never have broader ramifications for the "system." It may be impractical to attempt to implement sweeping changes to the fundamental structure of the system, but it is not unrealistic to believe that the system can be held accountable through exercise of the collective political will. State crime has flourished under a veil of secrecy, the maintenance of which is largely attributable to the inertia of apathy that has long characterized the association between the Canadian public and its leaders. Overcoming that inertia would provide the impetus for a far more equitable relationship, simultaneously asserting more consequential controls over state crime.

THE CHANGING NATURE OF STATE CRIME IN CANADA: THE FUTURE OF CONTROL

While there are clearly aspects of the Canadian political system that need to be improved, there is presently no need for fundamental structural changes. In some respects, the Parliamentary system contains elements that, if properly utilized, is quite effective in controlling official misconduct. In contrast to the U.S. system, where members of the political elite are protected from direct confrontation by the separation of the executive from the legislature, the nature of Parliamentary debate in Canada subjects the government to the potential for immediate and dramatic embarrassment. Moreover, in light of the damaging exposés of Mulroney's tenure (e.g., Cameron, 1994; Simpson, 1988), the ability of the state to engage in some forms of classic corruption has declined. Despite the concerted efforts of the Reform Party to uncover misconduct of any kind, there have as yet been no significant scandals associated with the present Liberal government. It is possible that the massive excesses of the Mulroney government were finally enough to shake the collective apathy of the Canadian public and initiate the requisite changes in political culture. There is hope yet that more drastic structural modifications may be avoidable.

This is not to suggest that the relative stasis in the level of political corruption could not become unbalanced in the future. For example, many government contracts are still extremely lucrative and offer the potential for serious political manipulation. Because of the overwhelming temptations in this area, the fairness of bidding procedures for public contracts should be subject to an independent review panel that would include non-political appointees (such as judges). Beyond these review panels, the theme of *political independence* generally should serve as the cornerstone for prospective state crime controls. There is significant evidence that Canadian prosecutorial agents, or Crown Counsels, came to be heavily influenced by the Mulroney government (Cameron, 1994). Consequently, one can advance a strong argument in favor of independent prosecutors and a police force independent of malicious political intervention. The success of the independent prosecutorial system in the U.S. provides a solid guide in this regard. Prior to attempting drastic structural changes, it is more appropriate to first provide the criminal justice system with the autonomy necessary to properly perform its function.

In contrast, there is reason to believe that changes in the context of national security and intelligence could increase the incidence of state crimes in the near future. The end of the Cold War and the decline of violent Québécois nationalism have prompted a shift in the nature of the threat from the state. Since 1917, and particularly since the defection of Igor Gouzenko in 1945, the thrust of illegal state activities have been anti-Communist in nature. In the late 1960s, the focus shifted briefly to Québécois terrorists. But as we enter the 21st century, the nature of espionage and subversion has changed in several discernible ways. First, with the advent of computers, subversive activities of all types have reached unprecedented levels of sophistication. Second, with the increasing internationalization of economic structures, industrial espionage, organized crime and corporate crime are but a few of the new types of crimes that now represent threats to the *national* interest. Third, changes in immigration patterns and the massive influx of foreign capital have resulted in the emergence of several new and powerful crime groups, including the Japanese Yakuza, Chinese Triads and the Cali drug cartel. Fourth, other non-traditional threats, such as the Hells Angels and additional outlaw motorcycle gangs, have gained prominence. Finally, with its extended coastline and open border, Canada may come to serve as a crucial landing and transit point into the U.S. All of these changes have raised serious questions about the appropriate role of the state apparatus in the new order.

Collectively, the trends identified above serve to substantially increase the difficulty of carrying out the intelligence gathering and investigative functions of CSIS and the RCMP. Greater sophistication means that traditional police methods must be modified. This process of change operates on a lag effect that tends to leave enforcement officials in a position of perpetual "catch-up." The emergence of new ethnic and subcultural criminal organizations also poses a dilemma, in that these groups are much harder to infiltrate; accurate intelligence on these groups, necessary for effective monitoring and control, is largely absent. Consequently, in those instances where authorities feel compelled to employ very aggressive techniques in the name of national security, the probability of illegalities and misconduct is enhanced. The use of informants, agent provocateurs and plea bargaining, for example, brings the CSIS and RCMP into moral and ethical gray areas where a fine line separates the legitimate and illegitimate exercise of authority. Canada has thus far managed to avoid the worst excesses of "witch hunt" behavior evidenced in the U.S. during the Bureau of Alcohol, Tobacco and Firearms (BATF) siege at Waco, Texas or the Randy Weaver incident in Ruby Ridge, Idaho. It is imperative that we endeavor to avoid crossing that line in Canada.

In a pluralist democratic society, there is a tenuous balance between oversight that holds the state responsible when it crosses the line and interfering with the state's security function. The trick is maintaining that balance. For routine activities such as warrants and wiretaps, the courts, particularly since the advent of the *Charter of Rights and Freedoms* in 1982, have been effective in emphasizing individual rights and restricting the power of the state. It is presently impossible to assess the potential efficacy of adequate oversight in the Canadian context, because review mechanisms have never been properly implemented. In contrast, the Security Intelligence Review Committee (SIRC), the formal watchdog of CSIS, "has proved to be a failure: it has no teeth, and its part-time non-experts don't have the knowledge or access to the information they would need to be effective" (Cleroux, 1990:287). Structurally, the SIRC should be replaced with multi-party oversight committee with independent powers. Moreover, Parliamentary supervision must be engaged in and reinforced routinely, rather than simply used to respond to crises as they become apparent. A suitably designed system of Parliamentary oversight should precede the adoption of more extreme measures for controlling state crime in Canada.

SUMMARY

Because of the central role they play in the Canadian perception of state crime, the discussion here has focused on two specific forms of state crime: political corruption and the illegal activities of national security officials. These forms of state crime, which have a long and established history in Canada, continue to present a serious problem. As the opportunities for profit associated with government increase (particularly in the areas of lucrative contracts), so too will the incentives rise for illicit dealings between the political and economic elites. The changing context of intelligence operations in Canada further magnifies the potential for state crimes perpetrated in the name of national security.

Canadian responses to state crime have generally been predicated on the tenets of the representative democratic perspective; that is, they have overwhelming concentrated on the individual perpetrator through legislation or criminal trials. Because they are based on an oversimplified understanding of the phenomenon, individualized controls alone are insufficient for controlling state crime. A more complete program of control must address organizational and systemic dynamics as well. While there is reason to believe that controlling the activities of subordinate political agencies such as police is largely a matter of political will on the part of the power elite, it is less realistic to suggest that the same elite would ever implement the type of fundamental changes required to properly address the structural context of state crime. Ultimately, controlling state crime may best be accomplished through changes in the Canadian political culture. Specifically, controlling state crime is intimately related to the extent to which the Canadian public is willing to actively participate politically and engage in what Inglehart has referred to as "elite-directed" politics. In the meantime, individualized strategies involving the criminal justice system and Parliamentary oversight committees must be formulated so as to include the political autonomy required to operate effectively.

NOTES

1. Senate positions within Canada do not carry with them the prominence afforded senators in the United States. The Canadian Senate rarely opposes legislation passed in the House of Commons, the principal seat of governmental authority. Moreover, Canadian Senators are political appointees, often chosen for their longstanding support for the party in power.

2. Gravel's case dragged out until 1988, when he finally agreed to guilty pleas concerning 15 of the original charges.

3. During the 1960s, Québec (mostly Montréal) experienced a wave of bombings aimed at symbols of the federal Canadian government (e.g., postal boxes). The bombings were attributed to Quebecois separatists. The October Crisis of 1970 occurred when one such group, the Front de Liberation du Quebec (FLQ) kidnapped Labour Minister Pierre LaPorte and British trade official James Cross. The former's body was subsequently discovered in the trunk of car.

FIVE.
CONTROLLING STATE CRIME IN ISRAEL: THE DICHOTOMY BETWEEN NATIONAL SECURITY VERSUS COERCIVE POWERS

by

R. Reuben Miller

THE FOUNDERS OF modern Israel had an idealistic and utopian view of the new state. They believed that Israel would shine "light unto all nations."[1] From its inception, the new state faced numerous challenges — to create political institutions, economic and social organizations, and military defense capability in the post colonialist era. Like many other modern countries that gained independence, the new Jewish state experienced crises, scandals, insurmountable difficulties, and repeated political, diplomatic, economic, and military assaults.

The most difficult task for the new state was, and still is, to guarantee national security. This responsibility was assumed by the Israeli Defense Forces (IDF) (i.e., the military) and the intelligence community.[2] Considering the geopolitical conditions of the Middle East region, the issue of national security in Israel became an obsession. This continuous political and military environment posed the basic dilemma facing any liberal democracy.[3] How to bridge the gap between guaranteeing national security that requires certain undemocratic measures while protecting personal freedoms? Could Israel ensure individual safety for its people without violating human rights and civil liberties? How can a democracy, with a free press and civil rights record for its citizens, conduct itself and keep the balance between protecting national security and preserving the primacy of the law?

There is a fine line between these challenges. Any liberal democratic state finds itself walking on a tight rope trying to preserve both ends without violating the other. Law and order are the root foundation of any stable political system. Public institutions have to abide by the rule of law, and civil rights will be determined by these laws. If that foundation is destroyed by extremist groups then the whole system is bound to collapse.

Over the years, especially since 1967, gradual ethical and moral deterioration has taken place among those who have defended the country. This chapter will outline this process in Israel, and initiatives to control the decline. The first section will present the dichotomy between Israel's national security and its use of coercive powers against Palestinians. Thus, attention will be given to the various security forces. They were guided by principles and attitudes as defenders of the country. Ultimately, their perceptions allowed them to make the transition to coercive and abusive force.

The second section will examine three cases that illustrate the use of extreme powers of the state and its security forces that operated in the name of national security. It will explore the BUS #300 Affair, the Nafsu case, and the Jewish Underground that attacked Palestinians. All three cases are the embodiment of the state's coercive methods directed at one target — the Palestinian population in the occupied territories. Different branches of government are culpable, but the General Security Services (GSS) are the main abusers of state power.

The third section will explore acquiescence to these abuses emerging from the culture and national trust in the security forces, the IDF, and the legal system that protected them. Finally, this chapter will review the work of parliamentary commissions (i.e., institutional/formal controls) that investigated the GSS's involvement in the above-mentioned cases. It should be noted that there are other mechanisms in Israel that check and control against abuses of the coercive powers of the state. Among them are: the state comptroller, a number of non-governmental agencies and "watchdog" organizations, human rights organizations, the media, independent councils and individual activists. The discussion below will reveal the importance of the "informal" agents in exposing the security forces and their abusive powers.

CONCEPTUAL FRAMEWORK

The conquest of inhabited land by military force generates abuses of power by the occupier (Harsagor and Stroun, 1992). The mere act of occupation, despite the causes and the origins of the process that led to the occupation, suggests that there is a disparity between two groups: (1) occupier, and (2) occupied (Gal-Or, 1990).

From the outset these two groups enter into a collision course, and confrontation between them is inevitable. The close and daily interactions between such groups do not guarantee that integration and cooperation will develop as functionalist theory suggests. Even if the time lapsed from the initial occupation is prolonged, such development is highly unlikely. On the contrary, one can argue that the emotional tensions between the two actors, victor vis-à-vis loser, increase, especially when the initiator of the hostilities has lost the war. The animosity is innate, deeply rooted in the mind of the occupied party and transferred to the following generations (Shalev, 1990).[4]

The historic record illustrates that in the aftermath of war the triumphant party, always enjoying the upper hand, asserts its superiority over the conquered. Hence, it exercises authority, and assumes legal, political, economic, administrative, social, organizational and other powers. Eventually, the victor dictates the terms of conduct and behavior to the occupied (Benvenisti, 1992).

During the 1990s this process took place in a number of countries. The breakup of the Soviet Union unleashed such long held animosities among the various republics. Azarbijanis vis-à-vis the Armenians have been battling each other. The Croats and the Serbs have been fighting each other since June 1991, as have the Bosnians and other nationalities in the former Yugoslavia; the Baltic States versus the Soviet Union, Tibetans vis-à-vis Chinese. Iraq had fought the Kurds for a long time. So did Shiites and Christians in Lebanon, Palestinians and Kuwait, and finally Palestinians and Israel.

Tensions between the victorious government and the defeated people only intensify over time (Harsagor and Stroun, 1992). Even a benevolent foreign ruler such as the U.S. is often being projected in the occupied community as an antagonistic and coercive. A sense of nationalism develops in the ranks of the occupied while a sense of threat develops in the mind of the occupier (Benvenisti, 1992).

One can argue that the longer the occupation lingers on, the more the animosity gains momentum, broadens its appeal in the community and fosters alienation in the hearts and minds of the occupied. By the same token, the occupier develops fear of the occupied. Suspicion rises quickly, and threat perception develops in the mind of the victor, although the occupier has the ultimate power (Benvenisti, 1992).

To enhance its own sense of security the occupier resorts to harsh measures. The government launches various methods of control — military, administrative and legal. Over time the government in power develops paranoia that in due time grows and perpetuates itself. Its own perceptions of threat from the defeated party and sense of insecurity will increase over time. On the other hand the occupied community takes countersteps and fights back (Benvenisti, 1992).

The occupied party is also the weaker actor in military capability, and therefore has to resort to other methods. In addition to covert actions, there are legal and ethical weapons. In this day and age, the simplest and cheapest tools to battle occupation forces entail the use of propaganda. With the availability of electronic media, telecommunication systems and instantaneous global media reporting, these methods serve well the occupied and deprived community by exposing the occupiers' abuses of power.

The conquered party can use a two-pronged strategy: to portray the occupied as victims of atrocities, injustices and violations of human rights, and to project the image of the foreign rule as a criminal and coercive force. For example, many acts of law enforcement are presented to the world community as illegal and as violations of human/civil rights. This may generate pressure through international public opinion. Ultimately, the intent is to defame and discredit the occupier by any possible means.

Thus the cycle of action-reaction is perpetuated (Ross and Miller, 1997; O'Brien, 1991). Both parties become entrenched in their own perceptual worlds of reality. Each party sees the other as the aggressor and a "Catch 22" situation develops without any resolution in sight. And, when examining state crimes that are one stage in the cycle of violence, we are often removed from the full context of the events that led to this dead-end situation. The cycle of violence seldom occurs in a political vacuum. Naturally, one may wonder what possible solutions can alleviate the deep-rooted suspicions and tension between the two communities. Both communities have lived next to each other for a long time, but have never gotten to know and cooperate with each other. Why? What is the root cause of animosity?

ISRAEL'S SECURITY DILEMMA — A UNIQUE CASE

The circumstances that led Israel to exercise coercive powers have a long history. For many years Israel developed a sense of paranoia over the issue of national security (Bar, 1990). The centrality of security in Israeli society is the single most important issue (Levite, 1988), and it is crucial to the very existence of its polity (Pinkas, 1993). Thus the common term "the security situation" combines institutions, security perceptions and creed. The Israeli idea of national security is not a product of cognitive and rational process alone. Therefore, Israelis are haunted by the sense of vulnerability to the threat of extermination, sensitive to verbal threats and actual behavior of their neighbors. These fears have left many Israelis reluctant to accept a territorial compromise (Kaufman, 1993).

No one can deny the importance of geopolitical considerations in the complex and hostile Middle East landscape (Kaufman, 1993). The conception of national security stems from the collection of national experience and accumulative sense of fears. The Jewish-Israeli frame of mind includes a collective memory, centuries old, of persecution culminating in the traumatic experience of the Holocaust. With this national memory in the background, Israel always feels vulnerable. It has experienced conventional and guerrilla warfare on its home territory and potential threats unlike any other country in modern times. Therefore, Israeli society turned into a fighting force (Kaufman, 1993).

Animosity and mistrust between Arab and Jew developed in the early 1900s. In the beginning, tensions between these two groups were accompanied by bloody confrontations and Arab massacres of Jews (1919, 1929, 1936). Since independence (1948), Israel has experienced a continuous state of emergency and war over the largest period of its autonomous existence: a war in each decade (1948, 1956, 1967, 1973, 1982, 1991) (Kaufman, 1993). Between these major wars, the Israeli national experience has included other border clashes, infiltration of saboteurs, localized conflicts, sporadic wars of attrition and continuous terrorism.

In the Six Day War (1967), Israel conquered vast Arab territories inhabited by Palestinians (Muslims and Christians). Since then, the term and the idea of national security have been broadened to include the territories, incorporating the threat-security equation (Pinkas, 1993). According to Benvenisti, the Israeli-Palestinian conflict is internal in nature (*Ha'aretz*, 17 September 1991). Since 1987, the Intifada has served as a constant reminder of a violent existence. In February and March 1993, for example, the Intifada intensified. The public's perception was that no place was immune from attack and viewed it as a continuous "quiet war." The public accused the government of not doing enough to protect Israelis. Increased killings, knifings, shootings, vehicular homicides and other forms of assaults by Palestinians against Israelis have raised the public's level of frustration and impatience. Israelis often view Palestinian violent actions as a continuation of the anti-Jewish pogroms in Erez (the land of) Israel before 1948 (*Ha'aretz*, 17 September 1991). The cumulative effect of these events led Israel to become a garrison state (Lasswell, 1941). A siege mentality dominated the decision-making of Israeli governments. The "Masada Complex,"[5] and the "Samson Syndrome"[6] enhanced national security concerns and ultimately national survival.

The Israeli control of Palestinians differs from other domination of Arabs by Arabs — Egyptians, Jordanians, or Lebanese. The ethnic distinctions, culture, language, traditions, religion, national history and memory, all carved the demarcation lines between the Israelis and Palestinians. Therefore, these two very different groups of people are on a confrontational plateau and bound to clash.

The Israeli case is unique because it developed due to regional conventional military confrontations. In this context, all Israeli governments — Labor or Likud — have used similar arguments and methods in their treatment of the Palestinians. The Israeli case is atypical since it is directed at other people (Palestinians who were recognized as occupied).

The Israeli case also differs from other conflicts elsewhere because it is a continuous legal state of war. As long as this situation remains, it perpetuates the perceived threat to Israel's national security. These fears and perceptions are widely shared by the people and its leadership. The lingering legal status of war between Israel and its neighbors places its Israeli-Arab citizens under suspicion of disloyalty. Despite the fact that most of them have displayed loyalty to the country over the years. They are marked as a potential fifth column if and when the tides of war change in favor of the Arab states. Thus the regional conflict mars the status of the Israeli-Arabs (Rekhess, 1993).[7] During the Intifada Israeli-Arab youths expressed Palestinian nationalist feelings. These nationalist expressions, never openly displayed before, evoked hidden fears among Israelis.

Not only the Intifada, but the Gulf War (1991), and many other violent incidents such as political assassination attempts[8] of national leaders in the Middle East constantly enhance the Israeli perception of destruction and threat to national security. Therefore, Israeli governments have developed and adopted defensive, although aggressive policies. Often, certain measures and methods were identified as oppressive (Stohl and Lopez, 1984).[9]

CASE STUDIES

The abuses of the GSS have been exposed domestically by the Israeli media, and internationally by Amnesty International in its annual reports.[10] The following section will highlight three case studies that epitomize the evolution of Israeli aggressive behavior and coercive practices against Palestinians. These cases compounded each other and the impact of criticism.

They reflect on the spreading acquiescence among politicians, the security forces, and the public to the use of forceful measures. The cases reveal that Shabak attempted to manipulate and deceive the judicial system. Also, they expose the political echelons of Israel, members of the Likud government at the time, as guilty by acquiescence and emotional association with the perpetrators, who were receptive to such practices. Furthermore, they exhibit the public's psyche and attitude toward abuses of state powers against the Palestinian population in the occupied territories. Further examination of these incidents reveals various existing mechanisms that overlook the branches of government and their practices. These cases are not presented chronologically.

Yet, together they revealed the Shabak in full view of the public. The exposé later became known as "The Shabak Affair."

The Bus #300 affair will be examined first although chronologically it was the last incident in this sequence of events. This case was the key that opened the pandora's box leading to the ultimate exposure of the GSS. It also was the first one to have provided substantive material against the GSS. The documentation pertaining to the bus incident presented indisputable evidence (Rachum, 1990)[11] incriminating the GSS in its illegal and coercive methods.

The Bus #300 Incident

On April 12, 1984, four Palestinian youths from Han-Yunis, in the Gaza Strip, boarded bus #300 at the Central Bus Station in Tel Aviv. It had about 40 passengers aboard and was destined to travel south to Ashkelon. When it reached Ashdod, the four Palestinians threatened the driver and commandeered the vehicle. The bus broke through three road blocks. It came to a halt after soldiers shot out the tires about 10 kilometers south of Gaza near the Dir Al-Balach refugee camp. Israeli security forces (GSS, IDF, and police) surrounded it. The place was swarming with high ranking officials and military commanders. Besides the various security experts in bargaining and negotiations, a large number of reporters, photojournalists, and electronic media (Israeli and foreign) personnel surrounded the site. At 4:50 a.m. soldiers from an elite unit — Sayeret Matkal — stormed the bus and killed two of the terrorists. Some military personnel led the remaining two off the bus to be interrogated. At that point, a group of photojournalists took pictures of the terrorists as they were separately escorted. During the short and brutal interrogation they were badly beaten, tortured and ultimately killed. The Israeli military radio reported about the incident in the next two days. However, the first report did not mention the remaining terrorists. The second report on April 13 announced that the four terrorists on the bus were killed. The following day, April 14, the military spokesperson reported that the remaining terrorists died on the way to the hospital (Rachum, 1990:42-62).

The military radio spokesperson's reports contradicted the information that circulated among the news media representatives who witnessed the incident. Questions surrounded the fate of the Palestinian hijackers. News photographers and reporters on the scene saw only two terrorists dead in the bus, and initial reports said that the other two had been captured (*New York Times*, 15 April 1984). *Ma'ariv* (the largest Hebrew circulation newspaper in Israel at the time) (13 April 1984), reported on its front page the death of two terrorists, and the capture of two others alive. Additional evidence included a photograph of one terrorist held by four Israeli military personnel.[12] Meanwhile, several photos were transmitted to Europe to be published in *Stern*, a German weekly. From that point on, the Israeli print media did not reveal the existing evidence.[13] In essence, due to military censorship, the media was supporting the official version of the Israeli military radio and became unwillingly involved in the cover-up. In the first two days, the official version said that "Two were killed during the counter assault and two on the way to the hospital." Two days later the two executed terrorists were buried at night in Gaza, and not in their home villages. One person from each family was allowed to attend the funeral (Rachum, 1990:50).

Izat Nafsu

Lieutenant Izat Nafsu was an officer in the IDF and a Circassian (i.e., a small ethnic minority in Israel). He belonged to a very small unit that operated in southern Lebanon. His duties included communicating with local communities in the area, collecting intelligence, participating in reconnaissance operations, transporting weapons and small arms to collaborators and providing them with medical supplies. Weeks before his military discharge, on January 4, 1980, the IDF called him to duty. Under the pretense of being called for a secret mission, he left home and a new wife. Instead, he was accused of dealing with an agent of the enemy — a commanding officer in the PLO and interrogated by Shabak (Rachum 1990:35-41 and 160-171).

The GSS treated Nafsu harshly. His interrogation lasted 40 days and up to 17 hours a day of questioning. Besides torture and continuous humiliation, he was subjected to psychological pressures, including constant threats upon his family (Raviv and Melman, 1990). Ultimately, he confessed to treason, spying and collaboration with the enemy during the time of war. His trial began in August 1980 behind closed doors.[14] On June 29, 1982, a military tribunal found him guilty and sentenced him to 18 years of prison and demotion to the rank of private (Rachum, 1990).

In January 1987, the Nafsu file was reopened due to the revelations made in the aftermath of the #300 Bus incident. The investigation of the bus case exposed the GSS's interrogation methods. The probe revealed GSS's misconduct and frame-up of Nafsu. Furthermore, it uncovered physical and legal abuses due to its power and ability to mislead as well as influence the justice system in Israel by carrying out disinformation practices. On May 24, 1987, the Israeli Supreme Court cleared Nafsu of the most serious crimes — espionage and treason. The only charge he was found guilty of was of a much lesser weight (Raviv and Melman, 1990), of having met with a foreign agent of the

PLO in southern Lebanon. However, Nafsu did not pursue this contact and never reported it to his superiors, the act for which he was found guilty (Straschnov, 1994). He was released that evening, retaining his former military rank. Later he was financially compensated and received his military back pay.

Jewish Underground

Since 1980, a small group of settlers participated in clandestine activities against Arabs in the occupied territories of Judea and Samaria (Gal-Or, 1990; Segal, 1987).[15] The individuals involved were a splinter group of Gush Emunim (Bloc of the Faithful) (Efrat, 1994).[16] For lack of a better name, this group was labeled the Jewish Underground. On April 27, 1984, 27 settlers were arrested and accused of terrorist activities against Palestinian Arabs on the West Bank. The main goals of the group were to engage in retribution against Palestinians in the occupied territories, and to destroy the Dome of the Rock Mosque in Jerusalem. The group operated infrequently and never claimed responsibility for its activities. According to Israeli media sources and court records, several attacks were attributed to the Jewish Underground. These operations included:

(1) planned attacks on Temple Mount, 1980-84;
(2) an attack on three Arab town mayors in the territories, June 1980;
(3) placement of explosives in the Hussein school in Hebron, 1982;
(4) planting of explosives in Mosques in the Hebron area, 1983;
(5) an attack on the Islamic College in Hebron, July 1983 (three killed, many people were wounded); and,
(6) an attempted armed attack on six Arab buses in Jerusalem, April 1984 (Gal-Or, 1990:16).

The GSS arrested members of the group shortly before the last operation (Shprinzak, 1987). The agency made the arrests two weeks after the #300 Bus incident. Was the timing of these arrests accidental or was it a tactical move by the GSS? Could it have been an attempt to divert the inquiry away from the Bus #300 incident? Was it an attempt to disguise or cover-up for the Bus incident by drawing attention to another highly explosive and visible case (Rachum, 1990)?

Until their arrest, the Jewish Underground considered and felt that the security forces in general, and the GSS in particular, were their secret supporters. They felt that the GSS tacitly was receptive to their activities. However, during their trial, members of the Jewish Underground felt betrayed by the GSS and were shocked because of the GSS testimonies (Gal-Or, 1990). Why did such a sense of betrayal develop by the Jewish Underground?

ABUSES OF STATE POWER

The security forces (broadly defined) operated in the occupied territories under different sets of rules. There were double standards — one for Israelis and the other one for Palestinians. Over the years, the pattern of abuses developed and became rooted in various echelons and branches of government. Among the many institutions responsible for Israeli security and defense, only three were identified by several commissions, and acknowledged publicly as abusers of their powers: the GSS, IDF, and the State Police's Department of Special Operations.

Due to the overlapping responsibilities among the security forces in the territories, it is difficult to specifically identify which of the security forces was responsible for which particular incident. At times it appears that all were culpable and responsible for different violations of Palestinian rights.

Since the early 1980s, Amnesty International has listed various violations by the Israeli security forces. Among those mentioned are: torture of suspected Palestinian prisoners; indiscriminate beatings of demonstrators; ill-treatment of detainees; use of live ammunition, rubber or plastic bullets against protestors; and use of tear gas. Most of the methods were applied by the IDF after the Intifada broke out on December 8, 1987.[17] Other methods of coercion against Palestinians in the occupied territories often include: demolition of suspected houses, long term curfews and deportations (O'Brien, 1991).[18] In more recent years, the IDF used undercover units who have killed Palestinian activists.[19] Amnesty International charged that the Israeli Justice system also was involved in summary trials of Palestinians, and imprisonment without trials. But, for the sake of balance, it should be pointed out, that even Amnesty International did not place Israel at the top of the list of abusive states against political opposition.[20] Also, the Amnesty International 1988 report does not mention Israel among the countries that exercised political massacres, systemic tortures, mass detentions without trials and disappearance of political opponents. Israel was not listed even among those countries that had unfair legal systems.

The General Security Services (GSS)

From the early days of statehood, certain institutions and branches of government in Israel have enjoyed unquestionable trust and credibility. Among them were the secret services, the upper echelons of the IDF and the military at large, the judicial system, and the police (Rachum, 1990).

Until the exposure of the Bus #300 incident the GSS had survived public criticism, while various scandals had exposed different political institutions including the police and military for improper conduct. Also, high ranking officials in different branches of government were accused, charged and found guilty of corruption. Such violations of public trust included bribes, embezzlements, misuse of funds and use of influential positions for personal gains.

In contrast, the security services held a special aura in the hearts and minds of Israelis as protectors and defenders of the state. Members of the GSS were held in the highest esteem in Israeli society (Raviv and Melman, 1990). The trust in the security services was blind. They were considered untouchable. It had been practically forbidden to utter the name of the Shabak (Raviv and Melman, 1990). Also, it had been unacceptable to criticize the secret services (Raviv and Melman, 1990). Prime Minister Shamir labeled the Shabak as "Israel's diamond" (Rachum, 1990:24).

Due to the nature of its work, the GSS probably used abusive methods of interrogation in the 1960s and 1970s. However, these abuses were occasional and not systematic (Ronen, 1990). Because of the new geopolitical realities and recently conquered territories, in the years that followed the 1967 War, especially in the 1970s, the Shabak underwent some major changes. It became larger, younger, less experienced and brutal. By the 1980s, interrogation methods became well rooted and systematized (*Yediot Aharonot*, 15 January 1988). It was not until the Bus #300 Affair of April 1984 occurred that the GSS came under scrutiny. The incident challenged GSS practices, and its public image was badly tarnished.

All three cases revealed various facets of GSS's coercive powers. At least two common denominators emerge from these incidents: double standards of interrogation methods for Palestinians versus Israelis, and deceptive practices and coverups. When Israeli attacks against Palestinians occurred, the GSS was sympathetic and lenient toward the perpetrators. The Jewish Underground case illustrates this point. The investigation of the incidents, arrests and interrogation of members of the group were generally gentle and lacked vigor (Segal, 1987). And, in general, during investigations of Israeli attacks on Palestinians the GSS has displayed lack of interest and held a dismissive attitude, as if to say "they (the Palestinians) deserve it." Usually, the GSS did not allocate many resources to investigate such incidents. Pressure from higher-ups in the Israeli political echelons could have also contributed to the dismissal of such investigative efforts of these attacks (Raviv and Melman, 1990). In a way, it appeared that the authorities were condoning these attacks. In the bus incident, for example, Shabak's actions could have taken place with Prime Minister Shamir's knowledge all along (Raviv and Melman, 1990). However, there is no hard evidence to support this argument (Asimov and Homer, 1988).

By contrast, the GSS's attitude and practices were different when it dealt with Palestinians and other non-Jewish Israelis suspected of terrorist activity. On those occasions it showed eagerness to use abusive and brutal methods of interrogation, and did not spare any efforts to examine and find those responsible for the attacks. The bus and Nafsu incidents epitomize the practice of abuse and excessive force. Both interrogations were brutal, and the bus case was fatal.

These events also illustrate how the GSS systematically lied to the courts and other authorities. It is surprising to realize that nobody questioned the integrity and professionalism of the GSS. Even the courts, for years before the bus case, extended blind trust to the GSS. When defendants claimed that they were coerced into confessions, the military judges rejected those charges as false accusations and accepted the GSS versions (Raviv and Melman, 1990). Hundreds of terrorists received harsh sanctions after military prosecutors read aloud the confessions obtained and submitted by the GSS. Those court hearings were conducted without juries.[21]

In the bus case, the GSS initially denied the execution of the two hijackers and blamed the IDF for the torture and killings. In the Nafsu case it forced a confession, lied about it to the court and fabricated evidence to incriminate the officer. In the Jewish Underground incident, the deception operated in a reverse direction. The GSS had infiltrated the group (Raviv and Melman, 1990) earlier, and it withheld information about the organization's activities as long as it could. Instead of arresting members of the Jewish Underground earlier, the GSS enabled the group to operate for almost four years. In the bus and Nafsu cases the GSS lied about those held in custody. But, with the Jewish Underground, it lied in an attempt to reduce their prison terms. In all cases they concealed information, covered up their abuses and deceived the courts and the public. Ultimately, GSS employees placed themselves above the law (Raviv and Melman, 1990).

By comparison to other democratic states, Israeli censors have unusual powers over the media. Due to Israel's sensitivity in security matters, military censors can forbid the publication of any story or any news items they deem necessary. It is justified on the grounds that such publications can endanger the security of the state or badly reflects on its policies or the security services. Despite such powers, foreign correspondents have found various methods to bypass the censors. The most exercised method is to file their reports abroad, rather than transmit their stories from Israel. Reporters used this method widely during the Lebanon War (1982-85). Foreign photojournalists and reporters recorded some of the war's horrors and smuggled them through Syria, Northern Lebanon, or Cyprus. During the bus incident ABC News reported in the U.S. that Avraham Shalom, head of Shabak, ordered the killings of the terrorists (ABC Nightly News, April 13, 1984). Thus, it violated another strict censorship order not to reveal the identity of the head of Shabak. ABC News also reported that the government was trying to cover up the entire case. At times foreign correspondents filed their reports directly to their home offices counter to the instructions of the Israeli military censors. Such violations caused their expulsion from Israel. The most recent expulsion occurred on January 3, 1994, when the Reuters News Agency transmitted pictures of Israeli undercover agents arresting Palestinian activists.[22]

In summary, the three cases illustrate the gray areas of responsibility shared by Israel's security services. While they are all responsible for defense and security, there are no clear demarcation lines in operational and legal terms. Apparently, because of security interests, the GSS has abused its stature and the public's blind trust. Over many years, these problems have been incorporated into daily routines and thus an evolutionary process became institutionalized practice. Even the government's pathology institute has been involved in the coverup, distortion, and alteration of facts.[23]

ACQUIESCENCE TO THE COERCIVE POWERS OF THE STATE[24]

Once these events were exposed, they were bitterly condemned and widely criticized by the media, the political left and the civil rights and peace movements. Of the three case studies discussed above, the bus and Nafsu incidents distinctly represented the culpability and active role of the GSS in coercive practices. By contrast, only the Jewish Underground case generated, and clearly identified levels of, acquiescence among different parts of Israeli society that included: (right-wing) politicians, the prison system, settlers, courts and public. Stohl and Lopez suggest that state acquiescence to terrorism "... occurs when terrorism is undertaken by third parties and while not explicitly supported by the interested state, the outcomes are neither condemned, nor openly opposed because they appear to serve the interests of the observing state" (1988:6-7). According to Asimov and Homer (1988), acquiescence goes beyond the passive acceptance of any assault. In other words, there is actual help expressed through emotional association, religious justification, political argumentation, and ideological approval. A background overview will provide the contextual framework that allowed the Jewish Underground to emerge. It will examine the complex interplay of various parts of Israeli society, its reactions and acquiescence to the rise of the Jewish Underground.

Background

The emergence of the Jewish Underground was symptomatic of the times — political uncertainties, indecision and hesitation by the Israeli governments about the future of the occupied territories. Labor governments, between 1967-1977, were indecisive about Jewish settlers on the West Bank. It allowed a limited number of settlements, which was lip service to their constituents. It always considered them as bargaining chips in any solution to the Israeli-Palestinian conflict. Likud's rise to power in 1977 legitimized the activities of the Gush on the West Bank and accelerated the pace of building new settlements. It was their policy of creating a bigger Israel that boosted the number of settlers. Since 1977, the Likud government wanted to sustain the status quo on the future of the occupied territories. Besides these distinctions between Labor, before 1977, and Likud after 1977, there were major gaps and overlaps in terms of responsibilities pertaining to control, administration and policing the territories. The military was not prepared or capable to administer the territories (Gal-Or, 1990). The military's role was to pacify the territories. But how? Who was ultimately responsible for the territories?

Due to unclear policies, political indecision and confusion over responsibilities, a window of opportunity opened up for the settlers. Thus, under the jurisdiction of military law, they assumed law enforcement responsibilities that included duties of: policing, patrolling, and various other security measures. Within this framework the settlers had practically a free hand to interpret and apply what security requirements were and established their own rules of engagement. Naturally, to exercise such needs, the settlers acquired arms. The IDF and police provided the weapons. Also, they received full support and tacit consensus from the GSS (Gal-Or 1990). Once the political reality in the territories was created, the settlers issued their own security cues to the authorities and established their newly acquired coercive powers. Later they used these powers on the Arab population. Once the distance between security needs for the settlers and pacification of hostile population narrowed, it was easy to accept certain practices. Thus, acquiescence was ingrained in the public's mind, political echelons, and to some degree even the courts. Therefore, duties were bent to adapt to political reality suiting the Underground.

General Atmosphere

Israeli society had a difficult time to accept the existence of the Jewish Underground and recognize its members as terrorists. Although the term "terrorists" carries a perception of threat, the notion of Jewish terrorism was very hard for the Israeli public to accept because they did not affect Israel's security. Instead, this terminology is implied and associated with the violent political actions of Palestinians and other Arabs (Sprinzak, 1986a). To reduce the image of Jewish terrorism, Israelis attempted to downplay the phenomenon through the use of tactful language and denying the association between Jews/Israelis and terrorism. For example, the Bloc of the Faithful consistently rejected the notion that they are an extremist violent group, and "It never openly embraced an ideology of violence" (Sprinzak, 1991:4). They proclaimed that they will never target the Israeli government, the Knesset, the Judicial system and the IDF. Their animosity was directed at the Arabs (Sprinzak, 1987). They never conducted covert operations. Gush Emunim's active agenda was to build settlements, engage in demonstrations, intimidate Palestinians, and use the media in order to expose its presence in the territories (Sprinzak, 1986b).

The general direction of the abusive powers of the state already generated a mood of dismay among the Left and the Peace Movements. The existence of a Jewish underground terrorist group enhanced the existing atmosphere (Asimov and Homer, 1988). By 1984, two years into the Israeli invasion of Lebanon, there were large anti-war demonstrations in Israel. The Peace Movements gained momentum. Among the military, over 2,000 reservists signed a petition asking that they should not serve in Lebanon. There was a pacifist and anti-militant atmosphere in the country. It was bad timing, from GSS's point of view, when the Bus incident was revealed. Shabak, which was familiar with the existing public's pulse and mood swings, understood the significance of the April 1984 killings. Shabak wanted to keep the case under wraps. That is why the GSS attempted so hard to coverup the incident, and its own practices. During 1985, sympathy for the Jewish Underground members rose when Israel was pressured by the U.S. to release hundreds of Palestinians who were captured in Lebanon and accused of terrorism and violent attacks on the IDF.

Rabbi Meir Kahane was the most well known and strongest advocate of actions against Palestinians. In the 1984 elections Kahane led Kach, a militant political party, to win one seat in the Knesset (Sprinzak, 1991). The party was small and had limited resources. It felt confident, viewed as legitimate and had strong a sense of justice in the public's eye. However, the public disapproved of Kach's harsh rhetoric and call for attacks on Palestinians (Sprinzak, 1987).

The call for random attacks were seen in Israel as a slippery road toward Israeli home-grown fascism (Sprinzak, 1991). Kach's party assaults on Palestinians were viewed by the Israeli public as repulsive, undermining and poisoning the political climate in Israel (Sprinzak, 1991). It could be argued that if this extremist element could have gained momentum and popularity it might have escalated into a very dangerous situation for the whole society, and even self destruction or anarchy.

Within Gush Emunim there was general help to take the law into their own hands and punish Arabs (Weisburd, 1989). Sixty-three percent of the Gush membership supported violent methods. Even if most of the Bloc's members disagreed with the deeds, at least most of them understood the motivation (Sprinzak, 1987). Weisburd argued that the Gush's reaction was a system of rational social control. This emerged due to the conviction that general law and order had collapsed or did not serve anymore. Accordingly, the Gush believed that its fight was legitimate. Also, they fully believed that the price they will pay will be low if caught, especially if their efforts were successful in reducing Palestinian/Arab terrorism (Sprinzak, 1987).

Public's Vacillation

In the early 1980s there were no clues that the security forces were engaged in systematic abuses against Palestinians. Hence, occasional vigilantism and revenge by Israelis against Palestinians, who were responsible for terrorist attacks, gained public acceptance. Acts of terror against terror appealed to some parts of the Israeli public. These efforts were intended to intimidate and harass Palestinians, and to avenge Israeli casualties. As long as they appeared to be isolated attacks, the public and the media acquiesced, rationalizing them as part of the harsh realities of daily life between occupier and occupied. The public believed these attacks were carried out by "crazy" Israelis. The public expressed high approval for such acts. Also, it reflected the public's frustration with the authorities' inability to stop Palestinian terrorism, especially after Intifada began in December 1987. More recent expressions and calls for vigilantism rose in March and April of 1993. A poll published in January 1984 reported that almost 20% of the Israeli public approved of the idea of striking Arab terrorism by Israeli counter-terrorism (*New York Times*, 30 January 1984) Another survey conducted a week later showed a rise in the approval rate (31%) of the Israeli public for anti-Arab vigilantism (*New York Times*, 6 February 1984). Immediately after the Bus incident, in an unscientific poll on the streets of Tel Aviv, four of five Israelis approved the killing of the hijackers (Rachum, 1990).

However, once the picture became clear that the state had used systematic abuse, the public was outraged. The Left, especially Peace Now, managed to arouse intense public reactions and demanded that the state apply legal and moral standards (Sprinzak, 1986b). In the aftermath of the bus incident the public widely criticized the method and timing of killing prisoners.

With the arrest of the Jewish Underground members, the Israeli public quickly identified with the group's motives (Gal-Or, 1990) The reasons for taking a violent course of action made emotional sense especially for some activities, for example the attempt on the Arab mayors in 1980. By contrast, the public condemned the attacks in Hebron, on the Arab buses in Jerusalem and on the Dome of the Rock Mosque in Jerusalem. Most Jewish periodicals criticized the acts (Asimov and Homer, 1988). Results from public opinion polls exhibited shock and dismay at the group's actions and the existence of such an underground (Gal-Or, 1990). What surprised observers in, April 1984, were the identities of the group's members. They were highly educated, some were reserve officers, middle-aged males and most had large families (Sprinzak 1986b).

Professor Yuval Neeman, a member of the right-wing Tehiya party drew distinctions between two kinds of attacks. Accordingly, the car bombs against the mayors were directed at individuals (i.e., selective targeting) who were involved in sedition and political incitement against Israelis (*New York Times*, 22 June 1984). On the other hand, the other assaults were wrong because they were indiscriminate and aimed at innocent Arabs (Asimov and Homer, 1988). These fine distinctions reflect the political bias of the political right in order to serve their own ideology, and justify their deeds.

Political Echelons

When the new Jewish Underground emerged in the 1980s they discovered an emotional cord that connected them with the old guard. Most members of the Israeli government (Likud) at that time were also ex-members of Jewish underground groups in the pre-statehood years (Gal-Or, 1990). This newly found bond established, in the minds of the Jewish Underground, ideological continuity, sense of legitimacy,[25] and tacit acquiescence from people like Shamir (*Ha'aretz*, 3 November 1985:3, and 9 November 1985:2-3).

The Jewish Underground was supported — ideologically, spiritually, and politically — by four political parties: Hatchia, Likud, National Religious Party, and Kach. Also, Gush Emunim which was helped in political circles but did not possess power, applauded the Jewish Underground. In other words, the Jewish Underground did not operate in a socio-political vacuum or isolation.

It enjoyed a sympathetic atmosphere (Gal-Or, 1990). By contrast, other Israeli attackers of Palestinians did not enjoy such recognition in the institutions and among politicians.

After the arrests, various members of government, Knesset members,[26] the GSS and other prominent politicians (Gal-Or, 1990) spoke on behalf of the Jewish Underground. All tried to apply pressure in order to reduce the sentences, pushing for pardon and amnesty. The Prime Minister Yitzhak Shamir actively solicited pardon for the Jewish Underground members (Ha'aretz, 28 June 1985:7). Shamir and President Haim Herzog tried to pass a parliamentary law that would grant the Jewish Underground amnesty or pardon (Gal-Or, 1990). On the other hand, Herzog called the attacks of the Jewish Underground "treasonous acts" and condemned them in public (New York Times, 9 May 1984:13). Shamir called the deeds "lunatic." He denounced the attacks saying "it is worrisome and regrettable that ... there are still those among us who deny the authority of the state and do not accept the fundamental principle that the Israeli government, and it alone, is responsible for security" (New York Times, 9 May 1984:3). This repeated involvement on behalf of the Jewish Underground members was indicative of the existing mood and the levels of sympathy they generated. Also, it reflects the distinction drawn between the terrorist deeds and the persons involved.

Sprinzak identifies this high level of intervention on behalf of the Jewish Underground as illegalism from above. Accordingly, such conduct involves high governmental echelons who are aware of the legal system and yet they violate it continuously. Such illegal behavior is dangerous because these echelons disobey and violate the legal system whenever they choose or disagree with the legal constraints. They find ideological or other rationales to bypass the system (Sprinzak, 1987). Sprinzak warns of the dangers in adopting illegalism since it leads to rationalization of such acts. And ultimately, it provides the seeds to violent extremism and acquiescence to such activities.

Ten of 27 members of the Jewish Underground plea bargained in order to receive reduced prison terms. However, in principle, the courts did not have to plea bargain. All members of the group fully confessed during the investigation by the Shabak. Group members provided to their interrogators detailed information about their activities and crimes. This high level of cooperation emanated from the fact that they already had been cooperating with the GSS for several years. The Jewish Underground felt comfortable working with the GSS because it generally sympathized with their cause. When the court declared the members of the Jewish Underground guilty, they were shocked by the verdict. A wide range of people felt disappointed at the court's decision.

Ultimately, the President pardoned 12 of the 27 members of the Jewish Underground. The remaining 15 members received reduced terms.

Prison System

All branches of government demonstrated strong sympathy for members of the Jewish Underground (*Ha'aretz*, 2 June 1985). For instance, while in jail, members of the Underground received preferential treatment that other prisoners did not have. Ultimately, the prison conditions were relatively easy for them to bear (Segal, 1987). Again, the trial and imprisonment situation proved the double standards and ambiguity pertaining to members of the Jewish Underground versus other non-Jewish terrorists.

In summary, the Jewish Underground case showed double standards applied by the Israeli authorities, and the ambiguity in emphasis on legality of deeds versus emotional reaction to practices. All condemned the attacks, yet they were supportive of those who carried out the attacks. A general atmosphere of forgiveness and "understanding" of the acts of the Jewish Underground also surfaced among many Israelis. During the mid-1980s many officials abused their positions and political contacts in order to intervene on behalf of the convicted Jewish Underground. They violated the ground rules for the separation of powers in an established democracy. Acquiescence was evident in the Jewish Underground case but not in the other two incidents.

CONTROLLING THE COERCIVE POWERS OF THE STATE

Despite the evolution in the coercive powers of the state, some mechanisms exist to check such abuses. Among them are: public opinion, media, civil rights movements, the courts and state appointed commissions.

The media was instrumental in exposing the Bus #300 incident. Once the story got out, despite military censorship, it provoked a close examination of GSS's practices. Initially, the media conveyed the affair abroad, but later it revealed the story in full view of the public in all Israeli newspapers.[27] The media persisted in its investigations unmasking the doings of Shabak. In due course, the relations between the media and the security forces, especially GSS, deteriorated and grew very tense. The Shabak accused the media of treason and betrayal. Ultimately, the media and public opinion forced the government to form investigative commissions.

Civil rights groups[28] and peace movements also did not spare criticism of the Likud government in general and the Shabak in particular. The Peace Now Movement,[29] Yesh Gvul (in Hebrew — There is A Limit) Movement,[30] and

others criticized the government. They extended their publi
to Israel's policies to the cases mentioned above. Among
many political activists. One of the most prominent indivic
still is active, is Felicia Langer, an attorney and a long-time
tinian rights. She defended many Palestinians in court, lor
gence of the peace movements and other civil rights group
is her success rate in defending Palestinians suspected of
including the families of the two dead hijackers from the

One of Langer's accomplishments was to establish
rights. Through the court system she challenged the state
Arab lands intended for Israeli settlements. The Israeli cou
of the Arabs and required the government to return th
government did not appeal those decisions, even if it did r
decision (Sprinzak, 1987).

Another mechanism of controlling the state's powers is the Israeli court
system, which has displayed a high level of moral and ethical integrity and
professionalism. The Supreme Court and the Court of Appeals deserve the
highest level of recognition since they upheld the law, and established legal
norms of conduct and order despite the tremendous pressures from the Prime
Minister, the President and other individuals in the top political echelons.

The last mechanism for controlling the state's coercive powers is the appointment of investigative commissions. They have been created due to public
pressure and Israel's free press and media. Often they have been very critical
of that very government that commissioned the investigation. Four investigative commissions were created — the Zorea Commission, the Blatman investigative team, the Karp Commission and the Landau Commission (Raviv and
Melman, 1990) — that were involved in the case studies listed above.

The Zorea Commission

Due to mutual accusations between the IDF and the GSS about the Bus
incident and the death of two terrorists, Moshe Arens (then Defense Minister)
appointed an internal commission of inquiry. Its goal was to unravel what had
happened in that event, and who was responsible for the deaths. The commission was formed on April 26 1984 and headed by Major General (Reserves)
Meir Zorea. It operated secretly and interviewed many witnesses: military
personnel (officers and soldiers), police and GSS personnel and journalists
(Raviv and Melman, 1990). Yossi Ginossar, a GSS representative, was officially
serving the commission and its inquiry. However, he provided the investigation
with misleading information about the Shabak's role in the incident in order to

defuse suspicions of misconduct by GSS. A month later, on May 24, 1984, the Zorea Commission submitted its report, which ultimately concluded that the IDF was responsible for the deaths (Rachum 1990) thus clearing the GSS. However, it was not able to identify specifically who in particular inflicted the final deadly blows that killed the two terrorists. Hence, the Zorea commission recommended to proceed with the investigation by the police and the investigative arm of the military police. According to Israel's Chief Military Prosecutor, Amnon Straschnov, the commission did a thorough investigation under the circumstances and information available at the time (Straschnov, 1994). Apparently Ginossar deceived the Commission, the Defense Secretary, the Israeli Cabinet and the whole country. Later, in August-September 1986, during a follow-up police interrogation, Ginossar did not deny the inherent intentions to deceive the Zorea Commission. He admitted that such practices were not unusual in order to deflect criticism of the GSS (Straschnov, 1994).

The Blatman Investigative Team

As an outcome of the Zorea report, in July 1985, the Blatman team charged Brigadier General Yitzhak Mordechai[31] for being responsible for the two deaths. He was court-martialed. But, due to inner disagreements within the Shabak's leadership, new information was leaked out about its chief, Avraham Shalom, and included new details about the bus incident. It was revealed that the two terrorists were killed by direct order of Shalom. The investigation found that the GSS people involved in this affair intentionally lied to the Zorea Commission. It was an attempt to cover-up for Shalom and the Shabak (Straschnov, 1994).

The Karp Commission

There were two different commissions headed by Assistant to the Attorney General, Yehudit Karp. Because of the new information and infighting in the Shabak leadership, a new commission was assembled. Yehudit Karp, Edna Arbel, and Yitzhak Eliasuf — Assistants to the Attorney General — were assigned to investigate the Bus #300 incident more closely. The new Karp commission was assigned to finally figure out who was responsible for the deaths of the two surviving hijackers (Rachum, 1990), and who derailed the Zorea Commission's investigation.

In its December 20 1986 report, the Karp Commission wrote that the head of Shabak lied during the investigation and ordered his aides also to follow suit. It also stated that it had "altogether pulled the wool over the eyes of three previous investigations — Zorea, Blatman, and by the GSS disciplinary court" (Raviv and Melman, 1990:288). The Karp report also identified Ginossar as a Trojan horse who undermined the initial investigation. The report concluded that the military elite unit who stormed the bus handed the two hijackers alive to the GSS for investigation. They were killed later by the Shabak (Raviv and Melman, 1990). Furthermore, the Karp report examined the relations between the political echelons and the Shabak during the bus incident. It concluded that there was no evidence to associate Prime Minister Shamir with the bus incident or to intervening with the investigation. The commission stated clearly that Avraham Shalom, the GSS chief, did not receive any orders from the Prime Minister about how to treat the terrorists (Rachum, 1990).

From this sequence of events and follow-up commissions, it became obvious that the Shabak, in addition to actually torturing and killing the two terrorists, was deeply involved in a multi-layer coverup. It interfered in several investigations, and actively and consistently deceived the government. To deflect criticism, GSS engaged in a campaign of disinformation and fabrication of evidence that led to accusing the IDF, and a high ranking officer, General Mordechai. This complex and interwoven affair reflected the gross abuses of powers by the Shabak and its ability to operate above the law and manipulate its procedures.

An earlier commission led by Yehudit Karp wrote a report in 1982. In February 1984, the Israeli Ministry of Justice released the report criticizing the authorities for ill practices in the West Bank and Gaza. It claimed that police had not shown "proper effort and diligence" in restraining Jewish settlers from committing offenses against Arabs. It accused the responsible authorities for ignoring, and turning away attention from the occupied territories. According to the document, such practices were creating "the beginning of a dangerous process whose end cannot be foretold" (Ha'aretz, 29 May 1984:7). The report made allegations that the Likud government tacitly accepted and indirectly approved of random Israeli vigilantism against Arabs. The Karp report studied many incidents of Jewish violence and, for balance, also listed a comparable number of unsolved cases of Arab violence against Jews (New York Times, 8 February 1984).

The Landau Commission

On May 31 1987 a commission headed by former Supreme Court President Moshe Landau was appointed to investigate the intelligence community and its methods. On October 30, 1987 the Commission published its report about the coercive powers of the state. It found that the GSS had used harsh methods of interrogation on Palestinian detainees (i.e., physical and psychological pressure) to elicit confessions from suspects. It said that "the GSS had committed perjury in proceedings related to the admissibility of confessions in order to conceal its interrogation methods and to ensure that the accused were convicted" (*Jerusalem Post International*, 7 November 1987:1-2). The Shabak had systematically perjured itself in denying to the courts that torture had been employed. Such practices were widely exercised, although there was nobody in particular who ordered or guided the GSS agents to lie to the courts. This method snowballed and became a practiced "tradition" without being spelled out by any specific orders from any particular authority (Rachum, 1990). Apparently these practices became self-serving and tacitly approved by the top GSS hierarchy. The Landau commission discovered that this "tradition" started approximately in 1971, although it was not often exercised in the 1970s. GSS operatives lied to Israeli courts as a matter of habit, though Israeli law imposes a "penalty of seven years in prison for perjury" (Raviv and Melman, 1990: 297).

The report argued that the use of limited and clearly defined psychological and physical pressure during interrogation of terrorist suspects was legitimate (*Jerusalem Post International*, 7 November 1987). It explicitly stated that the GSS had the right to interrogate suspected Arabs and apply pressure. However, the report refrained from defining the pressure (Raviv and Melman, 1990). The Landau Commission stated the supremacy of the rule of law despite the terrorist threat. The report deplored and criticized the GSS leadership for misleading and deceiving the courts in the name of national security.

In summary, it could be argued that a combination of mechanisms, pressures, and above all public exposure forced the truth out of the secretive Shabak. The commissions, after a lengthy process, revealed a new and negative reality in which the GSS operated above the law.

SUMMARY AND CONCLUSIONS

The Israeli self-image rests on the idea that it is a democracy and models itself after the West European socialist democracies. It takes pride in being the only democracy in the Middle East.

For more than 40 years, Israel survived a regional threat to its national security. While the subject of national security dominated the political arena, and was ingrained in the Israeli psyche, the leadership lost its clear view of this subject. Those national goals became obfuscated and wrapped in ideology. Members of the new Israeli elite reinforced each other's attitudes rather than counterbalancing them. Two factors contributed to the world view of the GSS, IDF and the police. One was the geopolitical reality that developed in the territories and in the Middle East region. The other was the existence of this new hawkish mood at the top echelons of government. Therefore, the security forces gradually developed and changed their modus operandi. Ultimately, the most trusted and reliable agencies in the country lost face and public confidence. How can the public put their faith in the hands of politicians, generals and secret agents, especially when some were exposed as having lied to their own superiors and government? Will the leadership stick to a strict interpretation of the law?

In the 1980s, Israel entered the twilight zone between security requirements and democratic values. Over the years, various leaders who were committed to defending the country gradually violated the cardinal rules guiding that society from its inception. They planted the seeds that ultimately led to the slow erosion of Israel's social, political and military fabric. The home-grown deterioration could be Israel's worst nightmare. Ben Gurion, Israel's first Prime Minister, outlined such a scenario in the early 1950s. He argued that the external threat brought strength and cohesiveness to the country. But, he warned, Israel's demise will occur from within due to internal division and discord.

The Shabak Affair opened a pandora's box. It exposed an ugly reality and practices that began a sequence of events that left Israelis shaken. The case studies previously reviewed identified the GSS as responsible for systematic abuses and practices of coercion, deception, manipulation and cover-ups. Beyond the cover-ups and deceptions, intricate investigations and a series of commissions exposed that two prisoners were murdered (Rachum, 1990). It also revealed that GSS's leaders behaved as if they were above the law (*Hadashot*, 23 September 1987). The cases above illustrate that the business of defense and intelligence matters can be controlled by a handful of politicians. One of the Shabak deputies involved in the affair summed it up by saying "... people holding a world view of power and control should not be placed in charge of institutions that exercise power. Such placement leads to abuse of power of these privileges" (*Hadashot*, 6 May 1988:2). The scandals of the 1980s illustrated the inherent dangers when small groups of people in high places or a state adopt coercive methods in the name of security. The cases above demonstrate how security agencies can fail because of misjudgment and access to power (Raviv and Melman, 1990).

Beside the abusive powers of GSS, the case studies pointed out confusing administrative and jurisdictional duties. There were endemic problems of demarcation lines among the different authorities and their responsibilities (Gal-Or, 1990). Often there were overlaps, competitions and gaps among the various authorities. The Bus #300 incident and the Nafsu case reflected on the institutions. Because of its special and high stature, the GSS frequently interfered with IDF's operations. In the bus incident the GSS took charge immediately after the military counter-attack. The event was transformed from a military operation into an intelligence matter, and was not handled by military intelligence. In the Nafsu case, the GSS interfered in a military affair. It framed a military officer, and was responsible for his prosecution in military courts. Again, the GSS, a non-military establishment, intervened in an issue that could have been handled by military intelligence or the investigation department of military police. The Jewish Underground case reflected on gaps and overlaps among various authorities, the judicial process and transformation of climate in parts of Israeli society. Also, the Jewish Underground case confirms the pattern of GSS involvement and assuming responsibility in the territories where the army operated. However, when the cases became public the GSS attempted to clear itself by using those areas of overlapping responsibilities and frame the IDF for blunders and abuses of power.

The rise of the Intifada created a new mood in Israel. First, it distracted public and media attention from the embarrassing Shabak Affair. Second, it crystallized the need for the services of the GSS. Simultaneously it proved that Palestinian violence against Israelis had to be dealt with and stopped.[32] The Intifada emphasized the GSS's important role of state security and public safety. These issues became tangible rather than a hypothetical situation with ethical overtones.

While Israelis began to worry about personal safety within the Green Line of pre-1967 borders, it appeared that the GSS's methods went beyond Israeli law. Ultimately, it revived the old dichotomy between public order and individual freedoms. It is only natural to realize that there was no equality between Israelis and Palestinians. When subjected to personal safety threats or when they fear for national security, Israelis often are willing to forgo freedom. Yet, they are still guilt ridden by such practices.

The security perspectives of the GSS, the IDF and other security forces did not change due to the rise of the Intifada. On the contrary, it enhanced their argument that the answer to the violence is to exercise harsh policy and coercive powers. Frequency of Palestinian attacks on Jewish settlers and the general increase in level of violence may have contributed to the security forces' attitude toward the Palestinians. The dilemma of reconciling due process with the requirements of protecting intelligence sources seems to be intractable. GSS investigators continue to claim that they have to use psychological and physical pressures as part of their investigations and interrogation techniques. The security forces argue that the nature of their work requires preventive and preemptive action. The GSS is often engaged in preventive intelligence, which dictates the use of coercive methods to elicit vital information at "real time."

Within the context of security and ethics "Torture is an issue that has never been satisfactorily resolved in any revolutionary war, including those engaged in by France, The United Kingdom, and the U.S." (O'Brien, 1991:260). In the final analysis, any method is justified since such information will save lives (Wardlaw, 1984). "When it comes to matters of life and death, and high politics, the officials defend vehemently their right to lie. (However), problems arise when officials abuse their power" (Raviv and Melman, 1990:415). Ultimately, there need not be a contradiction between the openness of democratic society and harsh measures exercised by its defense forces and agencies. The real issue is how to minimize and control those measures.

Since the rise of the Intifada, the IDF became the center of attention and criticism due to its use of harsh measures against the Palestinian civilian population. Unlike the Shabak's practices, the IDF was exposed to the media — domestic and international — and subjected to daily scrutiny for its coercive practices. Many of these measures were filmed regularly by foreign correspondents and aired world-wide.

Until a solution to the regional conflict is found, the Palestinians are bound to persist with their national aspirations. In turn, these desires will not assuage the Israeli fears for national survival. As long as the occupation continues, Israel is bound to exercise its powers over the Palestinians. Perpetuation of these relations occupier/occupied will prolong the mutual suspicions, animosity, and conflict. The only visible solution to break this hostility is through political means. The Israeli-P.L.O. Accord of 13 September 1993 established the first step toward that direction.

The Israeli-P.L.O Accord confirms the fate of these two peoples, that they are bound to live next to each other. The agreement has been a unique historical stepping stone because it made the psychological leap of mutual recognition and removed the notion that these communities are linked by mutual destruction. Until the terms of the accord are made workable the animosity will continue, while mutual fear will not disappear either. Thus, we find two antagonistic societies, one deprived and occupied, while the other plays the role of the occupier.

Israel experienced domestic scandals, various embarrassing situations, and often was subjected to different criticisms from within and from the outside world. One can argue that instead of becoming "a light to all nations," as the founding fathers of Israel imagined, it was transformed and became a nation-state like all others, with their prerogatives as well as their faults.

NOTES

1. It will project high moral values and ethical standards.

2. The intelligence community includes five bodies: (1) Military Intelligence, (2) General Security Services (GSS), (3) Police Special Operations Department, (4) Center for Political Research in the Foreign Ministry, and (5) Mossad.

The General Security Services (in Hebrew: Sherut Bitahon Klali - Shabak, from here on GSS) is also known as the internal security forces. It resembles the FBI in the U.S. in terms of duties and scope. The terms GSS and Shabak will be used interchangeably in this chapter.

Mossad is known to have operated abroad. Its operations focused on Palestinian terrorism, securing Israeli dignitaries and embassies, spying, and counter intelligence.

3. This subject has been widely explored in the literature of terrorism. See, for example, O'Brien (1991); Wilkinson (1986), Wardlaw (1984); and Lodge (1981).

4. For a review of the causes of the Intifada see, for example, Shalev (1990).

5. The Masada Complex is named after the fortress in the Judean wilderness overlooking the Dead Sea. Masada was the site of a climatic Hebrew resistance against Roman legions that ravaged Jerusalem in A.D 73. Masada fell to General Flavius Silva's army after more than three years of siege. However, the Jewish warriors put themselves and their families, more than 900 defendants, to the sword. They chose to die as free people rather than be enslaved by the Romans. Since then, the heroic epic of the last stand was ingrained in Jewish history and Israeli psyche as an event that shall never be repeated.

6. The Samson Syndrome is based on the Bible. Samson had been captured by the Philistines after a bloody fight and put on display, with his eyes torn out, for public mockery in Dagon's Temple in Gaza. He asked God to give him strength for the last time and cried out, "Let my soul die with Philistines." With that, he pushed apart the temple pillars, bringing down the roof and killing himself and his enemies in the process. This story reflects Israel's possible choices at time of total war. If Israel were to be abandoned by the U.S., or any other guarantor, and overrun by Arab armies, the Israelis would fight to the end. It would fight with nuclear weapons, if necessary, to destroy its enemies.

7. Rekhess, Elie. "The Arab Minority in Israel - On Verge of Change," a lecture delivered at Tel Aviv University, The Moshe Dayan Center for Middle Eastern and African Studies. 26 December 1993.

8. Political assassinations in the Arab world can change the political landscape and relative peace. The assassination of Egyptian President Anwar Sadat in October 1981 generated fears in Israel, as have numerous other attacks on Arab leaders.

9. Stohl and Lopez (1984:7) distinguish between repression and oppression. They define repression as "the use of coercion or the threat of coercion against opponents or potential opponents in order to prevent or weaken their capability to oppose the authorities and their policies."

10. For more details see, for example, *Amnesty International Annual Report* 1991, 1990, 1989, 1988.

11. A set of photographs is presented in Rachum (1990:80-81). This collection initially appeared in Israeli newspapers — *Hadashot, Haolam Hazeh, Koteret Rashit*, and others. Other photos were kept by photojournalists who took the pictures but were not published.

12. The photograph clearly showed the face of the terrorist, who was identified (unmistakably) as Subhi Abu Jama.

13. It is a common practice in Israel to request permission from the military censor for the release of any information or material pertaining to security and military affairs.

14. His family was not allowed to attend the proceedings.

15. For two different views of this case see Gal-Or (1990) and Segal (1987).

16. Gush Emunim (meaning "Bloc of the Believers" or "Bloc of the Faithful"). An extra-parliamentary movement of Jewish settlers who decided to reclaim land on the West Bank and build their homes there. The Gush's approach to the territories is religious, if not messianic. It believes in the sanctity of the "Land of Israel" (i.e., the land of the forefathers). They maintain that through settling in its historic homeland, the Jewish people, and not only Israel, were nearing salvation (Efrat, 1994; Aronson, 1984; Rubenstien, 1982).

17. Since the beginning of the Intifada, a large body of literature has appeared and detailed the IDF's practices in the territories. The IDF attempted to put down the uprising by exercising the Iron Fist Policy and suppressive measures (Hunter, 1993; Peretz, 1990; Schiff and Yaari, 1990).

18. The most important act of deportation occurred on 17 December 1992. Israel expelled 417 Palestinian activists and provocateurs to Lebanon. They were not allowed to enter Lebanon and remained on the Lebanese side of the border for eight months.

19. Members of these units wear Arab dress as a disguise to track down and kill militant Palestinians. These units are called Mista'arvim (in Hebrew). For more information about these special units see: *The Denver Post*, 4 May 1993, p.2; *Time*, August 31, 1992, p.49-50; *Washington Post*, 29 June 1993, p.3; *Middle East Policy*, Vol. 1, No. 3, 1992, p.182-193; and Cohen (1993).

20. In its reports on the Middle East, in the early 1980s, Amnesty named Syria at the top, and then Iran, Iraq, Egypt and South Lebanon Army in Lebanon as the most coercive. The 1988 report identified many European countries, among them Britain and Poland, that exercised coercion and abusive methods as part of their police work.

21. In Israel, terrorists, and others who are charged with security violations are always tried in military courts before a military judge. See Straschnov (1995).

22. On January 3, 1994 Reuters did not ask for clearance from the Israeli military censor and televised these pictures. The photos were printed on the front pages of many newspapers. Among them were Israeli papers *Ha'aretz*, *Ma'ariv*, and *Yediot*. The Israeli military censor was outraged because it violated the strict censorship code. It argued on Israeli television (1.3.94) that exposing the identity of these individuals would endanger their lives. These soldiers were marked men, according to the Israeli military. Besides, the televised clip exposed their method of operation in the Gaza Strip and identification system.

23. The forensic experts were responsible for determining the death causes of security suspects who died in custody. However, their reports were altered in order to complement those issued by the GSS (Raviv and Melman, 1990).

24. I owe this observation to Ken Menzies and Jeffrey Ian Ross who commented on an earlier draft of this chapter.

25. For more details and background about the rise of the radical right in Israel see Sprinzak (1991).

26. For example, Geula Cohen, Rehavam Zeevi and others were strong supporters of Gush Emunim.

27. For example, see: *Hadashot, Ma'ariv, Yediot Aharonot, Ha'aretz*, 29 May 1984; *Haolam Hazeh*, 39 May, 5 June, 13 June, 1984; *Davar*, 30 May 1984; *Ha'aretz*, 1 June 1984.

28. B'Tselem is one example. Ratz was a Civil Rights Movement at the time and at present is a member of the Labor coalition government since the June 1992 elections. Its most prominent members are Shulamit Aloni, and Amnon Rubinstein. Another recent peace movement is called "Dor Shalem Doresh Shalom" (in Hebrew) meaning a "Whole Generation Demands Peace." This nonpartisan social movement was established after the assassination of Prime Minister Yitzhak Rabin on 4 November 1995. His son, Yuval Rabin heads the movement. The movement of young Israeli citizens speaks out against the deep rifts and indignities in Israel's social fabric. The movement is founded upon three fundamental principles; peace, democracy, and social equality that promotes opportunities for all.

29. Peace Now is a movement of reserve officers concerned about the challenge of peace. It emerged in 1978 after Prime Minister Menachem Begin's failure to respond

to peace initiatives from U.S. President Jimmy Carter. In the 1980s it objected and actively protested against Israeli settlements in the territories (Bar-On, 1985).

30. Yesh Gvul emerged as a protest movement in the background of the War in Lebanon 1982-85. It reflected on widespread sentiments in Israeli public, including the military, who did not agree with the policies and various practices in Lebanon. After the Lebanon War, the movement diverted its attention to the territories and protested against many of the abusive practices by the security services, including the IDF.

31. He was the commander in charge of the army's rescue operation.

32. During the Intifada, many Palestinians were targeted by fellow Palestinians. The Intifada created an atmosphere of fear among the Arab population in the territories. Many Palestinians were executed for being suspected collaborators with the Israeli security services and IDF. Others were killed due to personal vendetta or family feuds. Some women were executed because they were accused of violating Islamic code and considered prostitutes. Hence, the Intifada was directed at the Israeli public at large, Palestinians, as well as the Israeli military and security services (Shalev, 1990).

SIX.
CONTROLLING STATE CRIME IN FRANCE

by

Jim Wolfreys

IN FRANCE SINCE the revolution of 1789-1799, the rule of law and the separation of executive, legislative and judicial power have supposedly formed the mainstay of Republican rule's safeguard against patronage and privilege. In the two centuries since revolutionary France proclaimed its fidelity to Montesquieu's belief that power, if society is to function properly, must curtail its own abuses, and the Chapelier Law laid down clear lines of demarcation between general and private interests, the French political elite has established a legacy of criminal activity. Leaving aside the human rights abuses of the Vichy régime (Marrus and Paxton, 1981; Paxton, 1972) and the state anti-Semitism exposed by the Dreyfus Affair (Cahm, 1996), the history of modern France is littered with examples of corruption (from the Panama scandal and the Rochette, Oustric and Stavisky Affairs under the Third Republic[1] to the widespread malpractices of the Fourth),[2] massacres (in Sétif, 1945, Madagascar, 1947,[3] and Paris, 1961[4]), kidnappings and assassinations (e.g., of Ben Bella and Ben Barka).[5] This legacy survives today to fuel a continuing debate about the nature of French institutions.

The constitution of the Fifth Republic, drawn up by General de Gaulle in 1958, was nevertheless designed to eradicate the dangerous autonomy of sections of the state apparatus, notably the army, which seriously undermined Republican rule during the Algerian war;[6] to end the ministerial instability which plagued the weak governments of the Fourth Republic; and to create a respected, democratic and centralized regime based on the strengthening of executive power at the expense of the legislature. Opponents of the new constitution believed it was undemocratic. One of its harshest critics, François Mitterrand, denounced it for having established a regime of an almost totalitarian nature (Mitterrand, 1964).

When Mitterrand took office himself in the 1980s, however, such criticisms were then used against his own Presidency, adding to a climate of widespread public scepticism about the probity of public office holders, which has plagued successive governments over the past decade. Indeed, in the run-up to the 1995 Presidential election, a series of damaging scandals led to the resignations of three cabinet ministers, the trial of a major party leader and, indirectly, the suicide in 1993 of the former Socialist Prime Minister, Pierre Bérégovoy. As the curtain fell on Mitterrand's 14-year reign the question of state crime, which first emerged to threaten his own position in 1985 with the Rainbow Warrior Affair, had become one of the key issues of contemporary French politics. Indeed, numerous commentators articulated the fear that if the scandals continued the existing lack of confidence in the political elite would develop into a more generalised disaffection with the institutions of French democracy (Lorenzi, 1995; Suleiman, 1991; Pontaut and Szpiner, 1989). Under Mitterrand's successor, Jacques Chirac, this fear was dramatically reiterated: in May, 1997 five leading constitutionalists called for sweeping reforms in order to "make the state impartial" (*Le Monde*, 7 May 1997), and the following week 103 magistrates launched an appeal that denounced "the degradation of public life" and called for an independent judiciary (*Le Monde*, 13 May 1997).

Explanations for the apparent increase in corruption scandals[7] have focused on a number of factors: the subordination of judicial and legislative power to the executive, enshrined in the 1958 constitution and accentuated by the "monarchisation" of presidential power under Mitterrand; the intensification of political rivalry between parties of the left and right, bringing with it increased spending and the extension of existing networks of patronage and favour intrinsic to the pursuit of electoral office by weak and fragmented political parties; the Socialist government's decentralisation policies of the 1980s which, in giving more power to local authorities, made them more vulnerable to corruption; and the predominance of unelected technocrats and administrators who operate unfettered by the constraints imposed on politicians by their electorate (Birnbaum, 1994; Howarth and Cerny, 1981; Suleiman, 1979; Crozier, 1964).

This chapter recounts a number of abuses of power that have occurred under the Fifth Republic, in particular those that have precipitated the current crisis, before examining both the reasons offered for the apparent increase in state crime and the solutions put forward to deal with the problem. Although the present volume of state crime is unparalleled, and despite the fact that certain features of contemporary French society undoubtedly encourage the abuse of power, it will be argued that the French experience reveals illegality to be an integral part of the modern state, which the rule of law serves to legitimize.

The various forms of state crime to dominate public debate can be divided into three categories: (1) crimes justified on the basis of state sovereignty or *raison d'état*, embracing state-sponsored acts of terrorism (bombings, hostage taking, assassinations), cover-ups and illegal phone-tapping; (2) "politician crime" (Friedrichs, 1995:73), defined as illegal acts, such as the fraudulent financing of political parties carried out in the name of the "common good;" and (3) the more prosaic realm of political white collar crime, whereby state representatives abuse their position for personal gain or act illegally through sheer incompetence. Although these distinctions provide a useful framework, it will be seen that in contemporary France these categories frequently tend to blur and that the analysis of state criminality, as Barak acknowledges, also calls for "a structural critique of the state" (Barak, 1991:280). The question of the state's relationship to democracy will be dealt with in the final section of this chapter.

EXAMPLES OF STATE CRIME

I) RAISON D'ÉTAT (REASONS OF STATE)

Many of the scandals that took place during the early years of the Fifth Republic were a product of France's colonial engagements. These years saw de Gaulle's regime wage a vicious struggle against both the independence activists of the Algerian Front de Libération Nationale (FLN) and dissident sections of the army, who formed the *Organisation Armée Secrète* (OAS) to continue the fight against decolonisation. On February 8, 1962, eight people were killed by police during a demonstration against the OAS in Paris. The outrage brought half a million Parisians onto the streets the following week and is now commemorated by a plaque at the Charonne *métro* station where they died. Another atrocity, more bloody yet seldom commemorated, took place the previous autumn. On October 17, 1961, thousands of Algerians took part in a demonstration called by the FLN against the curfew in force in Paris. The unarmed protesters were confronted by the police. Over 200 Algerians were beaten to death, shot or drowned,[8] and over 10,000 arrested and interned. Fifty demonstrators were executed in the courtyard of the *Préfecture de Police*.[9] In the weeks that followed, hundreds of those arrested were deported, and on the banks of the Seine, between Paris and the surrounding towns, dozens of corpses were washed up (Einaudi, 1991).

The official account of events recorded three dead (two Algerians and one European) and 77 injured, among them 13 policemen. Subsequent research has established that over 200 Algerians were killed and that, despite police claims to have acted in retaliation, not a single policeman was shot. The repression was overseen by the chief of the Paris police force, Maurice Papon. As late as 1988 he repeated the story that the police had been provoked, that nobody had been drowned by the police and that only two Algerians died (Papon, 1988). In 1997, he claimed that those drowned, numbering no more than 15 to 20 people, were the victims of a faction fight between rival Algerian groups (*Le Monde*, 17 October 1997). With few exceptions the French press at the time repeated the official version of events, and the massacre provoked little reaction. Access to the official archives relating to the events of October 17 was restricted until 1997.[10] None of the policemen who took part in the massacre have ever been disciplined.

Four years later, in October 1965, Mehdi Ben Barka, a leader of the Moroccan opposition, was kidnapped in Paris. Ben Barka was visited and, according to one of his captors, the gangster Georges Figon, tortured by General Oufkir, the Moroccan Interior Minister,[11] and then killed. Ben Barka's kidnappers included two French policemen and a member of the French counter espionage service, the *Service de Documentation Extérieure et de Contre Espionage* (SDECE), raising questions about the involvement of the French state in the affair.

Speculation has surrounded the role of de Gaulle's special adviser on African affairs, Jacques Foccart, coordinator of the President's intelligence operations. Williams, however, argues that the Gaullist government had no interest in Ben Barka's death, and that any involvement of the French forces must have been the result of a section of the state apparatus acting independently of de Gaulle, an eventuality "at least as plausible under the strong Fifth Republican government as under its weak predecessors" (Williams, 1970:115).

In 1987, France became the only Western democracy since the Second World War to confess to perpetrating an act of terrorism in peacetime. Two years earlier, in July 1985, two French secret service agents working for the Foreign Intelligence Service, *Direction Générale de la Sécurité Extérieure* (DGSE), were arrested by police in New Zealand following the sinking of the Greenpeace ship Rainbow Warrior, which was to have been used to hamper French nuclear tests in the Pacific (Bornstein, 1988; Dérogy and Pontaut, 1986; Dyson, 1986; Gidley and Shears, 1986; The *Sunday Times* Insight Team, 1986; Lecomte, 1985). A Portuguese photographer was killed in the incident. The two explosions that destroyed the ship marked the successful culmination of an operation overseen by Defense Minister Charles Hernu, the head of the DGSE, Admiral Pierre Lacoste and a third figure, General Jean Saulnier, President Mitterrand's personal military attaché. The ship, it was later discovered, had been destroyed on the orders of the French state to protect France's nuclear defense capacity.

In 1987, Hernu admitted to the *Le Monde* newspaper that the bombing had been carried out on his orders and that he had subsequently attempted to cover the matter up. Hernu's confession, however, came after two years of denials and systematic lying by those involved. The inquiry into the affair, ordered by the Prime Minister at the time, Laurent Fabius, and headed by the Gaullist Bernard Tricot, exonerated the DGSE, the foreign intelligence service, and left many questions unanswered, largely, as Tricot himself intimated, because he had been lied to by DGSE officers. Tricot revealed that the surveillance operation had been approved by both Saulnier and the Prime Minister's staff. Press speculation alleged that contrary to Tricot's findings, not only had high ranking DGSE officers been involved in the bombing, but the Defense Minister and the President (via his principal advisor, Jean-Louis Bianco) had also played a leading role. In the wake of mounting evidence of their involvement in the affair, both Hernu and the director of the DGSE, Lacoste, were obliged to resign their posts in September 1987. Questions still remain concerning the extent to which Mitterrand and Fabius were involved in the bombing; in a book published in 1997 Lacoste confirmed that the sabotage had been ordered by Hernu and that Mitterrand had been kept informed of developments throughout the operation (Lacoste, 1997).

The Rainbow Warrior affair was by no means an isolated incident. During the 1980s, Luchaire, a French armaments firm,[12] exported 450,000 shells to Iran, contravening the embargo imposed by the French government in 1980. According to Admiral Lacoste, Mitterrand had been informed of Luchaire's activities shortly after taking office in May 1981. The French President had told Lacoste to speak to his Defense Minister, Hernu, about the matter. Hernu took no action. In 1986, when the Gaullists came to power, the government commissioned an inquiry into the affair, which produced the Barbu report, revealing that Luchaire had paid up to three million francs to the Parti Socialiste (PS). The incoming Defense Minister, André Giraud, was reluctant to declassify the report, only doing so once it had been leaked to the *Figaro* newspaper in November 1987. Former right-wing Interior Minister Michel Poniatowski declared that this was a case of "high treason."[13]

In 1988, as the Presidential election approached and the pressure on the two main contenders, President Mitterrand and Prime Minister Chirac, increased, fighting broke out in Ouvéa, New Caledonia, between independence activists and the *gendarmerie* (local police). Four *gendarmes* were killed, two wounded and several more taken hostage, along with six members of the armed wing of the President's anti-terrorist unit, the *Groupe d'intervention de la Gendarmerie Nationale* (GIGN) (Plenel and Rollat, 1988). The French state's response was angry and brutal. Chirac denounced the barbarism and savagery of the rebels. Mitterrand sent a unit of 50 men to Ouvéa. The unit's first task was to locate the hostages, one facilitated by means of beatings and electric shock treatment administered to adults and children alike. On May 3, Mitterrand consented to an assault on the cave where the hostages were being held. The attack, carried out by members of the GIGN and the DGSE equipped with flame-throwers and machine guns, resulted in the death of 19 rebels and two French officers. In the weeks that followed, reports in *Le Monde* alleged that at least five of the rebels had been killed *after* being taken prisoner. Philippe Legorjus, commander of the GIGN at the time, later admitted that four rebels had been killed while prisoners of his unit (Legorjus, 1990). None of those responsible for the atrocities have ever been punished.

More than a dozen separate police forces are currently operational in France. The multiplication of these units can be seen as both a symptom and a cause of illegal state activity.[14] The existence of a parallel police force controlled by the President and operating outside the law has long been the subject of vociferous criticism: "Above and beyond the Interior Minister and the relevant highly ranked civil servants, he leads his own enquiries from the Elysée.... Members of his entourage, independent of any hierarchy and entirely devoted to him, inform him, pull strings, head the parallel networks..." (cited in Plenel, 1994:96). This attack on the powers of General de Gaulle was made by Mitterrand in 1964. In 1993, the activities of the President's own parallel force, the anti-terrorist unit, or *cellule antiterroriste*, came to prominence when Edwy Plenel, a journalist with *Le Monde*, found that he had been the subject of an illegal phone-tapping operation (*Libération*, 4 March 1993). In February 1995, it was discovered that the *cellule* had recorded and transcribed the private conversations of journalists, such as Plenel, along with lawyers and politicians, including collaborators of Charles Pasqua, and civilians, such as the actress Carole Bouquet, none of whom had any involvement with terrorist groups (*Le Monde*, 21 February 1995). Between 1983 and 1986, the President's so-called anti-terrorist branch recorded the calls of over a thousand different telephone lines, operating, as *Le Monde* pointed out, like "a *cabinet noir* worthy of the *ancien régime*" (*Le Monde*, 19/20 February 1995).

The chief architect of Mitterrand's covert operations during the 1980s was the former commander of the GIGN, Christian Prouteau. In 1982, the GIGN arrested three Irish citizens in what was hailed as an important breakthrough in the fight against international terrorism. Yet after nine months of imprisonment, all three were released and the evidence of the bombing mission they were supposedly on the verge of carrying out proven to have been fabricated. Prouteau was put on trial. In September 1987, Mitterrand, in an extraordinary development, took it upon himself to speak to then Justice Minister, Albin Chalandon, regarding the Prouteau case.

> Your duty is to let the examining magistrate do what he wants to do; and there must be no brake on the part of the executive, that is not its role. If it were to ignore its role this would be a major error... That said, I am obliged to tell you that I have the greatest esteem for Colonel Prouteau, that I like him very much, that he is my collaborator and that ...I have absolute confidence in him... The French will learn to respect and to like Colonel Prouteau who is for me the prototype of what our army is capable of producing. I believe him to be disinterested and I have confidence in his courage and in his truthfulness [cited in Plenel, 1994:83-84].

Mitterrand's remarks testify to the President's scant regard for his obligation to remain aloof from judicial matters. Prouteau himself, having led Mitterrand's *cellule* from 1982 to 1988, was rewarded in 1988 with the post of prefect[15] and put in charge of security for the 1992 Winter Olympics in Albertville.

II) POLITICIAN CRIME

The corruption scandals, on a scale and a frequency unparalleled in French history, which have beset France's political elite over the past decade have had devastating effects for parties of both left and right. By the end of 1991, two-thirds of the French population considered politicians to be dishonest (Mény, 1992). The problem is not simply that corrupt politicians exist, but that political parties have been able to interfere in the judicial process, either to protect their friends or to incriminate their rivals.

One of the first major corruption scandals of the Mitterrand years was the Carrefour affair (Garrigou, 1989). In 1983, the Socialist Cooperation Minister,[16] Christian Nucci, responsible for relations with former French colonies, set up *Carrefour du développment*, an organization whose role was to inform the French public of development programmes taking place in newly industrialising countries. Over a three year period 81 million francs[17] of government subsidies were given to the association. More than 26 million francs were embezzled for various ends, including Nucci's electoral expenses (and his party dues!) and the personal expense account of Yves Chalier, the Minister's *directeur de cabinet*, which included cars, an apartment and a chateau. According to Chalier (1991), Nucci was fully aware of where the money was going. Chalier was later tried, but Nucci, who feared having to appear before the High Court, was given an amnesty under the terms of legislation, discussed below, ostensibly aimed at combatting corruption.

The Socialists were hit by a further scandal in the spring of 1989, when investigations began into falsified accounts involving a subsidiary of France's third largest construction company, the *Société Auxiliaire d'Entreprises* (SAE). Enquiries led investigators to the Marseille offices of a consultancy firm known as Urba, a bogus association set up to facilitate the illicit financing of the Socialist Party. Companies seeking contracts were obliged to pay a commission to Urba and the money would then be split three ways, 40% would cover Urba's running costs, 30% would go into party funds, while the remaining 30% would be paid to the party's local elected representatives.

When the investigations into Urba began, leading Socialists instructed the local prosecutor's office in Marseille to sit on the file. The cover-up incurred the wrath of the judiciary, which refused to let the affair subside (Gaudino, 1990). Eventually, in March 1995, the General Secretary of the Socialist Party, Henri Emmanuelli, and two former directors of Urba were put on trial. Emmanuelli, party treasurer from 1986 to 1988, was charged with the trading of favors and receipt of stolen goods. When the scandal broke, Emmanuelli was President of the National Assembly, the fourth most highly ranked post in the French state. In May 1995, he was given a one-year suspended prison sentence and a 30,000 franc fine (around $6,000 U.S.).

Political interference in judicial affairs was also a feature of two major scandals involving the RPR in the Paris region, firstly in the Hauts-de-Seine, to the west of the city, and secondly in the RPR-controlled city hall itself. In February 1994, it was discovered that huge sums of money were finding their way into RPR accounts via a number of spurious consultancy firms. A major construction company, the *Société d'Application et de Revêtements* (SAR), was found to have been falsifying accounts relating to public housing contracts issued by the local authorities in both the Hauts-de-Seine and the municipal administration in Paris. Politically, the enquiry into RPR finances was extremely sensitive and threatened the party's entire system of funding and patronage in both the Hauts-de-Seine, where the regional council was led by RPR Interior Minister Charles Pasqua, and Paris, where Jacques Chirac was mayor (until he was elected President in May, 1995).

The enquiry was led by Eric Halphen and claimed its first victim on November 12, 1994, when Michel Roussin, Cooperation Minister in the Balladur government, resigned following reports that he had accepted briefcases stuffed with cash from a leading protagonist in the affair, the property developer and former RPR central committee member Jean-Claude Méry. In January 1995, Halphen was alerted to the activities of Didier Schuller, RPR regional councillor in the Hauts-de-Seine. In a bizarre twist Schuller informed the police that he had been the subject of an extortion attempt by Halphen's father-in-law, Dr. Jean-Pierre Maréchal, who had allegedly offered to intervene in the case on Schuller's behalf in exchange for money. Maréchal's telephone was immediately tapped. According to French law the *Groupement interministériel de contrôle* (GIC), answerable to the Prime Minister, is authorized to monitor telephone calls provided they are specifically related to the fight against organized crime and terrorism or where national security is at issue. Yet on December 15 1994, Interior Minister Charles Pasqua signed an order authorizing the monitoring of calls made by Maréchal, a man with no connections whatsoever either to organized crime or international terrorism. Conversations between Schuller and Maréchal were recorded, during the course of which Schuller agreed to pay Maréchal one million francs to bring his influence to bear on Halphen. Maréchal was arrested having received the sum from Schuller, who fled abroad. The criminal appeal court accused the police of setting a trap for Maréchal. The whole affair seriously undermined the Presidential campaign of Edouard Balladur, whose Interior Minister was suspected of abusing his authority in order to undermine an examining magistrate.[18]

In June 1996, Halphen was again at the centre of a major controversy when, during the course of the same enquiry into the RPR's handling of public housing accounts in the capital, he attempted to search the home of RPR deputy Jean Tibéri, Chirac's successor as mayor of Paris. On the orders of Olivier Foll, director of the Paris *Police Judiciare* (PJ, or Criminal Investigation Department), the policemen accompanying Halphen were instructed not to assist him in his search. Foll, a former advisor to Edouard Balladur, was severely censured by the criminal appeal court, which suspended him from his functions as an officer of the PJ, an historic ruling which Pasqua's successor at the Interior Ministry, RPR deputy Jean-Louis Debré, effectively overturned by supporting Foll's actions and declaring that he would remain in his post as director of the PJ, despite the suspension.

III) WHITE COLLAR CRIME

White collar crime and misdemeanors committed through negligence or for personal gain emerged to destabilise the government of Pierre Bérégovoy in the run-up to the 1993 parliamentary elections and continued to plague his right-wing successor, Edouard Balladur. In the run-up to the 1995 Presidential election, Balladur lost both his Industry Minister, Gérard Longuet, who left office following accusations that he had abused his status for personal gain and contravened rules governing the financing of political parties, as well as his

Communications Minister Alain Carignon, mayor of Grenoble, implicated in a racket involving contracts granted by the municipal administration for his town's water supply.[19] Under Bérégovoy, the high-profile Minister for Urban Affairs, Bernard Tapie, was forced to resign, first as a minister and then as a deputy, and undergo five separate corruption trials.[20] Bérégovoy himself, who as Prime Minister instigated a series of inquiries into the problem of corruption,[21] was accused of having profited from the affairs of a known insider dealer on the stock market, Patrice Pelat.[22] Aggrieved by the allegations, he committed suicide following the Socialist party's election defeat in March 1993.

The man who led the PS in the 1993 election campaign, Laurent Fabius, was also under investigation at the time for his part in the contaminated blood affair. This episode, one of the most tragic in recent French history, revealed the ease with which leading politicians and officials are able to exist in a shadowy area between crime and legality, independent of any control or sanction. During the mid-1980s the French Blood Transfusion Centre, the *Centre National de Transfusion Sanguine* (CNTS), which controls the importation of blood, while fully aware of the risk of allowing blood that had not been tested for HIV to be used for transfusions, did exactly that with the result that thousands of hemophiliacs were exposed to the risk of contamination. The Health Minister, Georgina Dufoix, appeared to articulate the contemptuous disregard of the political elite for those who suffered as a result of its actions when she declared herself to be "responsible but not guilty." Dufoix was later put in charge of the French Red Cross. Her superior, then Prime Minister Laurent Fabius, had given his word in June 1985 that all blood supplies would be tested for HIV. By this time contaminated supplies had been in use for four months. Even after Fabius's declaration, the use of a screening product was not authorized until August 1985. Both Dufoix and Fabius denied any knowledge of what had been going on.

In June 1983, a circular was sent from the Director of Health to all transfusion centres recommending that a selection process be applied to all donors, given the risks of HIV infection through contaminated blood. The recommendations were not followed up systematically. Indeed, a report published in November, 1992 revealed that transfusion centres had continued to accept blood from France's prison population even after the existence of high-risk groups had been acknowledged (Hirsch, 1993). Neither was any attempt made to import pasteurized blood. This, despite the fact that heating blood plasma was known to be effective in killing the HIV virus and despite the American firm Travenol's offers, made in 1983 and again in 1984, to provide enough pasteurized plasma to satisfy the entire French market.

Why was this so? Recent technological developments in the blood deriva-tives industry, combined with the need to provide the means to screen blood for HIV, had massively inflated the market for blood products. In 1981, Michel Garretta, director of the CNTS, unveiled plans to build a new production unit that would give France an unrivalled production capacity but not the ability to produce pasteurized plasma. Faced with having to pay for uncontaminated blood and acknowledge that its expensive new unit (whose cost had meant cutting back on imported blood products) was obsolete before it had even been completed, the CNTS chose instead, on the pretext that there was a shortage of foreign pasteurized plasma, to release contaminated stocks for use. Untested and untreated blood was thus given to hemophiliacs in the full knowledge of the CNTS on the grounds that if the contaminated stocks were not sold, the CNTS stood to lose seven million francs a month (Bettati, 1993). Garretta, replying to a letter stressing the need to use heated blood products, argued that, "The pasteurization of blood plasma is an effective way of killing off viruses.... We could indeed treat some patients with such plasma, but certainly not all hemophiliacs, because these heated products are made by foreign firms that have only one aim, to conquer the French market" (Garretta, cited in *Valeurs actuelles*, 7 February 1994. See Laughland, 1994).

The same protectionist considerations were also to delay the setting up of an effective screening system for donated blood. By the spring of 1985 the need for such a system was becoming increasingly apparent. One method of testing, marketed by the American firm Abbott, was already being used abroad. The French equivalent, to be produced by the Institut Pasteur, was not yet ready for use. The authorities simply refused to authorize the registration of the American test, thus preventing the American company from taking advantage of the delay in the completion of the Pasteur system and flooding the French Market (the Abbott test, costing 15 francs, was eight francs cheaper than the French equivalent; Bettati, 1993:59), despite the fact that only the American company was in a position to offer screening for all blood products and amid reports that 50 inhabitants of the Paris region alone were being infected every week with the HIV virus through contaminated blood.

Fabius announced, on June 19, 1985, that screening would be introduced immediately. Two days later the Pasteur test was finally registered. On June 27 the director of the transfusion centre in Toulouse wrote to then Health Minis-ter Georgina Dufoix informing her that despite the Prime Minister's promise that systematic screening would be introduced, no such instructions had been received and the tests were not taking place. His demand for a meeting with the Health Minister received no reply. It was almost a month later, on July 23, that a ministerial order decreed that automatic screening would come into effect beginning August 1, 1985.

In order to protect the interests of the French blood transfusion industry, therefore, the population was denied access to both safe treated plasma, and to a cheap system for screening donated blood. Garretta, the man largely responsible for the tragedy, was released from prison in May 1995 after serving 30 months for "deception," still to face charges of "*ingérence*" (interference) and "*empoisonnement*" (poisoning). By this time, details of 40 separate cases of contamination had reached the judge investigating the affair. In March 1997, proceedings began against seven doctors, all hemophilia specialists, who had carried on prescribing unheated blood products to hemophiliacs after it was known that they were contaminated. This brought the total number of people under investigation to 21, including three former ministers, Edmund Hervé, Georgina Dufoix and Laurent Fabius, whose fate by late 1997 had still not been decided.

EXPLAINING STATE CRIME

The issues raised by the contaminated blood affair — the ease with which the prerogatives of political power, profit and national sovereignty take precedence over morality, the lack of accountability of the officials concerned, the difficulties experienced in punishing the guilty — illustrate the extent to which the three types of state crime outlined above overlap. Those seeking to explain the occurrence, and in certain cases the growth, of state crime in France have focused on a number of factors, some relating to recent political changes: the pressures that heightened party competition has brought to bear on politicians covetous of office, the decentralisation policies of the 1980s and the increasingly monarchal Presidential style of François Mitterrand. Others are structural: the influence of an unelected administrative elite, the subordination of legislative to executive power, the lack of a truly independent judiciary and the historical weakness of political parties in France. The explanations offered for the apparent increase in abuse of power by politicians and state functionaries, discussed below, have far-reaching implications that, as we shall see in the following section, the various attempts to counter the problem of state crime have so far failed to address.

I) POLITICAL RIVALRY

The intensification of party political struggle following the emergence of the Socialist Party as a viable party of government during the 1980s was accentuated by Mitterrand's own political acumen. His readiness to use the growth of the extremist *Front National* as a means of splitting the traditional right, as evidenced by the introduction of proportional representation in 1986, ensuring Parliamentary representation for the *Front*, his tendency to reduce the appointment of ministers to transparent exercises in public relations (notably, and disastrously, the populist Bernard Tapie and Edith Cresson, the first woman Prime Minister) and his skilful use and abuse of patronage caused increasing disquiet and generated a debate over the constitutional role of the President, dealt with below. One result of the heightening of party political conflict has been the increasing tendency of partisan rivalry to impinge upon matters of state.

The Rainbow Warrior affair is one such example. The relatively limited consequences of the affair can be explained in part by the manoeuvrings of politicians prior to the 1986 elections (Bornstein, 1988). The right-wing leaders Jacques Chirac and Valéry Giscard d'Estaing, mindful of Raymond Barre's considerable lead in the opinion polls, would scarcely have benefited from Mitterrand's resignation at this juncture.[23] Thus a government that had ordered the destruction of a Greenpeace vessel in a friendly port in peacetime and that then proceeded to lie about events to anyone who asked, was nevertheless able to see out its term of office. The Ouvéa outrage, perpetrated in the heightened political atmosphere of a Presidential election campaign, provides further evidence. Indeed, during the 1986/1988 *cohabitation* period between the Socialist President and the right-wing Prime Minister, Jacques Chirac, government was effectively reduced to an unedifying sparring match between two politicians each with their eye on the 1988 Presidential poll.

II) DECENTRALISATION

The soaring costs of electoral campaigns as a consequence of this intensification of political rivalry have been cited as a major cause of corruption (Lorenzi, 1995). The cynical attitude of France's political elite toward the funding of parties is summed up by the claim of Alain Madelin, Vice-President of the Parti Républicain, that "the false invoice is as necessary to the world of politics as clean air is to men of a normal constitution."[24] It is in this context that the policies of decentralisation are seen to have contributed to the proliferation of illegal practices.

Decentralisation was one of the cornerstones of the Parti Socialiste programme in 1981. In giving more power to local administrations, the Socialists created a situation where corruption was already flourishing. Under the terms of the Royer Law of 1973, all companies were obliged to submit construction proposals involving over 1500 square metres for authorization by a departmental commission on urbanism made up of nine locally elected representatives and nine members of the private sector and non-voting prefects. This legislation not only exposed the conflicts of interest that invariably beset local dignitaries who combined political responsibilities with their own business ventures, it also opened the door to bribery.

In the early 1980s, when the decentralisation programme was implemented, the decision-making responsibilities of local authorities were greatly increased. It became common practice for businesses to bribe local politicians, either in the manner described above in the Hauts-de-Seine and Urba affairs, or by offering to contribute to public works initiatives. Links between political parties and the private sector therefore grew closer. One RPR politician has freely admitted that if his party is able to help a supermarket, or a trader, or a distribution company, they will return the service whenever possible (Eric Raoult, cited in Coignard and Lacan, 1989). François Léotard (PR), Mayor of Fréjus in the south of France, openly boasted that in his municipality, "no road, no building, no roundabout, no lamppost will have cost the town a penny" (cited in Mény, 1992). It has been claimed that French democracy is financed by four major public works companies. One of these, the *Compagnie générale des eaux* (CGE), was found to have made donations to all parties, some of which exceeded the 500,000 franc ceiling on contributions imposed in 1990.[25]

PRESIDENTIAL POWER

The most controversial aspect of the constitution of the Fifth Republic was its revision of the role and status of the President. The President was given the right to veto legislation, to dissolve the National Assembly and to assume emergency powers in a crisis. In 1962, for the first time, the President was elected by universal suffrage. "The indivisible authority of the state," declared de Gaulle, "is entrusted entirely to the President by the people who have elected him. There is not a single authority, whether ministerial, civil, military or judicial which is not entrusted to him or upheld by him" (cited in Plenel, 1994:240). The nature of Presidential power in France led Suleiman to argue that, "if the term 'imperial presidency' can be applied with any degree of validity one might choose to apply it to the President of France rather than to his counterpart in the United States" (Suleiman, 1980:103-4).

Having based most of his career on a vehement critique of the concentration of power effected by de Gaulle, Mitterrand, once elected, was expected to introduce limits on Presidential power. Indeed, he had pledged in his 1981 election manifesto to curtail the term of office for the head of state to five years, or make the post non-renewable. Mitterrand eventually departed 14 years later, leaving behind his *cabinet noir*, a series of opulent monuments to his reign (the Louvre pyramid, the Opéra-Bastille, the Grande Arche de la Défense) and a network of patronage testifying to his personal influence within the French state,[26] not least within the legal system.

The *Conseil Supérieur de la Magistrature* (CSM), which oversees the appointment and promotion of judges and is responsible for disciplinary measures, has been termed the "nerve centre of political control" (Plenel, 1994:115) of the judiciary. In 1958, the CSM was placed under the direct control of de Gaulle who, as President, was the guarantor of judicial independence. The Secretary, along with nine of the ten remaining members of the *Conseil*, were chosen by the President (three directly, the remainder chosen from a list drawn up by the Court of Cassation). In this way the CSM reflected the general thrust of the 1958 constitution, giving predominance to Presidential influence over that of the legislature and judiciary.

Under Mitterrand the extent of this influence became clear. In 1987 four confidential memos sent by Danièle Buguburu, a Mitterrand ally appointed General Secretary of the CSM in 1981, to the President, were leaked. They contained extensive details on the political views of candidates nominated to sit on the CSM and spoke volumes about the control exercised over the judiciary by the Presidential Elysée Palace. A subsequent inquiry into the bugging of the apartment of the man responsible for the leak came to nothing despite Gaullist insistence that the investigation be carried out by the *Inspection Générale de la Police Nationale* (IGPN), whose director was known for his right-wing sympathies, rather than the Police Judiciare.

The continuing Presidential hold over state institutions was confirmed by one of Mitterrand's last acts in power, which was to appoint his long-time friend and collaborator, Roland Dumas, to head the Constitutional Council. The Council, set up by de Gaulle to ensure respect for the 1958 constitution, has been responsible for giving France the kind of constitutional controls on legislation that exist in other democratic states. This development followed a 1971 ruling when the Council censured a law on the rights of association on the grounds that it contravened the Declaration of the Rights of Man (Bigaud, 1994; *Le Monde*, 24 February 1995). The Council has subsequently intervened to modify legislation concerning the right to asylum in 1993 and to block measures introduced by the Balladur government in 1994 to increase state funding for private schools. Opinion as to the merits and effectiveness of the Council are divided. Despite claims that it exists to safeguard the constitutional rights of French citizens, the Council has long been the object of criticism because ordinary citizens do not have the right to appeal to it and because of the extent to which it is a politically dominated institution. The right's frustration with the body was manifested by its nomination of two figures[27] known for their opposition to the role played by the institution to sit on the Council. The appointment of a highly political figure to head a body responsible for pronouncing on matters of constitutional law underlined the extent to which the upper echelons of the French state have become politicised. By entrusting Dumas with the task of passing judgement on legislation passed by the right-wing National Assembly, Mitterrand, as *Le Monde* remarked, had ensured that *"la Mitterrandie"* would survive him (*Le Monde*, 24 February 1995).

THE STATE BUREAUCRACY

This politicisation of the institutions of the French state, and in particular the civil service, has been the subject of a number of studies (Birnbaum, 1994; Howorth and Cerny, 1981; Suleiman, 1979; Crozier, 1964). In Britain, the civil service is based on the theoretical principle of political neutrality. The primary responsibility of those in public service is therefore meant to be in the public interest rather than the party of government. In France there is a considerable overlap of political and administrative elites.[28] This is due to several factors. In the first place the upper echelons of the French state are dominated by a comparatively small number of graduates from the hierarchical and highly competitive *grandes écoles* system made up of specialist schools, such as the *École Nationale d'Administration* (ENA), which exist independently from the university system and offer graduates access to the state administration via the *grands corps de l'état*. The principle of *détachement* allows members of the *grands corps* to take leave from their post in order to work in the private sector or in politics. This system means that a tiny elite is able to exert its dominance over the principle institutions of government, business and finance. Although it would be an exaggeration to claim that the French state is dominated by a conspiratorial old-boy network, the narrowness of French elites and their preponderance in government and industry, along with the widespread practice of political appointments (every change of government in recent years has precipitated a thorough purge of the state administration), has blurred the distinction between government and administration and undoubtedly increased the possibility that conflicts of interest and patronage may compromise the ability of state functionaries to operate in a detached and neutral manner. Former Prime Minister Pierre Messmer, referring to complicity between politicians and civil servants as a factor in the scandals of 1987, stressed the need for greater separation of political and administrative functions, arguing that, "little by little at the State's summit a politico-administrative complex is formed in which an American-style 'spoils system' becomes the norm" (cited in Frears, 1988:309).

THE JUDICIARY

In recent years, political interference in the legal system has become a major issue, as we have seen in our discussion of the role of the President, and as the Urba, Hauts-de-Seine and Paris city hall affairs illustrate. The Urba episode marked a turning point in the struggle between the political elite of the country — backed up, it appeared, by the prosecution service — and the judiciary. Having refused to succumb to the pressure exerted upon him by the political establishment, Judge Jean-Pierre opened the way for further investigations, notably the unprecedented search of the Parisian offices of the Socialist Party in January 1992 by Renaud Van Ruymbeke, a leading magistrate. A shift had clearly taken place in the balance of forces between the political establishment and the judiciary, largely because judges had been able to win broad approval for their actions as the volume and gravity of the scandals threatened seriously to destabilize political life. When Alain Carignon, Mayor of Grenoble and Communications Minister in the Balladur government was imprisoned, at no point did Pierre Méhaignerie, the Justice Minister, attempt to intervene on behalf of his colleague, a decision taken by some commentators as evidence of the changing relationship between the executive and the judiciary. The judges, it was claimed, "can from now pursue their investigations to their conclusion. They will certainly not hold back. The wheels of justice will not stop rolling" (Jérôme Dupuis and Jean-Marie Pontaut, *Le Point*, October 1994).

Immediately after his election as President in 1995, Jacques Chirac seemed to vindicate this optimism when he promised to ensure the "total independence" of the judiciary (*Le Monde*, 15 May 1997). Moreover, Justice Minister Jacques Toubon told France's public prosecutors that he would never instruct any of them to cut short legal proceedings (*Le Monde*, 26 July 1996). Yet within months the government had appointed Alexandre Benmakhlouf, a former advisor to Chirac, to the post of public prosecutor to the appeal court, and François Burgelin, Gaullist Albin Chalandon's former *directeur de cabinet*, as public prosecutor to the Court of Cassation, reviving accusations of political interference, which appeared to be confirmed by the Foll affair of October 1996, when the intervention of the Interior Minister posed once again the problem of political interference with the judiciary and led one commentator to predict that France's judges would soon be in "a state of revolt against the political authorities" (Philippe Alexandre, *Le Monde*, 23 October 1996).

CONTROLLING STATE CRIME

Mitterrand's 1981 election manifesto had contained a number of proposals aimed at giving more weight to the legislature and judiciary at the expense of the executive: the Presidential term of office would be reduced from seven to five years, Parliamentary powers would be increased, the independence of the judiciary would be achieved through a reform of the *Conseil Supérieur de la Magistrature* and public figures implicated in scandals would be brought to justice. In 1982, a committee was set up as the first step towards implementing these reforms, which were then swept under the carpet for nearly a decade. Towards the end of the 1980s, as France's political elite became increasingly conscious of the damaging effect that the steady stream of corruption scandals was having on citizen perceptions of public life, successive governments sought to legislate against malpractice. Proposals have focused on the areas given priority by Mitterrand in 1981. Measures introduced have so far been limited to the question of party financing and the role of the judiciary.

Three major anti-corruption laws have been introduced since 1988.[29] The first, passed in March, 1988, imposed a ceiling on party expenditure during Presidential and Parliamentary elections, established public financing of Parliamentary parties, and required all candidates to reveal the state of their personal finances. The law also declared an amnesty for the period prior to 1988. In January 1990, further measures were introduced as loopholes had become apparent in the existing legislation. The ceiling on expenses would now cover all election campaigns[30] and include expenses that were incurred by individual candidates and later reimbursed by the party concerned. Public funds were to be made available for candidates of parties not represented in Parliament and gifts from individual benefactors were legalized. Candidates whose budgets exceeded the legal limits would face disqualification.

Both the 1988 and 1990 legislation recognised a distinction between corrupt practices for party political gain and those indulged in for personal enrichment. As Mény points out, the distinction set France apart from other nations, such as Japan, Italy, Germany, Spain or the USA, where politicians implicated in corruption scandals were obliged to resign (Mény, 1992). By contrast, the 1990 French legislation granted an amnesty to politicians involved in cases that had not yet even come to court and was widely perceived as covering all politicians implicated in corruption scandals, an impression confirmed by the amnesty granted to the former Socialist minister, Christian Nucci, implicated in the *Carrefour du développement* affair.[31]

In January 1993, the so-called Sapin Law introduced measures to regulate the granting of public works contracts. The private financing of political parties, despite pressure from the government, was not banned, but details of private donations had to be published in party accounts. The legislation also provided for a *Service Central de Prévention de la Corruption* (SCPC), an interministerial administrative body charged with centralizing and analysing information relating to corruption cases before referring them, if necessary, to the prosecution service. The establishment of this body and the ambiguity of its status highlighted the problem of separation of powers since the SCPC's role appeared to be partly administrative and partly judicial. Judge Jean-Pierre denounced it as a parallel police force (cited in Lorenzi, 1995:181). Although the Constitutional Council ruled that the SCPC did not infringe the principle of the separation of powers, since its role was primarily administrative, neither did the new body satisfy the need for a single, centralized body combining administrative and judicial functions. Instead the SCPC became one more organization amid an expanding network, joining the *Mission Interministérielle d'Enquête sur les Marchés*, created in January 1991, responsible for investigating charges of favoritism in the granting of public sector contracts, and five separate bodies charged with combatting economic and financial delinquency.[32] In August 1994, further legislation undermined the Sapin Law by introducing a loophole. The original law laid down conditions under which contracts could be extended. In the 1994 measures, however, the word "work" (*travaux*) was replaced by a much vaguer reference to "investments, material or otherwise" (*investissements matériels ou immatériels*), which could refer to all kinds of consultancy work, research or allowances (*Regards sur l'actualité*, January, 1995:6).

The amnesties introduced by the 1988 and 1990 laws were controversial and, coming in the wake of the contaminated blood scandal, revived the debate over the question of ministerial responsibility for crimes committed in office. Under the terms of the 1958 constitution, ministers could be called to appear before the High Court only once both the National Assembly and the Senate had voted to refer the case to the magistrates who sat on the Commission of the High Court. If the Commission decided to send a minister to the High Court the case would be in the hands of deputies. Thus, in the interests of stability and according to the principle of the separation of powers, it was impossible either for the public to instigate the trial of a minister or for the trial to be conducted by the judiciary. The decision to start proceedings against a minister therefore rested with the Parliamentary majority. Since the minister would almost inevitably be a member of that majority, the system virtually guaranteed ministerial impunity (Bigaud, 1994).

Constitutional measures were introduced in July 1993 in an effort to address the exclusive, politicised and discretionary nature of the High Court. The new legislation preserved the existing High Court but limited its jurisdiction to the head of state. A new body was established to deal with ministerial crime, the *Cour de Justice de la République* which, unlike the High Court, would be composed of both deputies and magistrates and presided over by a judge. The procedure for bringing criminal proceedings against a minister was simplified.[33] Ordinary citizens were given the opportunity to approach the public prosecutor if they felt themselves to be the victims of governmental crime. The public prosecutor would then refer the matter to the *Commission d'instruction* of the newly established court. It was before this body that Georgina Dufoix, Laurent Fabius and former Secretary of State for Health, Edmond Hervé, appeared in September, 1994 charged with "complicity to poison."[34]

The July 1993 legislation also carried out the long-awaited reform of the *Conseil Supérieur de la Magistrature* (CSM). The 1993 reforms divided the CSM into two bodies, one for the prosecution service and one for the bench, each to be comprised of five magistrates, one State councillor and three non-magistrates, only one of whom instead of two was now to be nominated by the President.[35] The CSM was thus given greater independence from the head of state although, significantly, the President retained the right to nominate the Secretary. This prompted the leader of a moderate magistrates' association, the *Union Syndicale des Magistrats*, to declare that, having considered the reform a small but well-meaning one, it was now apparent that it was little more than "*une réforme en trompe-l'oeil.*"[36] The constitutional reforms also retained the Presidential pardon, a legacy of the *Ancien Régime*.

STATE CRIME AND DEMOCRACY

Having outlined a number of abuses of power and the various reactions to them, some conclusions can now be drawn about state crime by France and its control. It is frequently argued that the structure of French society, its lack of an effective, autonomous, democratic counterweight to a centralised executive and an unelected bureaucracy, means that France is the "classic land of the political scandal" (Williams, 1970:3). Furthermore, the emergence of the Socialist Party as a party of government has both increased the frequency of scandals (as a consequence of intensified party competition) and diminished the possibility of limiting the scope for abuses of power (because of the left's own misuse of executive power and its acceptance of the right's foreign and defense agenda; Bornstein, 1988).

Certainly, numerous crimes outlined in this chapter bear traces of experiences specific to France, notably the Second World War and the post-war decolonisation process. France's experience of occupation and resistance gave legitimacy both to underground and illegal methods and to unlikely alliances forged for the sake of expediency. The kidnapping of Ben Barka by agents of the French state, working in collaboration with gangsters, and the network of associations built up by the Gaullist SAC, whose members were involved in murder, burglary, arson attacks and international drug-running operations during the 1960s (Boggio and Rollat, 1988; Ferrand and Lecavalier, 1982), bear testimony to the links that apparently respectable politicians were prepared to nurture with altogether more disreputable elements. Those who escaped the post-war purge, moreover, were themselves able to make use of lessons learned through collaboration with the Nazis. Maurice Papon, who, as General Secretary of the *Préfecture* of the Gironde region in western France oversaw, between 1942 and 1944, the deportation of more than 1,500 Jews, without doubt drew upon this experience when organising the October 1961 massacre and mass arrest of FLN sympathizers.

One of the features of the Third Republic, the so-called *"République des camarades,"* was, according to one commentator, "that rigorously honest men were on good terms with fairly honest men, who were on good terms with shady men, who were on good terms with despicable crooks" (Denis Brogan, cited in Williams, 1970:123). The claim that the Fifth Republic represented a more just and honest regime than its predecessors was greatly undermined by the Ben Barka abduction and subsequent scandals. Indeed, as Williams scathingly remarked, "the worst features of the despised old *République des camarades* were revived, more dangerous than ever, in the purified new *République des compagnons*" (Williams, 1970:124). Although the Ben Barka affair prompted a reform of the French police force,[37] numerous aspects of the scandal were to resurface in later episodes, occurring long after the resolution of the colonial issue and testifying to the continued existence of an underground network of unaccountable secret service units (the DGSE, GIGN, GIC), the collusion of state officials with the illegal activities of these units (Rainbow Warrior), the rivalry between different police forces (CSM affair), and the secretive and clandestine nature of France's dealings with its former African colonies (*Carrefour du développement*).

However, while aspects of various crimes outlined in this chapter are a product of French political culture, many of the crimes themselves form part of a generalised international phenomenon. Breaking arms embargoes, as similar scandals in Britain (Norton-Taylor, 1995) and the United States (Kornbluh and Byrne, 1993) have demonstrated, is not a specifically French phenomenon.[38] Corruption scandals have taken on ever-greater dimensions in most Western countries over the past decade, particularly in those places where the existence of strong Communist Parties cemented alliances between establishment parties. These alliances have begun to break up as a result of the end of the Cold War, paving the way for revelations that would previously have destabilized the political system and weakened unity against the perceived Communist threat.

For obvious reasons the *rate* of crime committed by the state is difficult to quantify. Today, however, there is clearly a greater *perception* of state crime, attributable to various factors: the tenacity of certain judges, the readiness of political parties to reveal the existence of corruption as a consequence of increased party competition, and the development of investigative journalism.[39] Faced with greater awareness of abuses of power, governments have been forced to act in order to preserve their own legitimacy. The argument put forward by Williams (and later by Bornstein), that in France those implicated in scandals suffer no lasting consequences, has been undermined in the mid-1990s by the manner in which significant numbers of politicians have been brought to justice. By June 1995, 100 elected representatives were under investigation on corruption charges, with a further 60 cases pending, figures which bear comparison with the 200 deputies and senators who faced corruption charges in Italy during the early 1990s (Lorenzi, 1995). The extent to which those involved in major scandals will suffer any lasting consequences is unclear, although the careers of Tapie, Longuet, Carignon, Roussin, Arreckx and several other leading figures have been considerably damaged by the punishments meted out to them (Dupuis and Pontaut, 1995).

The reforms introduced, however, have so far proven piecemeal and have not addressed the structural aspects of the problem — the concentration of Presidential power, the subordination of judicial and legislative power to the executive, and the state administration's lack of neutrality. Measures introduced to control abuses of power have been overwhelmingly reactive rather than preventive. Moreover, despite the punishment of certain individuals, France's record on disciplining those guilty of state crime is poor, particularly with regard to Vichy. Indeed, after the war many leading collaborators either escaped justice altogether or served short sentences before resuming their careers. For example, Georges Albertini, former General Secretary of the fascist, anti-Semitic and collaborationist *Rassemblement National Populaire* during the Second World War, was condemned to five years of forced labour, completed three, and became political advisor to the Worms Bank establishing contacts over the following 30 years with various politicians, including former President Georges Pompidou and the present head of state, Jacques Chirac (Plenel, 1994; Lévy, 1992). It took almost 50 years for René Bousquet, chief of police under Vichy, responsible for overseeing the deportation of 12,000 French Jews to Nazi camps, to be charged with crimes against humanity. Following the October 1961 massacre, Maurice Papon continued as chief of the Paris police force until 1967. He went on to become Chairman and Managing Director of the *Sud-Aviation* aeronautical company and National Treasurer of the Gaullist *Union pour la Défense de la République* (UDR), under whose name he also served as a deputy in the National Assembly. In 1983 charges of crimes against humanity were finally brought against him for his wartime activities (Einaudi, 1991). In 1997 he eventually went on trial.

France has also escaped sanction by the international community for its crimes against humanity. At the end of the Second World War the demand for self-determination by France's colonies led to a series of uprisings brutally repressed by the French. There were to be no reprisals on the part of the international community for the Sétif massacre in Algeria of May and June 1945 (estimates of the numbers killed range from 1,500 to 45,000; Benot, 1994:29); the bombing of Haiphong, Vietnam, in December, 1946, which left 6,000 dead (ibid., 97-113); the repression of the Madagascan uprising of 1947-8, during the course of which 89,000 insurgents were killed (ibid., 114-145); or the torture, beatings and assassinations carried out by the French army during the Algerian War of 1954-62 (Vidal-Naquet, 1975). In 1988, France further exposed the ineffectual role of the international community in dealing with acts of state terrorism[40] by allowing the two agents who carried out the bombing of the Rainbow Warrior to return home, thereby breaking the terms of the international agreement signed between France and New Zealand in July 1986. On April 30, 1990, the Arbitral Tribunal dealing with this contravention simply ruled that France had acted illegally (Migliorino, 1992; Pinto, 1990). No further measures were taken.

The crimes examined above — politician and white collar crimes along with those committed in the name of *raison d'état* — should be seen not as aberrations, but as intrinsic features of statecraft in advanced industrialized countries. While individual crimes differ in scale and importance, there are factors common to each category of state crime. All were committed by state representatives acting on behalf of a nominal "national interest," whether protecting national security (Rainbow Warrior), defending colonial assets (Ouvéa, 1988; Paris, 1961) fending off foreign competition (the contaminated blood scandal), or funding the political establishment (Urba, Luchaire, Carrefour, the Hauts-de-Seine affairs). All were facilitated by the existence of a large and powerful state administration, whose traditions of secrecy and lack of accountability allowed crimes to become obscured behind the closed doors of the bureaucratic code of silence. All illustrate the extent to which various aspects of French society — the control which ruling parties exercise over institutions, facilitated and perpetuated by the nature of the administrative system, combined with the weakness of pressure groups and the party system itself — mean that there is little separation between state and government. "It is not just laws that are needed in the French political system," argues Suleiman, "but the independence of other institutions to call for their application and to apply them" (1991:67-68).

The need for an effective separation of powers is often invoked as a means of countering the abuse of executive power. But the principle of the separation of powers cannot be understood in isolation and should be seen as a means of balancing competing interests within the state,[41] itself defined by Poulantzas as "the material condensation" of the various tensions which exist among those who hold political and economic power within society. Contradictory relations, argues Poulantzas, are therefore "enmeshed within the state." Although it provides an apparently unitary framework for the different interests and factions within the ruling elite, sections of the state apparatus can thus become the tools of rival groups within the power-bloc (Poulantzas, 1978:128-132). We have seen how different political factions have made use of parallel police forces and brought their influence to bear on the judiciary, either to subvert the course of justice or occasionally to positive effect by exposing the illicit practices of a rival faction.[42] Many of the abuses of power outlined above are a product of the struggle between antagonistic elements within the French state. The incapacity of these elements, detailed in this chapter, to establish effective legislative and judicial counterbalances to executive power highlight the conflict between the need for democratic controls on power and the imperatives of effective government (Markovits and Silverstein, 1988). A solution to the problem will not, therefore, come from the separation of powers per se. Indeed, this principle can be seen to complicate, and thus to hamper, effective rule. Moreover, the separation of powers is frequently used as a constitutional device to ensure the independence of the executive from the legislature, thus effectively limiting the scope for controls on government.[43]

We have seen various illustrations in this chapter of the divorce between the state and society at large. The state, however, does not exist "suspended in mid-air" (Marx, 1968). Its role is primarily (although not solely) to defend the interests of the dominant class in society. This link, between the dominant economic forces in society and the state, is subject to tensions and contradictions. Draper compares it to the relationship between Caliban and Prospero in Shakespeare's *The Tempest*: Caliban is bound to serve his master, but strives for independence, Prospero needs his slave, but remains wary of him (Draper, 1977).[44]

In order to defend the interests of the ruling class in society the state will, if necessary, systematically break either its own laws or those of another country. At times this happens openly, evidenced by the numerous crimes and human rights abuses carried out in the name of *raison d'état*. "Democracy stops," as Pasqua readily acknowledges, "where the interest of the state begins" (*Le Monde*, 28 February 1987; cited in Bornstein, 1988:110). Otherwise it occurs covertly, via devices that provide for illegality: loopholes. Much of the legislation introduced to combat corruption is characterised by its vagueness and lapses. The 1986 law on the accumulation of elected offices was derided as "homeopathic" (see Mény, 1992:82), while the 1990 law on corruption was introduced largely because of the huge lapses in the earlier law of 1988. The Sapin Law of 1993 expressly included a loophole relating to public works contracts. (In this respect the French case is not exceptional. A consultant for the Democratic Party, referring to legislation passed in the United States relating to the financing of Presidential election campaigns, claimed that it contained a loophole "big enough to drive a President through," (cited in Drew, 1983:99).

Ultimately, then, the state acts as a barrier to genuine freedoms, combining "legality shot through with illegality" (Poulantzas, 1978:85). The potential for government policy alone to eradicate state crime is, therefore, restricted. Although government is inevitably the focus for reform, the limited power of governments to curtail abuse should also be recognised. Henry argues that "by failing to limit accumulation of private wealth at is source," capitalist governments are guilty of state crime "of omission" (Henry, 1991:266), resulting in the marginalisation of sections of society and so increasing the likelihood that they will resort to criminal activity. The experience of the Parti Socialiste after its election victory of 1981, however, graphically exposes the incapacity of governments simply to legislate away social inequality. Elected on the most radical left-wing programme of any ruling party in post-war France, unemployment was the central concern of the government. The Socialists pledged to create jobs, to free the state from the influence of big capital and to reduce the working week to 35 hours. Within a year of its election the new government, with the economy in recession, introduced the first of a series of austerity measures. By the middle of the decade unemployment had more than doubled. The 35-hour week was never introduced under Mitterand.

Behind the failure of the Socialists and of governments worldwide to limit the accumulation of private wealth, lies the acceptance of existing property relations, and the inequalities flowing from them, which binds governments to "preserving disorder"[45] and drives them to protect the interests of national capital in an increasingly competitive international market by whatever means necessary, to the detriment of their own electorate, as the Socialist austerity measures and the grotesque spectacle of the contaminated blood affair illustrate.

To control state crime, the solution lies neither with the separation of powers nor simply with government policy, but rather in the extent to which popular participation in the running of state institutions can be maximised. The anti-democratic nature of the divide between the executive and its bureaucracy from society at large, which gives rise to abuse of power, must be combatted by greater popular influence over public institutions. Based on this principle of democratic control, numerous constitutional measures could be introduced to increase the accountability of the executive and its administrative network, to reduce its scope for independent activity, and to maximise the influence of representative institutions in government. Such measures would include: limiting the Presidential term of office; subordinating the head of state to the legislature; granting the National Assembly greater powers to introduce and veto legislation; curtailing the practice of political appointments to key administrative posts; minimizing the role of unelected officials and increasing their accountability to parliament. The judiciary should be made truly independent of both executive and legislative power; its powers should be extended and judges themselves subject to democratic election and recallable.

The extension of popular control over the institutions of the state, in order to convert it from "an organ superimposed upon society into one completely subordinate to it" (Marx, 1976:326) involves a degree of democratisation that extends beyond the political need for checks and balances on state power, to raise fundamental questions about the social and economic organization of society. Full popular participation in the running of the state can only come about through full popular participation in the running of society as a whole. Yet capitalist property relations require the subjugation of the majority of the population in order that these relations are not threatened. When threats emerge, state power is used to defend the economic interests of the powerful ruling minority in society, and the machinery of the state used to obscure its crimes.

In contemporary France, as we have seen, measures introduced to combat state crime have been insufficient, concerned primarily with punishing misdemeanors rather than preventing them. The need for sweeping structural reforms to deal with the problem is double-edged. Firstly, an increasingly beleaguered political establishment has a growing need to assert its legitimacy in the face of mounting public disquiet about political corruption.[46] Secondly, controls are required in order to limit the potential for the state to cause harm and to increase the possibility of open government. In any society, capitalist or socialist, measures to ensure maximum accountability of elected and unelected officials to representative assemblies, to reduce the autonomy of executive power and to guarantee the independence of the judiciary, are crucial if abuse of power is to be curtailed and democracy achieved.

NOTES

1. See Jeanneney (1984); Ducloux (1958).

2. Williams (1970).

3. Benot (1994).

4. Levine (1985); Einaudi (1991).

5. Sarne (1966); Muratet (1967); Guérin (1991). See also Williams (1970).

6. In February 1958, the French Air Force, unbeknownst to the government, bombed the Tunisian village of Sakheit, suspected of harbouring members of the Algerian independence movement, the FLN, killing 69 people. Two years earlier, the FLN leader Ben Bella was arrested by army officers acting independently of the government.

7. Numerous commentators are of the view that corruption is more widespread now than ever before. See, for example, Gaetner (1992); Mény (1992); Minc (1990).

8. Exact figures relating to the victims of police violence are unavailable. Einaudi has drawn up a list of 74 Algerians killed during the autumn of 1961 and names a further 66 known to have disappeared. (See Einaudi, 1991:313-318.)

9. Headquarters of the Parisian municipal police force.

10. During Maurice Papon's trial for crimes committed against humanity under the Vichy regime, Catherine Trautman, Minister of Culture and Communication, announced that access to the files related to the October 17th events would be granted (*Le Monde*, 18 October 1997).

11. Figon later withdrew this allegation.

12. Luchaire was run by Daniel Dewavrin, son of Colonel Passy, head of the Free French secret services during the Second World War.

13. Poniatowski, cited in Gaetner (1992:205). Poniatowski had been Interior Minister in 1976 at the time of the assassination in suspicious circumstances of a centrist deputy, Jean de Broglie. Allegations that the Interior Ministry knew of the plot to kill de Broglie and had failed to protect him led to calls (which came to nothing) for Poniatowski to appear before the High Court of Justice. See Frears (1988:307-22).

14. On the French secret services, see Deacon (1990); Faligot and Krop (1985).

15. A senior local government official responsible to central government.

16. Responsible for liaising with former French colonies. Effectively, as Frears (1988) remarks, Minister for Africa.

17. Around $16 million.

18. Pasqua was no stranger to covert operations having played a leading role in the notorious *Service d'action civique* (SAC), an underground Gaullist dirty tricks unit. See Boggio and Rollat (1988).

19. Carignon became the first government minister to be imprisoned under the Fifth Republic. Released after six months in custody he lost no time in publishing an account of his ordeal (Carignon, 1995) before he was sentenced in July 1996 to five years in prison.

20. By mid-1997, having had his assets frozen and been declared bankrupt, he had been found guilty in all five and sentenced to several years in prison.

21. Notably the Bouchery report published in December, 1992.

22. Over a period of two decades Pelat donated a total of 8.5 million francs to figures connected with the Socialist Party. During the same period he amassed a fortune of 74.2 million francs "on the fringes of legality" (Plenel, 1994:298-9). See also Dupuis and Pontaut (1994); Marion and Plenel (1989).

23. Indeed, it was Chirac, on becoming Prime Minister, who negotiated the transfer of the two agents (found guilty of manslaughter rather than murder, in November 1985) to the French military base in the South Pacific. Chirac gave New Zealand an official apology, $7 million and an unofficial promise that the French veto on the renewal of New Zealand's trade agreement with the EEC would be withdrawn.

24. Madelin, cited in Mény (1992:260). After the victory of the right in the 1995 Presidential election, Madelin was appointed Minister of Finance and the Economy.

25. *Le Nouvel Observateur*, October 1994. (See Lorenzi, 1995:212.) It was also discovered that the *Parti Communiste Français* (PCF), relatively unscathed by the scandals, had received money from the CGE, paid to PCF-sponsored companies in exchange for water contracts. The companies then passed the commission (usually 3% of the total contract) on to PCF-controlled councils.

26. On the use of patronage by the Socialists since 1981 see Streiff (1990).

27. Etienne Dailly and Michel Ameller.

28. The proportion of *fonctionnaire* deputies in the National Assembly has risen from 17% under the Third Republic to 53% today. See Wright (1989:125).

29. Alongside these laws further measures, passed in December 1992 and December 1993, brought France into line with European Community legislation governing the granting of contracts in the water, energy, transport and telecommunications industries.

30. Except for municipal and cantonal elections in areas with under 9,000 registered voters.

31. Whatever happened in practice, as Lorenzi points out, Article 19 of the new law did specify *three* exceptions to the amnesty: cases involving personal enrichment, those where corruption or the trading of favors had been proven and those involving politicians who were deputies at the time the infringements took place. See Lorenzi (1995:163-4).

32. The *Direction Centrale de la Police Judiciaire* (DCPJ), the *Direction des Affaires Criminelles et des Grâces* (DACG), the *Direction Générale des Impôts* (DGI), the *Direction Générale des Douanes* (DGD), and the *Direction Générale de la Concurrence, de la Consommation et de la Répression des Fraudes* (DGCCRF). See Lorenzi (1995:179-86).

33. For an account of the means by which the judicial process deals with infractions committed by government ministers in Germany, Belgium, Denmark, Spain, Greece, Italy, the Netherlands and Portugal, see *Regards sur l'actualité* (February, 1994:32-3).

34. Along with the three ministers involved in the affair, six ministerial advisors, including Fabius's advisor, François Gros, also went before the new court.

35. The others were to be nominated by the president of the National Assembly and the president of the Senate.

36. "A reform which deceives the eye," Valéry Turcey, cited in Bigaud (1994:25).

37. In July 1966 the *Sûreté nationale* (state police) was fused with the *Préfecture de Police* (municipal police) ensuring that the latter, which hitherto had enjoyed a degree of autonomy, came under the jurisdiction of the Interior Minister. See Harstrich and Calvi (1991:130-132).

38. Neither, as the Belgrano affair illustrates, is the practice of sinking foreign boats in suspicious circumstances. See Dalyell (1987.)

39. It was with the media (and the judiciary) in mind that Mitterrand declared, in May 1993 that Bérégovoy's honour and life had been "thrown to the dogs."

40. For a discussion of the use of this term see Stohl and Lopez (1984).

41. On this view of the separation of powers see Marx and Engels (1976).

42. One feature of recent affairs has been their uncanny timing. The Maréchal/Schuller scandal, for example, emerged to embarrass Pasqua in the very week of the Urba trial.

43. Foreshadowing later criticisms of de Gaulle's 1958 constitution, Marx attacked the French constitution of 1848 for seeking to secure "moral" power for the National Assembly while giving actual power to the President. A personal relationship was established between the President and the "sovereign people" by allowing him to be elected once every four years through direct suffrage. The President was thus given "a sort of divine right." Since votes to elect the National Assembly were concentrated not on one individual but on 750, each representing a town or a party rather than the nation, the National Assembly enjoyed only a "metaphysical" relationship to the nation (Marx, 1968:106-108).

44. Draper provides an excellent summary of Marx and Engels's theory of the state.

45. "Our job is not preventing disorder. Our job is preserving disorder." (Mayor Richard Daley of Chicago, 1968. Cited in Widgery, 1989:[x]).

46. Within six months of Chirac's election in May 1995, his Presidency had fallen into the familiar pattern of its predecessors: constitutional reforms passed in July 1995 increased presidential powers by granting the head of state the right to by-pass parliamentary opposition in calling referenda, and Prime Minister Alain Juppé was engulfed in a corruption scandal relating to his own Paris apartment and the rent reduction given to his son while Juppé was finance chief of the Paris City Hall. As if such echoes of the Mitterrand years were not enough, Chirac's decision to resume French nuclear tests in the Pacific led to violent clashes between French forces and anti-nuclear activists aboard the Greenpeace vessel, Rainbow Warrior II.

SEVEN.
CONTROLLING STATE CRIME IN ITALY:
THE CORRUPTION OF A DEMOCRACY

by

Donatella della Porta

and

Alberto Vannucci

STATE CRIME REFERS to a wide range of illicit activities, including "cover-ups, corruption, disinformation, unaccountability, and violations of domestic and/or international laws. It also includes those practices that, although they fall short of being officially declared illegal, are perceived by the majority of the population as illegal or socially harmful" (Ross, 1995:5-6). These activities may be defined as state crime when they are "carried out by the state or on behalf of some state agency" (Friedrichs, 1995:54). In other words, state crimes are illegal activities performed by individuals invested with public power. In fact, for a discussion of state crime it is necessary to analyze the relationship existing in any organization between the *agent*, the person delegated to take decisions, and the *principal* on whose behalf that agent acts. A relation of this kind can exist in the private sector — as, for example, between the manager and the owners, usually shareholders of a firm — as well as in a political organization: between citizens and elected politicians governors and elective assemblies and functionaries of different grades. All public agents have private interests and goals that do not coincide with those of the principal, and they are in a position to exercise power that is to a certain degree discretional (Rose-Ackerman 1978; Banfield 1975).

In democratic systems, public agents act in the name of the collectivity. The instrument universally adopted for limiting the potential conflict between the private interests of the agent and those of the principal (i.e., the public) has been the creation of fixed and verifiable procedures restricting the discretional power of the agent (Pizzorno, 1992). Failure to respect the rules, verifiable through hierarchical, administrative, legal or political controls, is subject to (legal, political, social) sanction. One can speak of state crime, then, when the procedural or political constraints placed on public agents by legislation, customary practice, or international law are violated in order to favor the private interests of the agent or of specific organizations or groups. These illegal activities imply a failure to respect the (implicit or explicit) contract foreseeing the delegation of public responsibilities to the public agent who perpetrates state crime.

There are two main sets of variables that influence the overall level of state crime in a particular country. On the one hand, there are those determining the costs of and benefits expected from illegal behavior.[1] Mechanisms of control capable of influencing these variables, thus rendering illicit behavior inopportune, can be either *internal* to the state apparatus (control bodies, commissions of inquiry) or *external* (the mass media, public opinion, international organizations). The second cluster of variables are those that influence the so-called "moral costs," linked to individual aversion to committing illegal actions. This variable reflects both the "civic spiritness" of public servants and the public attitude towards unlawful behavior, which, in turn, are the product of complex processes of socialization.

In the history of the Italian Republic, state crime developed inside a (wide and relevant) hidden sphere of political activities. In general, it is possible to distinguish between two spheres of political activity: the public sphere, in which the different agents seek to gain credit and to stand out in the eyes of the citizen/voter, and the hidden sphere, in which, thanks to a position held in the state apparatus, favors are exchanged and activity of a frequently illegal nature carried on (Pizzorno, 1993). The past 50 years were marked in Italy by numerous sensational scandals (Turore, 1992; Galli, 1991) that clearly demonstrated the friction that can be generated by a major expansion of the hidden political sphere. According to the Italian sociologist Alessandro Pizzorno, the concealed, or occult level began to lay solid roots in the Italian political system with the terrorist threat in the 1970s:

> converging — perhaps with the intent of provoking, perhaps of controlling, these tensions — with secret activities whose inspiration lay within the state or its organs. Accompanying activities ... which aimed at controlling parasitic income were operations whose referents lay in illegal international markets rather than in the country itself. The resulting parallels between the concealed activities of the political class and those of organized crime are striking [Pizzorno, 1993:298-9].

In Italy, the frequency and magnitude of the scandals through which state crime has been brought to light (only to be swiftly covered up again in many cases) has noticeably increased in the past 25 years, culminating in the recent political upheavals caused by the *mani pulite* ("clean hands") investigations on corruption (on which we will return later). The perception of widespread illegality in administration of public power by Italian bureaucrats and politicians has thus found significant confirmation. Even the Transparency International Corruption Index, which gives a ranking of the levels of diffusion of corrupt practices in 54 countries, refers to Italy as the western democratic country with the highest levels of corruption (Transparency International and the University of Göttingen, 1996).

In order to understand the control of state crime in contemporary Italy, we begin by offering a brief reconstruction of the evolution of different forms of state crimes in this country. Attention will thereafter turn to the mechanisms favoring the widespread diffusion of political and bureaucratic illegality and the way in which these mechanisms have interacted with other, "traditional" failings of the Italian administration to create a veritable vicious circle. Finally, an analysis of the more effective means for preventing state crime will be offered. Our research is based on judicial documents concerning 40 episodes of corruption, the reports of Parliamentary Inquiry Commissions, the requests of judicial action against Members of Parliaments, and articles in the daily and weekly press (della Porta and Vannucci, 1998, 1994; Vannucci, 1997a; della Porta, 1992).

STATE CRIME AND CORRUPTION IN ITALY

Judging from the episodes that have been exposed, state crimes in Italy seem to be concentrated in the following areas: secret service involvement in terrorism and subversion; the covering up of such illegal activities on the part of the country's political leadership and, presumably, their employment for particularistic ends; administrative and political corruption; and the collusion of vast sectors of the state with criminal organizations such as the Sicilian Mafia. In this section, we will provide some information on these different forms of state crime, following the timing of their discovery and investigation.

THE SECRET SERVICE INVOLVEMENT IN TERRORISM AND SUBVERSION

Between the end of the 1960s and the beginning of the 1970s, Italy experienced a dramatic wave of right-wing terrorism. Neo-fascist groups attacked not only their political adversaries but the general public as well: in December 1969, a bomb in the *Banca dell'Agricoltura* in Milan killed 17 people; in July 1970, bombs on a train killed six people; in 1974, eight individuals died when a bomb exploded during a union's demonstration in Brescia, and another 12 people died when a bomb exploded on the train "Italicus." The repression of right-wing terrorism was so ineffective that the instigators and perpetrators of those crimes are still unknown. This inefficacy is explained, above all, by the protection that the neo-fascist groups received from the Italian secret services (De Lutiis, 1996, 1992; della Porta, 1995a, 1993, 1990; Violante, 1984). In the first three decades of the history of the Italian republic, the secret services were in fact characterized "first by lack of accountability to Parliament, second by dependence on the policy decisions and resources of Italy's NATO allies, in particular the United States, and third by a vigorous anti-communism" (Furlong, 1981:84).

In 1964, General De Lorenzo, the head of the military intelligence service *Servizio Informazioni delle Forze Armate* (SIFAR), was accused of planning a coup d'état and had to resign. Although reforms were passed, the reliability of the intelligence services did not improve. Between the end of the 1960s and the beginning of the 1970s, the strategy to deal with an increasing social and political conflict was the threat of the violent "opposed political extremisms" — communists and neo-fascists — to induce public demands for law and order (della Porta, 1995a). A main element in this strategy was the already mentioned protection of the right-wing groups. According to a study carried out on parliamentary acts: "More or less relevant signs of direct action or involvement by the secret services can be singled out in all the trial records referring especially to the most serious crimes of right-wing terrorism, such as the massacre of Piazza Fontana, of Piazza della Loggia, on the train Italicus, at the Bologna railways station, the attempted coup of the Rosa dei Venti and the Golpe Borghese" (Rodotà, 1984:83).

It has further been suggested that the action of the secret services was engineered by groups formed within the political parties (Galli, 1986). Although no strong evidence supported this hypothesis, at least until now, it should not be forgotten that the Masonic lodge P2 had important ramifications inside many parties.

FREEMASONRY AND POLITICS: THE LODGE P2

All of the different forms of state crime to be found in the Italy interacted in the case of the "secret" P2 Masonic lodge. In fact, the P2 offered a confidential arena in which entrepreneurs, members of the liberal professions, intermediaries, functionaries and politicians could meet, get to know each other, propose business deals, negotiate and work out agreements and guarantees.[2] Indeed, secret Masonic lodges generally represent a *market* for individuals disposed to and interested in making clandestine contacts, legal or otherwise. Freemasonry also presents characteristics that strongly reinforce the bonds of loyalty among members, reducing the risks involved in transactions. Being a member provides a "certificate of trust" in exchanges, and failure to respect agreements has a direct economic cost: the exclusion from future opportunities for exchange.[3]

The affair of the secret P2 Masonic lodge came to light in 1981, when documents were confiscated by the Milanese magistracy in a villa belonging to its Grand Master, Licio Gelli. Gelli's activities were geared towards *elite* concealed proselytizing on a national scale (Magnolfi, 1996). The lodge membership roll — a list of 962 affiliates discovered during the sequestration — was not deposited with the secretariat of the Grand Orient, the main Italian Masonic order. The lodge did not hold meetings or elect its officials. Secrecy inside the lodge was carried to an extreme through its tentacle-like structure. Members included three government ministers, 30 members of parliament, more than 50 generals (including the highest ranks of the secret services), high-level functionaries, diplomats, journalists, financiers and industrialists. At the center of the web stood Gelli, who maintained the contacts between the various members, thus ensuring his exclusive power as a mediator: "Able to capitalize on tentacles that linked bankers skillful at illegal financial dealings, virtually the entire top echelon of the country's secret services, the conspirators behind the right-wing 'strategy of tension,' and the world of organized crime, Gelli and the P2 had become — or were on the verge of becoming — the center of the system of 'occult power' that constitutes the dark underside of Italian democracy" (Chubb and Vannicelli, 1986:126).

An essential resource for Gelli was the control of *confidential information*. By way of the former chief of the disbanded secret service, Gelli received its confidential files that enormously increased his stock of compromising material on representatives of the political, economic and financial worlds. Moreover, at the moment of joining, Gelli demanded a "fee" from would-be adepts in the form of information regarding eventual injustices, abuses, persons responsible. The information in his possession steadily accumulated. In this way Gelli was able to create a *monopoly* of blackmailing power on a range of individuals and, thanks to that power, obtain access to further resources — in particular, through Roberto Calvi, the president of Italy's largest private bank, the Banco Ambrosiano:[4] "[the financier] Sindona in particular provided Gelli with the documentation that could have definitively exposed Calvi. From that moment,

Gelli's power multiplied because, with Calvi and the *Banco Ambrosiano* at his disposition, the Grand Master could conceive financial operations on a grand scale" (Galli, 1983:207). The *Banco Ambrosiano* became the financial arm of the covert lodge, acting as an intermediary in diverse transactions. The bank was used to extend the lodge's influence into the world of the media through the placing of P2 affiliates in prominent positions in Italy's leading daily newspaper, the *Corriere della Sera*. A number of channels of communication with the Mafia created the possibility of exercising violent sanctions (Parliamentary Committee of Inquiry on the Mafia, 1993).

Gelli used this mix of blackmail, corruption and coercion to enlarge the network of connections created in the economic and political realms. The P2 thus came to resemble a "state within the state," with the power to influence prominent sectors in both institutional and economic life (Teodori, 1986). As a result of the resources at his disposition, the role of Gelli on occasion exceeded that of simple intermediary. He frequently appeared as *guarantor* of deals he helped arrange, acting on a scale that transcended the confines of Italy itself.[5] The lodge operated in a plurality of, at times illegal markets: national and international finance, publishing, corruption and arms trafficking. In fact, the P2's Grand Master offered an extra-legal system of handling rather murky dealings (Parliamentary Committee of Inquiry on P2, 1984). The financing of political parties increased Gelli's power as a guarantor of illegal transactions.

Gelli's activities contributed to the production of the resources (compromising information, the web of reciprocal obligations between various centers of economic, political, financial and military power) which in turn permitted him to offer his services on an ever expanding scale. Whoever advanced in their careers or dealings in the public or private sector thanks to P2 affiliation in turn favored, through the filter of Gelli, the success of other members. Thus, the overall influence of the secret organization in the economic and political fields was extended.

ADMINISTRATIVE AND POLITICAL CORRUPTION

With the exception of the P2, political corruption is the only form of state crime for which sufficient information for a qualitative analysis is available. Even the information available on other forms of administrative and political illegality, such as collusion between sectors of the state and organized crime, has often emerged from the uncovering of specific cases of corruption. In other words, the investigation of the "hidden face" of public power demonstrates that the market of corruption has, for many years, represented the determining factor for a vast range of (frequently illegal) activities based on the appropriation of public resources by state functionaries, a group of entrepreneurs benefiting from political protection, and actors from the criminal world. The market for corruption, therefore, will be at the center of our analysis.

The secret dimension of public activity, and corruption in particular, has exerted a crucial influence on public policy since the immediate post-war period. In the 1950s, relations with leading politicians and the higher echelons of the bureaucracy were administered in a centralized fashion by the *Confindustria* (the industrial employers' association) and the electric companies, who generously financed pro-Western public exponents. Furthermore, a sort of competition to obtain a privileged position through corruption developed between the private and public sectors of industry.

Moreover, a powerful monetary impulse to corruption originated from *abroad*. Immediately following the war, Italy was contested terrain between the two dominant world power-blocs, and it was from them that the two principal Italian parties, the Christian Democrats (*Democrazia Cristiana*) and the Communist Party (*Partito Comunista Italiano*), took their political lead. Immense sums of money from both the United States and the Soviet Union financed the political life and electoral activities of the parties (Colby and Forbath, 1981).[6]

The drying up of American subventions to the Christian Democrats coincided with the beginnings of the policy of large-scale nationalization and growing public intervention in the economy. From then on hidden activities concentrated on this field of public action, in which the curbs and controls on an administration geared to the (often openly illegal) accumulation of political funding were steadily being eroded. Part of the budget of public entities therefore became the "property" of government exponents, who nominated their own men to the positions of command. In these years of notable expansion in the area of public entrepreneurial activity, a bountiful flow of bribes arrived from major public enterprises.

The concealed accumulation of financial resources for political activity was intensified, then, through the (mal)administration of public power. The "legitimation" for demanding (greater or lesser) political percentages also depended on electoral results, thus creating incentives to spare no financial effort in that field.

To augment the flow of financial resources and diminish the risks, politicians entered directly into the running of public agencies, further extending the sphere of direct political control. The system of bribes further expanded between the end of the 1970s and beginning of the 1980s. According to the entrepreneur Vincenzo Lodigiani, the simultaneous presence of the various circumstances described above made it "necessary for the parties to open a direct 'line' with entrepreneurs who intended entering the world of public supply and contracting" (Tangentopoli, 1993:41). In this market for corruption the opposition too would be more frequently involved in hidden bargaining, either in order to push sympathetic enterprises or, on occasions in more recent years, to receive bribes. Going on the information that has emerged from judicial investigations, the system by now thoroughly invested every sector of the state, local and central administrations, public agencies and enterprises, the military apparatus and the bureaucracy.

In the early 1990s, this system of corrupt exchanges was exposed by the judicial inquiry *mani pulite* ("clean hands"). On February 17 1992, the most serious political crisis in the history of the Italian Republic began in Milan, with the first of a long series of arrests of prominent politicians and functionaries, from virtually all the national political parties, accused of committing extremely serious crimes, among them extortion, corruption, receipt of stolen goods, criminal conspiracy and association in organized crime. The inquiries of Antonio di Pietro, the Milanese Assistant Prosecutor who would become a popular hero, resulted in the arrest of Mario Chiesa, an administrator belonging to the Socialist Party (PSI) and President of one of the city's public agencies, the *Pio Albergo Trivulzio*. The investigation subsequently mushroomed, laying bare the true nature of public administration in what was to become known as *tangentopoli* (bribe-city). Thirty-five days after his arrest, Chiesa started collaborating with the magistrates, triggering off a chain of confessions that, in the course of only a few months, would lead to the incrimination of hundreds of politicians, businessmen and bureaucrats operating in countless public entities in the Milan area.

From Milan, the investigations spread also to other northern and central cities, and starting in 1993 reached into the south of the country as well. Initially concentrated on local politics, the investigations quickly extended to the uppermost levels of major private and public enterprises, implicating important government figures as well as the secretaries of the various political parties. In a matter of months, the magistracy had unveiled a scene of corruption and political illegality involving the entire political class of the country and broad sectors of its business community. The official statistics, which nonetheless only provide a partial picture of the phenomenon, show a gradual increase in the number of offenses against the public administration such as corruption, extortion, embezzlement and abuse of office: from a national average of 252 acts and 365 people denounced per year between 1984 and 1991, to an average of 1095 acts and 2084 people per year between 1992 and 1995 (Istat, 1997). More than 500 ex-MPs, four ex-Prime Ministers, many ex-Ministers and thousands of local administrators, bureaucrats, military officials, judges, public managers were indicted for such crimes. Moreover, as the same statistics signal, the number of people involved in political corruption grew more than proportionally to the number of cases, showing the presence of more complex networks of corrupt exchanges.

These judicial investigations on corruption, besides sanctioning what both media and politicians have come to describe as the crisis of the "First Republic," provide an enormous amount of material for the analysis of what can be defined — paraphrasing Bachrach and Baratz (1962) — as the "other face of power." In fact, reviewing the information that has emerged from the *mani pulite* inquiry since 1992, to that slowly accumulated in earlier judicial inquiries, it is possible to reconstruct certain aspects of that "invisible" level of Italian politics that has had such an important influence on the "visible" one (Pizzorno, 1993). The everyday activity of principal government figures was so preoccupied with a ceaseless search for money that to understand the political history of Italy in recent decades — the true motivations behind public policy and action — it appears necessary to refer to the illegal dimension of political life.

COLLUSION BETWEEN THE STATE AND ORGANIZED CRIME

The *mani pulite* investigation shed also a new light on another form of state crime: the collusion between politicians (often, a public administrators) and organized crime, such as *Cosa Nostra* or the *Mafia* in Sicily, *'Ndrangheta* in Calabria, the *Sacra Corona Unita* in Puglia and the *Camorra* in Campania. In at least four Italian regions, these criminal organizations have exhibited perturbing links with sectors of the state. According to the former mafioso and now collaborating with investigators (*pentito*) Tommaso Buscetta, "the Mafia never relied on politics. The Mafia used politics for its own ends" (Buscetta, 1992:23). Mafia interest in politicians was purely instrumental but pervasive.

For *mafiosi*, politicians often represent an obligatory channel of access to the judiciary, for the purpose of obtaining legal impunity. While the objective of the Mafia is to conduct its illegal affairs without interference, politicians seek to maximize their power and electoral support at times by resorting to corruption. The terrain on which the two meet is the hidden market for bartering resources such as protection, public programs, restricted information, the use of violence and intimidation or electoral patronage (della Porta and Vannucci, 1995).

In the last two decades, the number of politicians and functionaries having regular contacts with Mafia bosses would seem to have multiplied to the point that, as the entrepreneur Aurelio Pino has remarked, "certainly, in any entities of interest to them, the Mafia has closely connected functionaries and employees in key positions" (PRP, 1990:34). Politicians and bureaucrats transmit restricted information, fix public competitions and confer favors of every kind in return for protection, money or votes (Ruggiero, 1996). A number of leading political figures have been involved in judicial inquiries in this respect, including the ex-Minister of the Interior, Antonio Gava, accused of collusion with the Neapolitan *camorra* (APN) and Giulio Andreotti, several times Prime Minister and accused by the magistrates of Palermo of having "engaged — in a manner neither episodic nor contingent — in conduct such as to effect a positive contribution to the protection of the interests and the realization of the aims of the organization *Cosa Nostra*" (Public Prosecutor at the Court of Palermo, 1993:9; Public Prosecutor at the Court of Palermo, 1995).

ON THE DYNAMICS OF EVOLUTION OF STATE CRIME IN ITALY

Different forms of state crime interact with each other in a series of vicious circles that eventually brought through a serious crisis the corrupted regime. Regarding the dynamics of corruption, a number of scholars have suggested paths along which the phenomenon can grow (see, for example, della Porta, 1995b). In the first place, corruption can seep down from above. As already noted, "leaders, by definition, play an important role in directing public opinion and social behavior ... the corruption of the leadership tends to reduce the confidence, loyalty and integrity of followers" (Werner, 1983:150). Secondly, corruption can reproduce from below: "Once the incentives for petty corruption have been created," "it tends to extend up the way through interest in complicity. This in its turn, by way of impunity, creates favorable conditions for the growth of corruption" (Cadot, 1987:239). Also, the constant movement of politicians from elective positions in representative bodies to posts distributed by the parties in public entities furthers the horizontal spread of corrupt practices from one institution to another. The diffusion of corruption, therefore, diminishes its costs, reducing both the sense of guilt and the risks of losing face, while increasing, on the other hand, the possibilities of finding dependable partners for corrupt transactions (Andvig, 1991).[7]

These mechanisms, already observed "at work" in the Italian case (della Porta, 1992:324-6), have undeniably favored the reproduction of corruption on a large scale. However, it is possible to take a further step in understanding the evolutionary dynamics of this phenomenon if the analysis is taken beyond its "internal" mechanisms, to look at the interaction between corruption and other pathologies — or forms of state crime — regularly mentioned in sociological and political studies of Italy. In fact, causal ties have often been noted between corruption and clientelism, maladministration, organized crime, secret Masonic lodge and deviant secret services (della Porta and Vannucci, 1998; 1994). These different problems have created a spiral of malfunctioning within the Italian political and administrative system.

In such a context, the generalized inefficiency of public structures, for which the functionaries themselves are in part responsible, permits them to "privatize" and sell the resources of their office in exchange for bribes. The discretionary power accompanying administrative inefficiency can be used to further the interests of aspiring corrupters: thus, corruption feeds on inefficiency. For example, when long delays in carrying out certain procedures become the norm, even a functionary who limits himself to performing his job within the time foreseen by the regulations can demand a bribe in exchange for this by now unanticipated "service." As observed by a Sicilian politician: "The administrative paralysis transforms all civic rights in favors. If you need a certificate or a building permit, and if you wait for them for two years or so, eventually you ask for them and pay for them as a favor" (*La Repubblica*, 17 October 1991). Corruption, in turn, promotes inefficiency. If one of the objectives of functionaries is to collect bribes, they have an interest in fostering the conditions of procedural delay, viscosity and unpredictability that widen the margins for corrupt transactions: "Many files are kept opened, because this is the better way to keep all under fire," so complains a Milanese entrepreneur (FIPE, 1992:54). Similarly, a Sicilian businessman recalls: "there was the frequent need to pay the politicians, ... in order to avoid to displease those who, with their influence and prestige, could eliminate the obstacles preceding and following the adjudication of public contracts" (CD, n.450, 1993:2). Finally, administrative inefficiency obstructs investigations into corruption by lending formal justification for a vast range of actions taken by corrupt functionaries before organs of control. The judges who investigated political corruption in Bari observed that: "the immunity [for corrupted politicians] derives from that involution in the bureaucratic course that insure the *post-hoc* demonstration of the claimed delays" (Court of Bari, 1985:267). At the same time, verification of administrative inefficiency is powerfully hampered by acts of corruption, which conceal both the real motives for and the outcomes of public decisions.

Thus, maladministration and corruption are interdependent. On the one hand, the investigations into political corruption have showed very clearly how maladministration (sometimes resulting from inertia, sometimes from able maneuvering) increases the discretionary and arbitrary power of the administrators in each phase of the process leading to the "purchase" of public measures by bribery: from the creation of artificial demand to the contamination of the system of adjudication and the weakening of controls (della Porta and

Vannucci, 1994). On the other hand, through arbitrary rises in the price of and distortion of the demand for public works, corruption increases maladministration. Maladministration causes a growth of mistrust in the public administration: as a result, privileged channels of access to public decisions are sought, irrespective of whether they refer to enjoyment of a service or competition for public contracts, jobs, etc. The necessity for privileged channels increases willingness to "buy" access by paying bribes, in other words, the demand for corruption. Through the diffusion of corrupt practices, in fact, a selective inclusion of those who pay is realized. Corruption therefore increases inefficiency, recommencing the vicious circle.

If "maladministration" increases demand for corruption, clientelism — another typically Italian phenomenon connected with the construction of networks of organizational exchange between political patrons offering protection and specific benefits and clients reciprocating with general support, consent, votes, etc. (Graziani, 1980) — increases the supply. The Italian politicians involved in illicit activities appear to have possessed notable networking capacity to which a "patrimonialistic" conception of public goods as private assets may be added. Both these characteristics, undoubtedly useful in organizing a system of illegal exchange or for successfully introducing oneself into an existing one, also favor the construction of a network of personal support formed both of clients and "friends" in the local elite (della Porta, 1992). Various testimonies have emphasized the ability of many defendants in distributing favors to a large number of individuals, privileging sectors and groups who could provide the greatest compensation in terms of electoral backing and collusion (della Porta and Vannucci, 1994). In synthesis, it can be said that corrupt politicians reinforce their electoral and collusionary feuds by developing both traditional forms of clientelism, based on localized patron-client relations, and client networks anchored in broader institutional contexts; both patron brokerage and organizational clientelistic brokerage (Eisenstadt and Roniger, 1984).

It is precisely the desire to expand the volume of bribes that induces corrupt politicians to increase the activity and spending of the entities they administer and with them the opportunities for distributing favors. To collect more bribes, in fact, they must employ an increasing amount of resources and spend more public money, at least in those sectors where the illicit rewards appear highest and the risks lowest. Reinvesting in politics the money collected from bribes, corrupt politicians are able to organize sophisticated client networks and to acquire political protection. As one of the judges involved in the *mani pulite* investigation, Piercamillo Davigo, observed: "A lot of the illicit funds were used by the politicians of the different factions to buy party membership cards... These membership cards were used to established power relations inside the parties... The parties were transformed into joint-stock companies, where bribes were used to buy shares in order to acquire the possibility to be re-elected" (Davigo, 1993:11).

To the vicious circles already described are added others, particularly in the south of the country where political corruption and common crime have fed off each other. The presence of organized crime reinforces the stability of the illegal deals that underpin political corruption and widespread maladminis-tration. The risk of incurring violent sanctions consolidates corrupt exchange, and the latter in its turn favors the spread of those conditions of generalized illegality that protect organized criminality. The criminal groups strengthen the position of corrupt politicians through the blocks of votes they control and the use of violence. According to the former Mafia associate Antonino Calderone, "We are talking about a terrifying, massive force, if you keep in mind that every *uomo d'onore*, can count on at least forty to fifty people who will blindly follow his directives. ... We can readily understand the significance of Mafia support in electoral competition" (DAP, 1993:39). As one state's witness has revealed, "It is important to know which political figures receive electoral support from the Cosa Nostra, because, if that is the case, it is possible to turn to them for the compensation for the electoral backing already given" (CPMF:16). In their turn, corrupt politicians use the power they possess to offer services enhancing the power and reputation of the criminal organizations that back them (della Porta and Vannucci, 1995). Moreover, by guaranteeing impunity and control of the territory, often secured through the regulation of public contracts, corrupt politicians have reinforced the power of organized crime itself. According to the former Mafioso affiliate Gaspare Mutolo: "The unanimous belief was that one could easily influence the action of the courts through politicians and that, further, the function of Sicilian politicians was critical for 'Roman politics' [national level political decisions] with regard to Sicilian matters involving the Cosa Nostra" (DAP, 1993:24).

It can be added that the relationships between organized crime and cor-rupt politicians were favored by the existing state of maladministration, and in their turn contributed to making it worse. Maladministration has also increased the dependence of ordinary citizens on crime. As the Parliamentary Organized Crime Commission has warned,

> where the public administration is inert or inept and administrative controls fail to operate, almost automatically a favorable situation is created for the mixing of organized crime and politics. Often, it is no longer a question of mixing but of the occupation of the public in-

stitutions by emissaries of Mafia groups, who administer power on behalf of the "family" to which they belong, against the interests of the public and, on occasions, undisturbed by the organisms of control, whether administrative or juridical (CPMF, 1993:18).

A similar vicious circle developed between corruption, deviant secret services and covered Masonic lodges. In a system of widespread illegality, Masonic lodges, such as the P2, provided resources for the implementation of the corrupt exchanges. Information on possible partners available for illegal deals reduced the risks that are usually involved in the search for accomplices. The potential for blackmailing could be used to insure the respect of the illicit agreements. Linkages with the organized crime increased the propensity to comply with the demands of the organization. On the other hand, the presence of political corruption increased the power of the Masonic lodge P2, as well as, of course, the individual patrimony of their members who could collect bribes and favors.

As Norberto Bobbio observed many years ago, in democracies the greater publicity for some public decisions went hand in hand with the displacement of several negotiations from political, visible institutions to a series of invisible networks, linked by personal relationships. In the Italian case, this "sub-government" interacted with a "crypto-government," defined as "those actions performed by subversive political forces that act in the shadows, linked to the secret services, or with part of them, or at least not impeded by them" (Bobbio, 1980:201). Not only — as revealed by recent investigations — secret service agents actively took part in corrupt networks, but the spread of illegal activities reduced the transparency of the political process, leaving space for those who wanted to use the information they hold on the many vices of the political class as a resource to blackmail those who could have opposed their plans. These linkages between various representatives of the "crypto-government" emerged, for instance, in such obscure cases as the hidden negotiations involving the *camorra*, the secret services, and the Red Brigades during the kidnapping of the Christian Democrat politician Ciro Cirillo, suspected of having being involved in the political corruption that flourished in the region of Naples (Tranfaglia, 1994), or the bomb attacks on a train near to Bologna in the 1990s, and, later on, in Rome and Florence, attributed to a network connecting Mafiosi, right-wing terrorists, former secret service agents and deviated Masonic brothers.

DIFFICULTIES IN CONTROLLING POLITICAL CORRUPTION IN ITALY

For more than 40 years, the history of controlling state crime in Italy has consisted of political cover-ups and obstruction rather than successes.[8] For example, some of the major scandals that have erupted in Italy's recent past have been produced not by control agencies but by the diffusion of compromising information (sometimes originating from the secret services) on the part of politicians with something to gain from implicating others.[9] In other cases, such as the notorious Lockheed scandal — which led to the resignation of Giovanni Leone, at the time President of the Republic, and the incrimination of two ministers who had accepted bribes from the U.S. corporation willing to sell its combat planes to the Italian Army — it was investigations conducted abroad that led to the uncovering of the affair. The impression of widespread illegality in public affairs since the 1950s, then, has found partial (but significant) confirmation. In Italy, at least until 1992, controlling organs and mass media proved ineffective — due to internal difficulties and external interference — in combating and denouncing corruption and other state crimes in at least proportionate measure to their real diffusion and gravity. Even the parliamentary commissions set up to investigate the most prominent episodes (the Mafia, P2, Sindona, misappropriation of post-earthquake reconstruction funds) have resulted at best in generic denunciations lacking in any practical consequences.

It therefore seems opportune to analyze, if only briefly, the factors that have determined the pervasive influence of such illegal activities, enlarging the opportunities for corruption or, to put it another way, contributing to obstructing and defusing the mechanisms of control. In fact, as has been noted "Italian scandals are the by-product of structural problems that are deeply rooted in the country's political, institutional and social fabric. ... It is no exaggeration to say that most Italian scandals are 'state scandals'" (Chubb and Vannicelli, 1986:125).

THE EXPANSION OF THE PUBLIC SPHERE AND THE DISCRETIONALITY OF POWER

Among the factors that may have favored the growth of illegality in the exercise of public power in Italy, there is the indiscriminate expansion, particularly from the 1960s, of the functions of the state and other public agencies in regulation and control. In general, the greater the amount of resources passing through the hands of politicians or functionaries who have a certain power of allocation over them, or who have access to restricted information concerning the criteria for their allocation, the greater (all other circumstances being equal) the opportunities for corruption (della Porta and Vannucci, 1994). In Italy, the range of public decision-making affecting economic organizations is particularly broad. A comparison of public spending, expressed as a percentage of GNP, shows notable differences between developed democracies: the lowest is Japan, at just, 15%; the highest are Great Britain (37%), Italy (41%) and France (43%).[10]

Of course, no direct correlation can be made between levels of public spending and levels of corruption. There is, however, a refinement that provides more reliable indications. Rather than the absolute level of public spending, it is possible to take the *rapidity* and *extent* of its growth. If a certain rigidity in adapting to new conditions on the part of public organizations, procedures and control agencies is hypothesized, rapid growth in the volume of resources offers public agents greater opportunities for illegal appropriation. The rapid extension of the "territory" to be covered makes administrative and legal controls more difficult (Vannucci, 1994). In comparison with other industrial democracies, Italy presents in the last two decades, the highest relative increase in levels of public spending. Between 1970 and 1990 the level of public spending as a percentage of GNP rose from 18% to 41%. Using slightly different figures, which measure the average annual increase in the cost of public policies from 1951 to 1980, Italy remains in first place (9.3%), followed by France (8.3%), Germany (7.8%), the United States (5.1%) and Great Britain (4.3%) (Rose, 1988:318).

The intensity of legislative production also seems particularly significant. In Italy more than 100,000 laws are currently in force, compared to little more than 7,000 in France. The average number of laws passed annually in Italy is 588, compared with 93 in France, 148 in Great Britain and 452 in the United States (Rose, 1988:20).[11] The *inertial force* of laws remaining in force for an indefinite period after their emanation increase exponentially the quantity of legally binding regulations to be obeyed. This creates an escalation in the number of contacts between individual citizens and public entities as a result of the extended range of pertinence of laws and regulations. As a consequence, there is a proportional increase in friction, confrontation and contention between citizens and the public apparatus. The statistics on the demands for administrative justice confirm this trend: in 1992 more than 85,000 appeals were presented at the regional administrative courts, the TAR (*Tribunale Amministrativo Regionale*), with an increase of 169% since 1977. The appeals referred especially to public employment (41.55%) and public buildings (31%). This overload of demands was addressed toward institutions that were not prepared to sustain it: the difference between appeals and decisions increased three times in the last 15 years, with an average duration of the proceedings of 3,077 days (Arabbia and Giammusso, 1994:283-4).

At the same time, the risk increases of normative overlaps, assimilation, partial abrogation, exceptions and contradictions needing to be resolved at the judicial level. In such a context, the rules of the game predisposed and guaranteed by the state lose their role as a stable institutional framework within which transactions can take place. Instead, they become a point of departure for successive rounds of negotiation between centers of political and economic power from which the rules themselves emerge altered. According to a Milanese entrepreneur:

> If we had to respect all the legal norms when we start an economic enterprises, we could forget about it ... According to the law, before starting any activity, you need to have all permits and authorizations under your own name. Obviously, this put the entrepreneur in a situation of direct dependency from the public officials, who can control or not control, enforce the rules or do not enforce them [FIPE, 1992:64-5].

Uncertainty thus grows regarding the effective extent of individual property rights and, in consequence, regarding the content of market relations. Even leading figures in the economic world, who regularly operate in the market, increasingly risk acting at the margins of legality:

> The administrative norms designed to protect monopolized goods (designed, that is, to pursue public ends) become more numerous and complicated exactly where they regulate those activities that are socially most relevant and essential to the existing mode of production ... The risk of incurring in penal responsibilities grows as the activity pursued becomes more central and socially significant and as the social status of the actor increases [Sgubbi, 1990:61].

The probability of having to face choices that involve violation of the law is greater for members of the economic-financial elite since they are involved in a larger number of transactions subject to legal restrictions. Thus, there is a reinforcement of the incentives to collude with the governing class (in other words, corruption), in order to acquire legal or illegal political protection. The very diffusion of corruption reduces its expected dangers and costs. Increasing the space for arbitrary activities on the side of the public bureaucracy, the high number of laws, often conflicting with each other, also provide resources for the hidden activities of deviant secret services. At the same time the overload of demands for an intervention of the judiciary reduce the possibility that the misconduct of secret services and the like are investigated and repressed.

We should add that, compared with France, the United Kingdom, Sweden and Ireland, Italian legislation presents a lower level of *importance*, as measured by the number of persons affected, the resources distributed and the kind of redistribution involved. The legislative initiatives regarding decisions of limited significance are those more likely to acquire a notable *exchange value* in the corrupt market, since they "satisfy a multitude of extremely sectorial and clientelistic demands" (Di Palma, 1978:107).[12] Sectional, micro-sectional and so-called "mini-laws" proliferate, allocating particularistic benefits to groups of small dimensions while spreading widely the external costs.[13]

THE SYSTEM OF ADMINISTRATIVE, BUREAUCRATIC AND LEGAL CONTROLS

In evaluating occasions for corruption, a further decisive condition must be considered: the nature of the restraints and controls on political and administrative activity. Systems of *civil law*, such as the Italian one, are characterized by a strong suspicion of discretionality, which is harshly limited by a series of intersecting *procedural controls*, that is to say, by a rigid and extensive predisposition of norms for putting into practice and verifying each individual action. These controls are mainly formal ones, addressing adherence to procedural rules, while there is a lack of substantial controls on the costs and quality of the product. In Italy, in fact, "[p]reventive controls occupy too large a sphere, and ask for a drastic amputation. At the present stage, they are suffocating, formalistic, and to a good extent insufficient to insure a 'good administration'. ... Successive controls are few and ill-organized" (D'Auria, 1993:233). Moreover, "as far as the local finance is concerned, a model of preventive controls remains intact, without any possibility of controls ex-post" (Guccione, 1993:28). This might seem an effective model of controlling state crime, and in particular corruption. However, it presents a weakness that emerged with particular evidence in Italy. The existence of a complex system of prescriptions for and constraints on the behavior of public agents, and the resulting uncertainty on the norms to be applied, can end up aggravating inefficiencies, delays and misconduct, favoring the reintroduction of discretionary power. This *vicious circle of guarantees* (Pizzorno, 1992:55) has been encouraged by the traditional failings of Italian administration. Lengthy delays weighing on citizens using public services end up by legitimating ex post a greater discretionary power of public agents. In this area of decision-making, opportunities for illegalities will be greater because *extraordinary* discretionality, not foreseen by the regulations, is more difficult to control. Widespread involvement in illegal activities increases the resources of blackmail in the hands of those actors who, like the deviant secret services or the deviant Masonic lodge, collect compromising information and use them for their — either political or economic — aims.

As incentives to state crime grow, as they do for any other illegal activity, the less the probability of being discovered and punished. The risk of incurring sanctions depends on the internal dynamics of illegal exchange and on the efficacy of external controls on obedience to legal or administrative procedures and norms. According to Sabino Cassese (1992), ex-Minister for Public Administration, the prime responsibility for the proliferation of political illegality in Italy rests with the system of administrative controls. Controls inside public organizations have all but fallen into disuse because "they were contrary to the interests of the politicians who should have been leading the administration but who instead were using it to their own advantage." As to external controls, they have been frustrated by a lack of resources and the "piling up" of overlapping controls without any real verification of their effectiveness, as well as by the politicization of the controlling bodies.

At the same time, there was a growth in the power of the politicians over the private agents, who could not rely upon impartial controls in their legal conflicts with public agencies led by party-appointees. In fact,

> The traditional procedures and powers (that is, the legitimacy controls in the broad meaning of the words, the controls on the single act, the semi-contentious forms, and, therefore, those of a co-decision nature) were given to a politically appointed, non-professional personnel. This type of personnel would perhaps be able to manage, with efficacy, other types of control. With the traditional instruments in its hands, it produces the worst results: the law was used for illegal aims; the examination of each act as retaliation; and the condition of efficacy as a threat [Cassese, 1993:16].

An uncorrupted bureaucracy represents an essential watchdog on, and counterweight to, the activities of politicians as well as other public agents. Civil servants are often in a position to denounce the illegitimate actions of politicians, or they can refuse to carry out the measures desired by the latter. For their part, the politicians define the essential lines of the public administration's activity, influencing both the opportunities and risks of bureaucratic corruption. In Italy the bureaucracy has undergone a process of *political fragmentation*:

The lack of alternation and the lengthy permanence in power of the same political personnel has led to forms of vertical alliances between politicians and bureaucrats which transcend the traditional separation between political personnel on the one hand and civil servants on the other. Here too, the cement has been provided by corruption, or at least by the use of public resources for private or partial ends [Pizzorno, 1992:59].

An intermediary class of bureaucrat-politicians, whose first loyalty lies with the political parties, has thus developed and expanded, and these bureaucrats have generated a dense exchange network with leading political figures in the public administration. In order to obtain easier career advancement, greater decision-making power or to collect bribes and other private advantages, bureaucrats require the protection, or at least the abstention from supervision of their political superiors. In return, they can offer the services of their office to particular private actors (for either economic or political aim) or divide the proceeds of illegal activities with their political protector. The Italian bureaucracy has traditionally demonstrated a conspicuous permeability to interest and pressure groups where these have close links with the governing political parties (La Palombara and Poggi, 1975). The politician, for his part, can devote himself to illegal activities with a high probability of immunity thanks to the complicity of the bureaucrat. Politicians and bureaucrats cohabited in fact the corrupted market. As a Milanese entrepreneur indicated: "The aldermen, who are politically nominated, deal with the big business; and, on purpose, they leave to the top bureaucrats the smaller business so that all of them can work without troubles in its own field" (FIPE, 1992:13-4). In the case of the deviant secret services and the P2 Lodge, dense networks of political and personal links intervened in the recruitment of "loyal" people in the most strategic positions in the state apparatuses.

Besides formal control, the loyalty of the public agents to democracy and "good government" is determined by their "political culture" or, in other words, by the presence of a "sense of state;" this influences the moral costs of illicit activity. If the recognized moral criteria of the public organization to which the individual belongs are analogous to those of the public authority, the potential *exposure* consequent on involvement in corruption or other misconduct will appear particularly costly. The internalization of norms depends on so-called *pride in position* and the prestige of public service. The more public roles are sought after and socially rewarded, the less desirable will appear as the violation of group norms. Compared with the German, British or French public administrations, which have traditionally shown a strong esprit de corp, the Italian bureaucracy is characterized by a generalized lack of the sense of the state, related to the importance of political protection (or, in the best of cases, seniority) in determining careers: "it is therefore impossible to create solid alternatives to rewards based, on the contrary, simply on the manifestation of wealth; which cannot but derive, in the case of state servants, from corruption" (Pizzorno,1992:69-70).[14]

All democratic systems foresee a set of political and institutional controls on the exercise of public power whose efficacy is subject to a continual process of adjustment corresponding to the expectations and choices of citizens, in their turn influenced by the efficacy of the controls operating in the preceding period. A certain quantity of criminal episodes must be exposed before the public becomes aware of the problem, and politicians have an incentive (in terms of gains in consensus) to propose and actuate effectual reforms, discouraging further transgressions. If this does not happen, the inefficiency of the controls sets in motion a vicious circle, progressively slackening the institutional curbs on political illegality. Given that illegalities committed by public agents are often also breaches of the criminal law, the "natural" adversary of corrupted and corrupters is the magistracy. The latter performs, in fact, a decisive function in the control of corruption, as well as of other state crimes. In fact, any eventual punishment of corrupted public agents in political terms is tightly bound up with the existence and visibility of a criminal prosecution. The efficiency and degree of independence from political authority of the magistracy marks the degree to which indulging in state crime is dangerous.

For many years, the action of judicial organs has represented the principal, if not the only, source of risk for corrupted and corrupter. With the already mentioned *mani pulite* inquiry of 1992, an evident change has taken place in the attitude of the magistracy towards political corruption. Leaving aside contingent causes, it can be hypothesized that the recent exponential growth in investigations that has also been due to a weakening in the complicity of some judges with political forces that hindered, in part, the activity of the magistracy in the years preceding the 1970s. Until the 1960s, the work of the magistracy seems to have followed prevalently the interests of the political forces in government, in return for compensation in economic or career terms (Moriondo, 1967). Class collusion as well as political alliances thwarted any attempt to shed light on the subversive, anti-democratic plans of the deviant parts of the state apparatuses, as well as in political and bureaucratic corruption. In the last 20 years, however, magistrates have displayed a new and tangible independence, in particular as they have taken on a leading role in contrasting political corruption (della Porta and Vannucci, 1997; Nelken, 1996; Guarnieri, 1991).

Various strategies based upon intimidation have been adopted against magistrates who pierced the circle of political illegality, including pressure by superiors more sensitive to "political needs," marginalization or transfer, and even assassinations, in the case of investigations unveiling the relationships between organized crime and politicians. Inquiries were removed as quickly as possible from the magistrates responsible for the initiative and transferred to judicial seats more inclined to suppress the matter.[15] As most recent investigations indicated, many judges received political protection as well as considerable economic "compensations" — more or less hidden forms of bribes — for their protection of corrupters and corrupted, powerful Masonic brothers, mafiosi and secret service agents. In particular, recent inquiries have described a hidden network of corrupt judges of the Tribunal of Rome who sold their sentences and acts in particularly valuable cases, and who were paid by "friends" lawyers and entrepreneurs who acted as brokers (*L'Espresso*, 12 June 1997:60-63).

At the same time, politicians under investigation or suspected of responsibility quickly hid themselves beneath the protective umbrella of parliamentary immunity, almost invariably an insuperable barrier. For instance, after his arrest for corruption in March 1985, the socialist politician Antonio Natali — considered by the judges as one of the main organizers of political corruption in Milan —received all the possible "expressions of solidarity" from the leaders of his own party where "the news produced reactions of very strong pain and indignation" (*Il Giorno*, 3 March 1985; see also CD n.202:12-3). As the very story of Natali — who was elected MP, and, thanks to his parliamentary immunity, avoided further investigations — shows, parliamentary immunity became the institutional device to avoid penal sanctions.[16]

THE ROLE OF POLITICAL COMPETITION AND PUBLIC OPINION

In a democratic system, political competition should help deter the "bad behavior" by politicians in power, limiting the willingness of public agents to indulge in illegal activities. Competition between different parties and individuals aspiring to govern (in order to realize objectives defined by contending programs), in fact, should help those who are most honest or more willing to denounce the illegal actions of others. Defeated parties and politicians have a definite interest, in fact, in exposing the misappropriation of resources and other crimes on the part of those in government. In this way, citizens can acquire the necessary information to inflict electoral retribution on parties indulging in illegal business at their expense.

The dynamics of the Italian political system, however, have powerfully limited this possibility. For over 40 years, the absence of turnover in the national government of the country has represented the principal "anomaly" of Italian democracy (e.g., Pasquino, 1991). The absence of alternation and the limited expectation of change in the short term have made the discovery and denunciation of corruption more difficult. Moreover, strong ideological identifications have limited electoral mobility, rendering voting behavior impervious to political scandals. The main opposition party, the Communist Party, was strong enough to challenge the majority effectively, but not to take on direct responsibility for government. On the government side, the absence of turnover weakened the capacity for planning, favoring instead the immediate interest in dividing up and occupying public offices for clientelist ends [*lottizzazione*]:

> Given that the parties occupy the parliamentary political institutions, constituting as a result the channel of access for varying interests, and also that they distribute the posts within institutions and public entities with notable impunity, they are subject to fragmentation into factions [*correnti*]. ... These internal divisions lead to organizational weakness, which in turn makes them all the more subject, in an apparently endless spiral, to the temptation of recourse to the system of *lottizzazione* to strengthen their position [Pasquino, 1985:14-15].

Both government and opposition seemed "condemned" to remaining in the same arrangement also in the long term: "in no western country and in general, in no competitive political system, has such a limited turn over taken place in the highest political offices" (Pasquino, 1982:51-2). The opposition's strength could not be ignored in either general or distributive political decisions precisely because of the weakness of the government coalitions and the fractionating of the parties. Continuous negotiation was necessary to avoid the danger of paralysis through obstructionism and head-on conflict. At the same time, the opposition (with no immediate prospect of winning power) found a way of "governing" from its minority position. The solution was thus clearly one of collusion: sharp verbal and public dissension was accompanied, in reality, by a practice of under-the-table negotiations and deals (Pizzorno, 1993). This related in the first place to legislative activity but, from a certain moment on, included also the political sharing of minor government posts.[17] A tenacious "consociational" equilibrium was thus created: formally opposed political forces became part of a network of relationships and connivance relating to their respective illicit activities, allowing as a consequence an extensive subdivision of the benefits of power. For instance, according to Valerio Bitetto, a counselor of the *Ente nazionale per l'energia elettrica* (ENEL), in the administration of that public agency there was an agreement among all the major parties: "each counselor had the task of collecting money for his own party. There was a tacit agreement: each cultivated his own kitchen garden, without interfering with the business of the others" (*Panorama*, 14 February 1993:46). These collusive agreements eliminated, even inside the elective organs, the normal controls between the majority and the opposition.

The increase in the number of persons involved in the division of the political spoils did not lead to any reduction in individual shares because complicity permitted, with almost unanimous agreement, further extension of the range of political power. The same distributional criteria were successfully extended to even wider sectors of activity, such as the health service, banks, public construction and the media. Guaranteed by the general political equilibrium, the quantity of resources controlled by the political structures and actors participating in the system of complicity grew.

As far as the potential control of the public opinion on state crime is concerned, the intrusion of political influence in the field of the media appears particularly dangerous. Beside contributing directly to the exposure of illegal practices, the media also represents the *filter* through which knowledge on state crime is divulged. The public's idea of the gravity of a scandal (and therefore its possible electoral consequences) depends on the *quantity* and the *kind* of information provided by the media. Links between politicians playing institutional roles and the press and television, whether the result of secret exchanges or of proprietor pressure, represent a serious contamination of the democratic political process. In Italy, mass media seem to be particularly receptive to political pressure (Giglioli, 1996). Public TV networks managers are politically appointed, while the main private TV networks are personally owned by Silvio Berlusconi, former Prime Minister and leader of the political party *Forza Italia*. Even before his direct involvement in politics, Berlusconi's TV channels (Fininvest) appeared to have been used, through their informative services, as a tool for informal political influence. As a Christian Democratic politician observed:

> Fininvest has ever helped our party, both at national and local level, with so called *TV contributions*. On every electoral campaign Fininvest gave to the party ... place for several spots on TV and other mass media. Secondly, Fininvest offered free spaces on TV and press to specific candidates that were considered particularly 'friends'. This strong help created in our party a hearty attitude toward Fininvest's industrial enterprises [*L'Espresso*, 9 May 1993:76].

PERSPECTIVES OF REFORM IN THE CONTROL OF STATE CRIME AND CORRUPTION

The passage from monocausal explanations to an analysis of the interaction between the different phenomena allows a better understanding of the dynamics of what the media and politicians have called the "crisis of the regime," largely determined by the *mani pulite* judicial inquiry. It was not those paying bribes who attacked the system in the first instance; the regime was not rocked by conflicts between corrupters and corrupted, nor even between "honest" and corrupt entrepreneurs. Rather, it collapsed through a crisis of legitimacy produced by the complex interlinkage of corruption, clientelism, maladministration, organized crime and "crypto-government," which reduced diffuse support, that is, a consensus towards the political regime and its institutions, for the system and increasing the need for specific support.[18] During the reconstruction of the 1950s, polarized political culture, the climate of the Cold War, and the direction taken in economic development prevented the spread of a diffuse support. As a consequence, there has been a tendency to substitute "specific" support — directed, that is, towards those holding power at a given moment in time (Mastropaolo, 1987). This can explain an apparent paradox, the fact that Italy has, if compared with other Western countries, a very high rate of electoral participation, and, at the same time, a very low confidence in the governing institutions (Morlino and Montero, 1994).[19] More than by civic spiritedness, electoral participation could therefore be explained by the clientelistic incentives that were used to capture specific consent. This solution contributed, however, in the long term to further undermine generalized support. In fact, "the clientelistic practice, based as it is upon a personalized use of power, impedes the disassociation between the roles and the role-holders that is the first characteristic of the institutionalized authority. Being based upon the anti-bureaucratic principle of the 'consideration of the person,' it undermines the confidence in the 'rules of the game' and in those institutions that should enforce them" (Graziano, 1980:53). Thus, a spiral has been created in which the absence of diffuse consent has extended the parties' occupation of civil society, and this colonization has, in its turn, produced state crime and maladministration, reducing the capacity of the system to inspire a diffuse consensus.

For some time now, the debate on the legislative changes required to cut down the endemic illegality existing within the state has been intensifying. Looking, either explicitly or implicitly, to the variables influencing individual calculations of the costs and benefits of participation in corrupt exchange, many of the solutions proposed in Italy, as elsewhere, aim to transform the utility function of corruption. The probable costs of corruption can be raised by increasing the penalties and improving controls on the public administration. A series of proposals have been made in different countries in this area: the creation of commissions of inquiry independent of the parties (Pinto-Duschinski, 1977); the reduction of the discretionary powers of the public administration (Gardiner and Olsen, 1974); and an increased coordination between its various branches (Banfield, 1975). In a comparative analysis the opportunity of "a change in the rules of the game between politicians and bureaucrats," has also been suggested, "[in such a way that] bureaucratic elites offset the power of politicians, the bureaucratic structures becomes more independent of political intrusion and party politics, with the consequent withdrawal of bureaucratic resources from the political context" (Pippig, 1990; Etzioni-Halevi, 1989:302). The introduction of competition between different bureaucratic structures would allow curbs on the monopolistic power which public agents usually find themselves exercising (Rose-Ackerman, 1986).

However, it seems necessary to go beyond the single causes of state crimes to consider the complex interconnections running between political illegality and other phenomena. From what has been said up to now, it follows that, alongside measures influencing individual costs and benefits, it is necessary to act on those macro-phenomena that favor the spread of corrupt practices. The control of corruption will be all the more difficult if, at the same time, the problems connected with administrative inefficiency, an electoral system favoring the buying and selling of votes and political protection of organized crime and crypto-government are not also confronted. The completion of the "virtuous circle" that leads to the overcoming of a system of generalized corruption demands not only specific remedies but also profound institutional reforms.

For this motive, the public debate on control has concentrated on the institutional reforms necessary to avoid a return to illegality. Among the changes to the "rules of the democratic game" that can favor competition within and between different centers of power and render more transparent public decision-making procedures are those relative to the division of tasks, with precise government responsibilities for those who win the elections and control responsibilities for those who go in the opposition. The main institutional changes after the *mani pulite* investigation were those brought about by the new electoral laws for the national elections, passed in 1993, that introduced several elements of the "first-pass-the-post" model. The reform of the local electoral system went in the same direction. The instability and growing conflictuality at the national level indicated however the limits of an electoral reform that could not suffice to change deeply rooted political behaviors.[20]

Moreover, in a political system still characterized by an uncertain majority and low levels of common consensus, serious reforms that could thwart state crime and corruption are difficult to pass. In October 1996, a Committee for the prevention of corruption presented a report to the Chamber of Deputies, where a commission has been instituted at the same time with the aim of elaborating legal proposals against political and administrative illegalities. The report contains a wide set of reform proposals, addressing the several and inter-linked causes of corruption (see par. 3). Its general recommendations include a more rigorous separation between political and administrative functions, the elimination of political influences on bureaucrats' careers, an increase in the technical and professional competence of functionaries, the reduction of the parasitic rents related to state intervention and regulation, the simplification of the normative system, the introduction in the public sector of ethical codes contractually binding, the regulations of conflicts of interest, and the creation of a data bank on the evolution of the patrimonial situation of some public officers (chosen at random from the bodies with higher budgets) in order to monitor suspect movements of capital (Comitato di studio, 1996). An increase in the — at present extremely low — salaries of bureaucrats and local adminis-trators might raise the level of "professional competence" of aspiring candi-dates, their social status and, at the same time, the moral costs of illegal activity. In fact, the risks of being implicated in judicial proceedings would then include the loss of a greater income and more prestigious social position (ibid., 60).

In this context, the *mani pulite* inquiry, which has temporarily halted the perverse ascending spiral of corruption and inefficiency, undoubtedly had beneficial effects. Nonetheless, the prospects for the future remain uncertain. The action of the magistrates has broken only one of the rings in the chain of reciprocal causation by increasing enormously the risks involved in corruption. Exasperating slowness, unjustified delays, normative complexity, procedural quagmires, clientelistic practices, organized crime protection — in other words, the components of structural inefficiency in public activity — continue to be present. As observed by one of the judges of *mani pulite*, Gherardo Colombo:

> It is nonetheless impressing, disappointing, and frustrating for pro-fessional effort, that in the last four years not a law nor a measure has been adopted to make inqueries easier or — at least to a certain extent — corruption more difficult. Not a measure to modify con-trols, making them more effective, not a measure to remove from public administration all those who for dozens of years have sold their function [Colombo, 1996:154].

In fact, it remains to be seen whether bureaucratic and political personnel (notwithstanding the drastic renewal of the latter) will be capable of radically reforming public procedures and behavior, relinquishing the incomes, power and privileges they have acquired. As Pareto observed, if the politicians A are corrupted, and the politicians B take advantage of the scandal in order to gain power denouncing their crimes, we do not have to expect radical changes in the nature of government:

> We have, in fact, to acknowledge that, usually, the B have no intention to take away to everybody the possibility to accomplished the lamented facts, but just to take this power away from the A. They aim not so much at changing the social order, but at turning it to their advantage, chasing away the A, and taking their place. For this reason, it is for them advantageous that the facts appear not as a consequence of the social order, but as a consequence of the perversity of the A [Pareto, 1916:626].

A real danger exists, therefore, that once the present crisis has passed, the market of corruption will expand again in Italy its hidden network of exchanges, as some recent scandals seem to indicate.

Acknowledgments: Translated by John Donaldson. Although the entire chapter reflects joint work, the first and second sections were written by Donatella della Porta, the third and fourth sections by Alberto Vannucci.

NOTES

1. According to the economic theory of crime, besides the probability of being discovered, the decision to undertake a given illegal activity depends on the severity of punishment expected and other variables, such as income to be derived, expectations of gain in other illegal activities and the propensity to unlawful action (Becker and Stigler, 1972; Stigler 1970; Becker, 1968).

2. In 1992 there were 597 official lodges of the Grand Orient of Italy, the most important Masonic order (a *Gran Loggia di Piazza Gesù*, originating from a schism in, 1908, also exists). According to the then Grand Master, in 1992 there were 18,000 masons "all at the top of their professions" (Mola, 1992:873).

3. In the case of one secret Sicilian lodge, whose members included various public functionaries, local and national politicians, entrepreneurs, bankers and *Mafiosi*, the magistrates noted that "the affiliates of this Masonic brotherhood interfered in public affairs, intervening in the award of public contracts and in the procurement of votes

during elections, attempting to maneuver judicial proceedings and corrupt friends in the forces of order" (CPMF, 1993:15).

4. After the bankruptcy of his financial empire, which had been a channel of reinvestment abroad for Mafia as well as Vatican capital (through the Vatican's bank, Istituto Opere Religiose), Roberto Calvi was found dead in London, probably killed, on June 18, 1982 (see Canosa, 1995; Cornwell, 1983).

5. Honorary Consul to Argentina, Gelli was one of the few Italians invited to the swearing-in ceremonies of Presidents Carter in 1977 and Reagan in 1981.

6. In many of the episodes considered below, bribes were paid not to public agents but to the political parties, that is, to the private organizations mediating political demands. These cases, too, can be considered as state crime, given the virtually complete overlap of the parties and the state (in all its branches) in Italy. It is not a coincidence that Italy has been considered a paradigmatic case of *partitocrazia*, characterized by the attribution to the political parties of an "extensive, diversified and capillary control over resources and decision-making processes" (Pasquino, 1987:55). Furthermore, the parties have "colonized" civil society and the whole network of semi-public agencies.

7. In economic terms, the market for corruption presents a number of important "economies of scale": the costs of offering illicit services increase in a manner less than proportional to the overall level of diffusion of the phenomenon. Where corruption is widespread the risk of being accused is extremely low, given that the organs of control must distribute their resources over a far vaster area. Moreover, they meet increasing difficulties due to the code of silence among corrupt agents or the greater ease of concealing evidence. In fact, since corrupt practices are usually closely bound up together, the number of people willing to testify or provide information becomes increasingly limited. The involvement and interests of leading politicians further discourages or obstructs controls and allegations. Given the absence of honest administrators to turn to, the incentives for entrepreneurs to pay bribes increase (Rose-Ackerman, 1978). The effect of these mechanisms is to make corruption systemic: a situation develops, that is, in which "the illicit becomes the norm and ... corruption so common and institutionalized that those behaving illegally are rewarded and those continuing to accept the older norms penalized" (Caiden and Caiden, 1977:306).

8. Corrupt politicians ensured their safety from incrimination by refusing to grant authorization to proceed against parliamentarians under investigation, or by acquitting implicated ministers in the Inquiry Commission, a body itself composed of politicians. It is perhaps not surprising, then, that up to 1987 only 19% of the requests for authorization to proceed made by the magistracy were accepted by Parliament (Cazzola, 1988:133) and of 400 requests, only one minister was indicted. The cases of

the secret funds of the IRI and the *Italcasse*, used for clandestine financing of politicians, provide illuminating examples in this respect.

9. In the scandal that erupted in 1961 over irregularities in the construction of Fiumicino airport, for example, "not even the Minister of the Interior escaped attempts at blackmail, carried out by the secret services using their dossiers and inspired by other Christian-Democrat leaders" (Galli, 1983:90-1).

10. These and subsequent figures are elaborated from data in International Monetary Fund (1993), unless stated otherwise.

11. These data refer to the 1970s; according to more recent data, the average number of laws passed annually in Italy from 1987 to 1992 is 295 (Arabbia and Giammusso, 1994:272).

12. Moreover, the wider the distribution of benefits expected from a given measure, the closer, that is, it approximates to the general interest, the greater the difficulties faced by potential beneficiaries in exerting pressure on the power that decides. In other words, a correlation exists between the distribution of public resources and the individual convenience of corruption. In fact, public action allocating individual benefits is more easily translated into monetary terms. In the opposite case, those who wish to corrupt are confronted with the problems of collective action described by Olson (1965). Individually, it is more reasonable for each to wait until when others, more eager to corrupt, take the initiative thus relieving them of the costs, given that the benefits of the measure "purchased" will fall indiscriminately to all.

13. For instance, 88% of the bills presented in the Italian Parliament have positive effects on direct receivers that, in 45.5% of the cases, are members of homogeneous and small groups of individuals (Di Palma, 1978:119-123).

14. In a comparative perspective, the Italian bureaucrats emerge as legalistic, illiberal, elitist, hostile to pluralistic politics and essentially nondemocratic (Putnam, 1973). In comparison to the civil servants of other democracies, the Italian bureaucrats are characterized by a mainly legal education (54% against 3% in Great Britain, and 18% in the United States) (Aberbach et al., 1981:52).

15. For instance, the judge who indicted, in, 1983, the socialist "boss" Alberto Teardo was invited by other judges, in higher hierarchical positions, to abandon the case, and was discouraged when he did not (Del Gaudio, 1992). A similar destiny had another judge, Carlo Palermo, who had mentioned in his investigation about the illegal traffic of fire arms the-then prime minister Bettino Craxi. The word *insabbiamento* (literally, "covering with sand") started to indicate the several cases in which delicate

investigations — among others, those on 243 billions liras illegally paid by the public enterprise IRI to political parties, politicians and newspapers — had been taken away from their natural judges, and advocated by the Tribunal of Rome (known for a long period as the "foggy harbor"), ending up with the acquittal of all defendants (Galli, 1991:255).

16. The former PSI administrative secretary Vincenzo Balzamo so instructed his assistant: "Never get money from anybody, because I have the parliamentary immunity, but you don't" (*L'Espresso*, 14 February 1993:53).

17. In the first five legislatures of the post-war period, the average percentage vote in favor of laws passed in parliamentary commissions was 91%. The percentage vote in favor in the chamber itself was not unanimous, but nevertheless high at 76.5% (di Palma, 1978:85-9). The difference between commissions and chamber is to be explained by the greater publicity of voting in the latter, which would have made clear pre-arranged agreements difficult to justify before the electorate.

18. For the distinction between diffuse and specific support, see Easton (1975).

19. According to the Eurobarometer opinion polls, in 1995 the percentage of citizens who were "not at all satisfied" or "not very satisfied" with the working of democracy in Italy — never below 60% since, 1973, the year of the first Eurobarometer polls — reached 85% as against 35% in Germany, 56% in Spain, 47% in Great Britain, and 51% in France. In 1982, different opinion polls indicated that only 31% of the Italian citizens trusted the Parliament, as against 53% in the U.S. and Germany, 48% in France, and 40% in Great Britain. Only 28% of the Italians trusted the public bureaucracy as against 64% in Great Britain, 55% in the U.S., 50% in France, and 35% in Germany (Rose, 1988:267).

20. As Lijphart observed, in ideologically heterogeneous societies the majoritarian model has negative effects when the minorities feel excluded and loose confidence in the political regime (Lijphart, 1984).

EIGHT.
CONTROLLING STATE CRIME IN JAPAN: A CASE STUDY OF POLITICAL CORRUPTION

by

David M. Potter

ON 8 APRIL 1994 Prime Minister Hosokawa Morihiro resigned his office amid allegations that in the late 1980s he tried to hide income for tax purposes. The ex-chief executive of the first seriously reform-minded cabinet in two decades, Hosokawa testified before a Japanese House of Representatives committee in June about his financial dealings. His reply to accusations that his actions were illegal was simply that he had never claimed to be completely clean. Three years later Hosokawa was at the center of a scandal in which it was alleged that he had taken a bribe from an upper-house candidate in his party in exchange for placing the candidate's name higher on the party list in the 1995 election. These are disturbing accusations against a man with a reputation as a political reformer, and they cast doubt on recent attempts to clean up Japanese politics. It also suggests how difficult it is for anyone in Japan to maintain a successful political career while staying within the letter of the law.

Political corruption is not the only kind of crime by Japanese state actors. Miyazawa (1992) argues that police procedures result in frequent violations of human rights in contravention of the constitution and the law, a situation alleged by Human Rights Watch (1995) in the case of prisons as well. Analysis of these types of state crime is difficult, however, because of the limited availability of data on them. Police and correctional authorities are reluctant to allow free access to researchers, severely limiting the depth of research on these topics. By contrast, the volume of journalistic and scholarly work on corruption allows complete discussion of the structure of this kind of state crime. More important, political corruption in Japan provides an enabling environment that abets the above-mentioned abuses of human rights by state actors.

State-organized crime has not been discussed in the academic literature on Japan. Yet, corruption has been such a feature of post-war Japan's political system that some authors use the term "structural corruption" (MacDougall, 1988; Johnson, 1986; Murobushi, 1981) to suggest the depth of the problem. Alternatively, "money politics" has become a term used by academics and journalists alike to describe the foundations of contemporary politics in that country (Hirose, 1989; Kyogoku, 1986). This chapter argues that the rules of post-war parliamentary elections in Asia's largest industrial democracy created incentives for widespread criminality among Diet (parliament) politicians. As Ross (1995; this volume) notes, legislatures are slow to respond to state-created crime. Since the Liberal Democratic Party (LDP) successfully capitalized on the contradictions between legal norms and the perceived reality of creating and sustaining political careers, it maintained those rules despite their direct link to political corruption. Finally, this chapter assesses the likelihood that political reform legislation enacted in 1994 will resolve those contradictions.

Before beginning an investigation of corruption in Japan, it is important to clear up two conceptual issues. First, what do I mean by the state and second, what do I therefore mean by state-organized crime? By state I mean the institutions and personnel of government, as separate from members of private organizations. As for state-organized crime, there is little agreement on its definition (Ross, 1995; Tunnell, 1993; Barak, 1991), but let me start with Chambliss's clarification: "The most important type of criminality organized by a state consists of acts defined by law as criminal and committed by state officials in the pursuit of their job as representatives of the state" (1989:184). There appears to be an emerging consensus, by no means complete, that state actions that cause social harm, even if only through negligence, can be considered criminal as well (Tunnell, 1993; Barak, 1991). This insight is important in assessing the problem of political corruption because it alerts us to the wider impact that a form of state crime has beyond the exchange of preferential access for money. Finally, I consider the problem of corruption in Japan to be a species of politician crime (Friedrichs, 1995), since personal gain usually takes second place to other reasons for engaging in illegal behavior.

It is useful to remember that there are different types of corruption. As Lowi and others point out, there is "Big Corruption" and "Little Corruption" (De Leon, 1993:19-20.) In this chapter I am concerned with the former because it extends to the highest levels of the Japanese government. Misplacement of campaign posters and other low-level infractions need not detain us here.

Corruption is not new to Japan. The classic eighteenth century tale of revenge in the Tokugawa era begins with the refusal of a provincial lord to bribe an official of the shogun's court in return for teaching the lord the etiquette that it is the official's responsibility to teach anyway.[1] Corrupt practices did not disappear with the Tokugawa-era government and its replacement by a modernizing Meiji government in the nineteenth century. Bribery was a stock tactic for ensuring parliamentary majorities and silencing dissent in the Imperial Diet after 1890. The links between big business and the political parties, coupled with the rising cost of campaigns resulting from adult-male suffrage during the period of Taisho democracy, furthered the problem of corruption. Although vote buying was illegal, candidates were expected to provide local leaders with money, part of which they retained and part of which they distributed to voters on the basis of their importance. The result was a long string of scandals in the 1920s (Mitchell, 1996; Duus, 1968; Scalapino, 1967).

The post-World War II Occupation reformed democratized Japanese politics in many ways. Not least, the 1947 constitution placed the Diet at the center of the formal political system and in theory removed important powers from the bureaucracy. Ironically, the movement of power to the Diet probably served in part to foster corruption in post-war politics since it recreated a group of policy makers who would be subject to lobbying by private sector interests and dependent on the largesse of those interests to fund the expensive political activities necessary to stay in office. Just after the Occupation years, as old political habits were beginning to die out, cases of vote-buying continued in small communities (Dore, 1978). It persists in at least some rural districts even today. For example, in recent years a Diet member from one rural district paid about 30,000 yen[2] per vote in especially close elections (Fukui and Fukai, 1992; Hrebenar, 1986).

STRUCTURAL SOURCES OF CORRUPTION

Corruption in Japanese electoral politics involves violations of campaign finance laws and related bribery and tax laws. Kawaguchi (1993) points out that 90% of all election violations in Japan are financial. Not all financial transactions in politics are illegal; candidates and parties in Japan rely upon donations from constituents and interest groups just as in any industrial democracy. What we are interested in understanding here is whether and why the electoral system as constituted creates incentives for large numbers of politicians and campaign contributors to cross the line from legal to illegal campaign finance. What are the political consequences of electoral laws (Rae, 1971)?[3] In the Japanese case, one consequence is inducement to widespread criminality by government representatives.

Kawaguchi argues that corruption in campaigns is the result of the insufficiency of the law (1993). I would argue that the law itself, coupled with the structure of the electoral system, is the culprit. The combination of multimember constituencies and restrictive campaign laws generates demand by elected officials for large amounts of money to maintain expensive campaign organizations outside the parties and the formal requirements of electoral laws. Lax enforcement of electoral and bribery laws, and public expectations of political behavior, do not provide sufficiently powerful negative sanctions to correct the temptation toward abuse.

How much money is there in Japanese politics? No one knows for sure. One scholar observes that "political contributions are like icebergs. What is visible to the public is only a fraction of the whole." He estimated, in the 1960s, that party leaders publicly reported only one-fifth to one-third of total contributions, with the rest hidden (Yanaga, 1968:80). In the 1990s, another observer put the actual figure at two to three times the official figures reported by the parties, individual politicians and other political groups (Yanagawa, 1994). The gold bars and unsecured debentures, with an estimated worth exceeding $50 million (U.S.), found in LDP kingmaker Kanemaru Shin's residence at the time of his arrest in March 1993 give an indication of the attempt to conceal political funds from public scrutiny.

Even the official figures are impressive. Official declarations of political funds reported to the Ministry of Home Affairs by all national political groups, parties and individuals in 1992 amounted to a staggering 1.74 trillion yen. That figure represented a more than twofold increase from 1981, a growth rate faster than both the GNP and the national budget in the same period (Yanagawa, 1994). On the supply side, the figures are equally high. In 1993, a year in which corruption topped the government's political agenda, the National Tax Agency calculated the top 500 corporations "*shito fumeikin*" — unreported money reserved for political donations, bribes and hush money — at $53 million (*Asahi Shinbun*, 28 December 1994:1).

From a non-Japanese perspective, it is difficult to understand why such sums of money are necessary. Japan's excessively strict election rules, in many ways unchanged from the original election laws of the 1920s, limit a candidate's ability to appeal to the public broadly during the campaign season and, it would seem, to spend money on conventional electoral strategies. The Public Offices Election Law proscribes door-to-door canvassing during elections; bans publication of candidate popularity polls, even by the press; prohibits the provision of food or drink to prospective voters and limits spending amounts for the same in campaign headquarters; bans parades or marches "tending to play up spirits," and restricts rallies and public speeches to designated areas; prescribes the number and size of campaign vehicles and loudspeakers; restricts the use of campaign literature; bans the purchase of radio, television or newspaper advertising space; and prohibits the provision of money or other benefits to media personnel for election purposes. The law also limits the coordination of campaigning by political parties and their candidates (Public Offices Election Law, 1958). Subsequent revisions have relaxed, but usually not rescinded, campaign rules (Japan Ministry of Home Affairs, 1995; Curtis, 1988).

The restrictions would appear to limit the need for money. Unlike the extended campaign season for congressional races in the United States, the campaign season for the Diet in the post-war era lasts a maximum of forty days. There are, of course, no direct elections for the prime minister, negating the need to build a public campaign organization for a candidate for that office. During general elections, limited media time is equally allotted to all candidates. Finally, since 1975 there have been limits on contributions to individual candidates (Curtis, 1988). Yet, Japanese elections have the distinction of being among the most expensive among industrial democracies. The nature of constituencies and party structure has had a great deal to do with the expense.

Until the 1994 reforms, House of Representatives elections in post-war Japan were conducted in multimember constituencies, with voters given a single nontransferable vote. Most districts elected two to six candidates based on population. A key feature of the electoral system was the continuous majority held by the LDP in the House of Representatives. In practice, only the LDP, the Japan Socialist Party (JSP) and the Japan Communist Party (JCP) contested elections in every district.[4] A typical election result in a district with five or six members would include more than one candidate from the LDP getting elected to seats. In rural districts it was common for several LDP candidates to win seats. Therein lay the problem. For many LDP members the biggest challenges to their candidacies did not come from the opposition parties but from rival LDP candidates. Because several candidates competed from the same party, the organization's endorsement could not act as a signal to voters. Candidates were therefore left to their own devices to ensure election. Their recourse lay in two directions. First, they could ally with a faction leader in the party in order to gain needed campaign finances. Second, they were forced to rely on personal candidacies with campaign organizations loyal to them alone.

Factions in Japan date back to the origins of the post-war conservative parties (Fukui, 1970). They serve a variety of purposes in the LDP, but procurement and distribution of money to faction members stands out among them. The need for political funds was a driving force in the development of the factions (Thayer, 1969). The original conservative parties' organizations did not provide for treasury or accounting positions specifically. As a result, a main task of conservative parties' secretary-generals, then and now, has been to raise money for the party (Fukui, 1970). Faction bosses retained the loyalty of members and court new ones by providing opportunities for career advancement and, more importantly, cash to run their campaigns. Faction bosses were expected to raise and distribute money to assist members' reelection efforts. They also introduced junior members to well-heeled businessmen (Thayer, 1969). Indeed, the senior members' fundraising efforts aimed at providing campaign money well beyond their own needs.

The scale of the need is well illustrated by one of the largest factions, composed of 91 members in 1990. The *Far Eastern Economic Review* estimated that a faction that size required almost $7.5 million a year to maintain its members' loyalty. That faction, facing the imminent death of its leader, was in trouble because it lacked a successor with strong fundraising skills (FEER, 24 January 1991).

The existence of multimember constituencies meant that the LDP could not guarantee funding to candidates because different factions supported rival LDP candidates. Diet members, therefore, relied on individual candidacies based on their own organizations, *koenkai*, to maintain the loyalty of the conservative electorate.

Loyalty was expensive. Because the campaign season is so short, candidates had to find ways to maintain their *koenkai* support between elections. The law, however, prohibits "campaign activities" at any time except during the official campaign season. That meant that politicians were induced to provide individual benefits to key constituents. Candidates and their staffs spent a great deal of time in "non-campaign" activities: attending weddings and other social events, sponsoring clubs, organizing trips for key constituents to tourist spots,[5] and holding political discussion meetings in which they carefully avoided mentioning anything having to do with elections (see Curtis, 1983:153-178). Such "non-campaigning" cost a great deal because most *koenkai* activities were heavily subsidized by the candidate. Constituents' membership dues and other fees were dwarfed by the costs of organization activities. Finally, Diet members often helped finance the campaigns of local politicians in their *koenkai* in order to maintain those key support bases (Fukui and Fukai, 1992).

Koenkai were not always enough. While every Diet member had one, big city districts were large enough that candidates had to reach beyond core constituencies. Even in mid-sized cities, where *koenkai* were most active, candidates faced the problem of appealing to uncommitted voters (Curtis, 1983). The combined impetus of organizing a "hard vote" while attracting the floating vote drove up the cost of campaigns. In 1991, for example, a group of first-and second-term LDP Diet members reported spending an average of 133 million yen per year on political activities. Most of those took place back in the districts. Running for a seat for the first time was estimated to cost between

300 million and 500 million yen and require two to three years of organization (Yanagawa, 1994; Mizuguchi, 1993).

BUSINESS AND THE SUPPLY OF POLITICAL FUNDS

Big business has been a source of campaign finance as long as there have been parties. The Mitsui and Mitsubishi companies bankrolled rival conservative parties in the 1920s and early 1930s. The dissolution of the industrial combines during the Occupation destroyed the direct connection between specific conglomerates and parties, a change furthered by the merger of the post-war conservative parties in 1955 into the LDP, but the connection between business and conservative campaign finance remains. Big business is still the largest contributor of political funds in Japan and in recent years has become even more important than faction as a source of campaign funding for individual LDP politicians (Curtis, 1988). Until 1993 the *Keidanren*, the federation of big business associations, acted as a collector of political contributions from member firms on the party's behalf, assessing a tax on member firms according to a set formula (Chapman, 1991). LDP requests ran into millions of dollars.

Why would big business feel the need to supply enormous sums of money to the LDP? The benefits that accrue to a firm tend to be indirect, such as a generally favorable macroeconomic policy, rather than specific and tangible. The problem for corporations was this: until 1994 they saw no alternative to the LDP. Since the prewar period, the conservative parties have been the guarantors of political stability in the face of the Left. Business federations have made it their policy to keep conservative parties in power (Yanaga, 1968). After 1955, that meant the LDP. While there were a number of other parties, most of them were unacceptable to big business either because of their ideology or their small size. Like it or not, the LDP was the solid mainstay of pro-business sentiment and policy in the Diet for most of the post-war period.

A major service the LDP performed for business stems from structural characteristics of the Japanese political system found in all democracies: the separation of economic and political power. LDP politicians have acted as brokers between the business community and the powerful state bureaucracy. It is that role, as channel of access to the bureaucracy, that was especially important to the corporate world (MacDougall, 1986).

The step into illegality is murky at best, and a number of powerful LDP politicians avoided prosecution by engaging in questionable practices that technically stayed within the law (MacDougall, 1986). Diet members became ingenious at circumventing the Political Funds Control Law of 1976. Since the law limited corporate contributions to individual candidates, but not to non-party political organizations, LDP members simply expanded the number of political organizations to which corporations contributed on their behalf (Curtis, 1988). In turn, individual firms distributed their donations through "individual" contributions made by their employees (Hirose, 1989). The fundraising party was another conservative response to the new funding rules since the 1980s. Corporations invited to the "party" would buy up blocks of tickets to support the candidates; when their representatives arrived they would provide a further donation (see, e.g., Chapman, 1991). The result was to make available to conservative politicians political funds at much higher levels than the original intent of the law. Hand in hand with the new techniques of money raising came new donors as companies outside the circles of high finance and big business established links with politicians in need of cash.

The construction industry has become an important source of illegal campaign funding for the LDP (Curtis, 1988). In the latter half of the 1980s and early 1990s it accounted for two-thirds to three-quarters of corporate "undisclosed funds" in any given year (*Asahi Shinbun*, 28 December 1994:1). In ways not found in other parts of the business community, construction firms rely directly on government largesse in the form of public works contracts. Illegal activities, including bribery, bid fixing and kickbacks are endemic. Inevitably, government officials become involved since they either controlled the disbursement of government contracts or had the ability to influence those who did (Woodall, 1993). The potential for bribery was clear. As one author puts it: "the politicians can not be elected without money but are able to attract projects; the construction firms can not survive without being contracted for projects, but have money" (Wilkinson, 1993:5). While corruption scandals involving the construction industry are more mundane than the recent Recruit or Sagawa Kyubin scandals (see below) they are widespread. They extend from the national to local government. Recent bribery scandals involving construction firms exposed a former Construction Minister, a House of Councilors member, two prefectural governors, a vice governor and former Ministry of Home Affairs official, and the mayor of a large northern city. A 1993 newspaper poll revealed that one-half of the members of the Diet had admitted accepting secret donations from construction firms. Cases involving key LDP politicians revealed that construction companies routinely paid bribes of 3% to 5% of project bids to those politicians in exchange for fixing contracts (Wilkinson, 1993; Chapman, 1991).

The construction industry is hardly the only culprit in the corporate world. In the 1980s the Recruit Cosmos Co., a business with interests including publication of employment news, systematically bribed members of the LDP as well as some members of the Finance Ministry by providing them with unlisted stock shortly before public issuance. Similarly, the Sagawa Kyubin delivery company made payoffs worth hundreds of millions of dollars to influential members of practically every party, national and local bureaucrats and to organized crime.[6] Such bribery was seen as necessary for new entrepreneurs to break into elite government-business circles with access to special economic and political privileges (Nester, 1990).

The LDP's need for money, collectively and individually, has resulted in questionable and often illegal financial transactions overseas. The most spectacular revelations came in late 1994, when United States government documents confirmed that the Central Intelligence Agency (CIA) had secretly funded the LDP and extreme right-wing organizations during the 1950s and 1960s in order to buttress compliant bilateral relations during the Cold War (*New York Times*, 9 October 1994).

Japan's foreign aid program has been characterized as rife with illicit financial dealings. Japanese companies provide indispensable technical expertise for the aid program and, in return, they have been given preferential treatment in the award of contracts for overseas development projects. This special access has allowed them to run bidding rings overseas in the same manner they do at home (Potter, 1996). Stories abound of close links between influential Japanese politicians, favored construction companies, and the award of contracts (e.g., Murai, 1989), all understood to benefit the politicians at election time. In the wake of the downfall of the Marcos administration in the Philippines in 1986, journalistic sources revealed that portions of bribes paid by Japanese contractors to President Marcos had been channeled to key LDP leaders. Subsequently, the LDP quashed Diet investigations of the aid program to the Philippines and the allegations were never proven.

What the relationship between the construction industry and conservative politicians has in common with Recruit Cosmos' and Sagawa Kyubin's relationship with them is that campaign finance is not free. In return for money, contributors seek preferential access to government rule-making. In particular, the construction industry seeks political protection from interference in bid-rigging schemes (see *Japan Times Weekly*, 21-27 March 1994). The chairman of the Recruit Co. received, among other things, access to Nippon Telephone and Telegraph licenses and stock. Herein lies the insidious aspect of corruption. If political influence can be bought, then it goes to the highest bidder.

SANCTIONS AND POLITICIAN CRIME

The Japanese case is interesting because of what it suggests about law as a source of sanction in a non-Western context. The problem of finding ways to control state crime, corruption in this case, takes on an added dimension when we understand that in Japan rule making and rule adjudication, and law in particular, are mediated through the mechanisms of particularistic, personalistic resolution of disputes. In Japan, the distinction between the rule of universal law and the rule of particular situations is ambiguous; cultural expectations that justice should fit the circumstances of specific situations mean that norms of conduct embodied in law can never be universal. "Case by case" adjudication of problems and conflicts permeates the understanding of public officials and public alike (Haley, 1991; Upham, 1987), meaning that rules are applied differently to like cases depending on the relationship between individuals within and without the state.

Within the Japanese criminal justice system there is a reluctance to rely on formal sanctions. Imprisonment is used rarely. Suspension of sentences is common, and fines are levied in the overwhelming majority of cases in which sanctions are applied (Bayley, 1976). Prosecutors are given extensive leeway in bringing cases to trial. Trials in Japan are analogous to sentencing hearings in the United States: prosecutors in the former will tend not to bring cases to trial unless there is a high possibility of obtaining a conviction. The law allows prosecutors to take into account the suspect's attitude toward investigators, age and other personal circumstances, likelihood of repeat offenses and gravity and circumstances of the crime in determining whether to prosecute or not (Castberg, 1990; Kubo, 1986).

Companies engaged in illegal behavior are rarely punished severely. In citing a recent case of political pressure brought to bear on the Fair Trade Commission to prevent the prosecution of a suspected bid-rigging case, the *Japan Times* noted that the FTC had not brought charges against such a group since 1974 (March 21-27, 1994). Corporations found guilty of bid fixing or bribery are prohibited from bidding on public works contracts for a few months, and their presidents are expected to resign to take responsibility. Few perpetrators go to jail, and fines are modest (Woodall, 1993; McMillan, 1991). Following revelations of collusion or bribery the officials in each company detailed to the task of fixing relations with other companies are given assignments in other bureaus as a sign of "housecleaning." From time to time a company executive will commit suicide. While individual careers may suffer, corporations do not.

Similarly, few elected officials end up resigning their positions as a result of allegations of wrongdoing. Fewer still are indicted or actually convicted. There is evidence to suggest that prosecution for "abuse of authority," a category of crime covered in the Penal Code, is rarely prosecuted (Castberg, 1990). The code makes it difficult to obtain convictions on bribery charges since the prosecutor must demonstrate that the public official received money, knew it was a bribe and then acted to influence public policy as a result of that bribe (MacDougall, 1986). In any case, the statute of limitations for bribery is three years: since politicians' personal secretaries handle questionable financial transactions, most can hide their actions for that long.[7]

The reluctance of the criminal justice system to enforce corruption laws makes it difficult to measure the rate of politician crime. In 1991, police arrested about 11,600 persons for election-related offenses (Keisatsuch, 1992). Even this figure is suspect, since it is based on cases cleared by the police rather than those reported. It is understood that the police warn many low-level violators without arresting them.

Most of those arrested would have been campaign staff at the street level. Cases involving politician crime at the level considered in this chapter are probably a small proportion of that. If anything, reported cases and convictions for bribery have declined since a high in the early 1950s, despite laws designed to control it (Shikita and Tsuchiya, 1992). Writing in 1986, before the most recent round of corruption scandals, Kubo put the number of Diet members indicted for wrongdoing, mostly financial, at 313. He estimated that the number of Diet members questioned by the police for such behavior was over 600. In other words, fewer than half of the Diet members investigated were actually indicted. Of those tried, the majority were found not guilty or received suspended sentences. Of 35 cases tried between the Showa Denko scandal of 1949 and the Lockheed crisis in 1986, 10 resulted in acquittals and 20 resulted in suspended sentences (Kubo, 1986; see also Flanagan, 1991). More recently, a prefectural governor convicted of violating campaign finance laws received a suspended sentence, while two staff members received sanctions of less than one year each (Sapsford and Kanabayashi, 1994).

In other words, the likelihood of going to jail for political corruption is so low that probably it does not serve as a sufficient deterrent when compared to the expected benefits of that corruption. Moreover, corruption is a potential hornet's nest for prosecutors, depending as they do on the willingness of the political authorities to tolerate thorough investigations and indictments (Kubo, 1986). During the shipping industry scandals of the 1950s, the public prosecutor's office issued an arrest warrant for one prominent conservative politician, only to see it overturned by the Minister of Justice. Later that same year, the politician was indicted for violating political donations laws, but charges were dropped. He later became Prime Minister and presided over yet another round of corruption scandals (Curtis, 1988). In September 1992, Kanemaru Shin was arrested, fined a paltry 200,000 yen for evading taxes on an illegal 500-million-yen loan from Sagawa Kyubin, then released before a public outcry prompted his rearrest in March 1993 on tax evasion charges.

Ultimately, elected politicians depend upon the voters to maintain them in office. Officially, there are no obstacles to citizen removal through elections of a Diet member who has lost the trust of his constituents. Yet there are powerful factors in Japan's political culture that often thwart the removal of a politician accused or even convicted of bribery, fixing contracts or any of a number of related offenses.

The belief that government is irresponsible, unresponsive to individual citizens and run primarily for the benefit of big business is widespread (Krauss, 1984). Survey data reveal that the public sees politics as dirty and dishonest work. Questions probing the public's view of corruption find that the Japanese rate their elected officials quite low, and see them as distant, arrogant and likely to break the law during campaigns (Martin and Stronach, 1992; Richardson, 1974). Moreover, Japanese citizens exhibit comparatively low levels of political efficacy, especially when it comes to effecting changes in national politics. They also tend to identify with local issues rather than national ones (Richardson and Flanagan, 1984). As a result, citizens' movements aimed at corruption tend to be local and aimed at particular individuals (e.g., Kubo, 1986:96-97).

Finally, Japanese citizens tend to tolerate corruption by their officials because those individuals spread the benefits of that behavior to constituents. The construction industry is not only national but local, and its financial power and potential for vote mobilization mean that local firms benefit from Diet members' pork-barrel efforts. Notably corrupt faction bosses are continuously reelected to office. The most famous case involves Tanaka Kakuei, a former prime minister convicted of accepting over $1 million in bribes from the Lockheed Corporation in exchange for fixing a government contract to purchase aircraft. Tanaka was returned to his Diet seat in 1983 by the largest margin in his career, a year in which his conviction in Tokyo courts was upheld. Similarly, all but two of the 16 Diet members implicated in the 1989 Recruit scandal were reelected in the House of Representatives elections in 1990: one of them had already been indicted (Flanagan, 1991). In short, Japanese citizens may dislike corruption in the Diet, but they love their often corrupt Diet members.

Corruption does not persist because politicians are successful at covering it up. Corruption, violation of campaign laws and other breaches of expected conduct are widely reported in the media. As a tool to dislodge the LDP or promote the reform corrupt practices, however, the media has two basic weaknesses. First, the established media rely on political leaders for news, making them reluctant to expose corruption because it might damage their access in other instances. And, the established media in Japan tend to pick up corruption scandals only after they are exposed in the tabloid or foreign presses (Farley, 1996).

Second, corruption is a valence issue, one that tends to be seen in terms of good and bad, rather than a position issue requiring a carefully thought-out stance. While valence issues can hurt a party in single elections, their stress on emotion and outrage means that they usually do not last. Valence issues thus tend to fade quickly. In the Japanese case, scandals have been the objects of media attention for up to a year, but once an election occurs, the scandals fade from view. Moreover, valence issues do not cause confrontation between vested interests and therefore are not attached to organizational resources that might keep them in the public eye in the long term (Flanagan, 1991). The corruption issue forced the LDP to make promises of change, sometimes real, in the face of elections, but until 1993 it was able to ride out the tempest until the issue faded.

CONTROLLING ELECTORAL CORRUPTION

Will electoral reform stop corruption? That is the perennial hope. The newspaper *Asahi Shinbun* in 1964 suggested that the creation of single-member constituencies would eliminate elections based on money and restore the parties to primacy in campaigns. It opined that election debate would center around policy rather than personality and appeals to private interest. Smaller districts with single winners would also reduce campaign expenses, resulting in less corruption (Thayer, 1969).

The House of Representatives elections in July 1993 marked a watershed in Japan's post-war political system. For the first time since the elections of 1958, the LDP lost its control of that house. A seven-party coalition spent the following six months hammering out a political reform package that has the potential to reduce campaign expenditures and consequent need for money. The changes, arrived at only with the cooperation of the LDP in 1994, reform the electoral system and, less dramatically, campaign finance. That package paved the way for subsequent reforms in the way political corruption is handled. For example, a bill introduced in the Diet in October 1994 would force elected officials convicted of bribery to resign their seats ("Today's Japan," Nihon Hoso Kyoku broadcast, October 25, 1994).

The major structural reform passed in 1994 involves redistributing the seats in the House of Representatives.[8] The number of seats in that House was reduced from 511 to 500. More important, the medium sized multimember constituency was replaced with a two-ballot system similar to Germany's Bundestag electoral system. Three hundred seats will be elected from single-member constituencies and 200 will be elected by proportional representation based on 11 regional blocs.

Both measures were aimed at simultaneously reducing the impact of money in elections and breaking the LDP's monopoly on the Diet as a result. Reduction in the number of seats, it is argued, would limit the effects of money in campaigns. As Wolfe put it, "the more politicians you have, the more money you need. Reduce the number of politicians and the proportion of the total contribution pool available to each would increase, decreasing the temptation to look for 'tainted' sources of campaign funds" (1992:777). If this is indeed the case, then the 1994 reduction in seat numbers will have at best a modest impact on money politics.

The replacement of the multimember constituency will have a much greater impact. As noted above, the existence of multiple LDP candidates in single constituencies was a prime motivator of factional organization and *koenkai*. The combination of weak party sponsorship and medium-sized districts in which no candidate could expect to garner the support of sympathizers on party identification alone stimulated the demand for money to run expensive personalized candidacies.

The introduction of single-member constituencies will help eliminate the competition between candidates of the same party for seats or at least push the problem of candidate selection back on the parties. Moreover, successful candidates now have to appeal to new constituents not necessarily tied to *koenkai* because the new district lines have largely obliterated the old support bases.

Second, the PR formula on the second ballot will strengthen the parties' sponsorship of candidates. The division of the PR seats into regional blocs, a measure included at the LDP's insistence, undoubtedly will allow politicians with regional reputations to use their local support bases as keys to inclusion in the second ballot party lists. It may also reduce the effectiveness of the changes in eliminating the factions because the struggles between them may simply carry over onto party decisions on the lists. Yet holding the number of such seats to two hundred will weaken factional infighting since the parties will no longer pit members against one another.

Two reforms aimed specifically at strengthening the role of the political parties in the electoral process. First, the new law provides for contributions to the parties while it limits the ability of individual candidates to create independent political organizations to act as shells for campaign funds. Second, it introduces public financing of the parties. In 1990, an advisory panel to Prime Minister Kaifu suggested public subsidies as part and parcel of reforms to control corruption. The 1994 bill proposing the same was supported by the Hosokawa coalition and the LDP as a way to strengthen party-centered campaigns at the expense of individual candidacies. Both coalition and opposition versions of the final bill provided for up to one half of public subsidies to the parties for support of individual candidacies (Yanagawa, 1994).

The cumulative effect of the reforms have important consequences for campaign funds. In particular, there will be less need for the large amounts of money required to support the *koenkai*, which are disappearing. Recent gains by the LDP's opponents in local elections may help sever the link between that party's Diet members and their clients in the prefectural and municipal assemblies, again reducing the need for extra campaign money. Smaller districts in general should have the effect they do in Britain and Germany — reducing the need for campaign finance in short election periods. Finally, the parties will not only have control over their candidates but will be in a position to provide them enough money to help run their less expensive campaigns.

It should be noted that in the past, reforms themselves have caused unforeseen problems, particularly in the area of campaign finance. The limitations on individual contributions to candidates, imposed in the mid-1970s, is held to be responsible for the diversification of funding sources in the LDP away from the business federations themselves. LDP members found that they had to court more potential contributors in order to pay for still-expensive *koenkai* (Curtis, 1988). In this climate, smaller companies and those outside of the major business federations found themselves in a position to seek political favors in exchange for political donations. The Recruit Scandal resulted not merely from politicians' greed, but from a situation engendered by previous reforms that allowed an unknown company to buy influence by its willingness to bribe cash-starved LDP members.

If this is the case, recent "reforms" may do nothing to stem the tide of money to conservative candidates. In October 1993 the *Keidanren* announced that it would no longer organize the collection of campaign funds from big business to the LDP. *Nikkenren*, the federation of construction firms, also suspended political contributions, but resumed them in December 1994. In 1995, the *Keidanren* followed. In any case, companies are welcome to make campaign contributions on their own, subject to the new rules, which means that the trend begun by the Miki reforms may accelerate as party bosses chase individual companies to maintain their political clout. Nikkenren's resumption of its policy of providing political funds suggests that the construction industry still sees political clout as important to its ability to maintain access to the public works market. As long as the political and economic elite in Japan are not the same people, this will undoubtedly continue. That said, there is some evidence of a modest decline in reported political donations in recent years (Shikin, 1998).

Some issues of corruption have not been raised in Diet debate at all. There is a curious silence in Japan about reform of the Public Offices Election Law itself. Clearly, provisions outlawing bribery of candidates or voters are a necessary part of a clean electoral system. The current ban on the private purchase of media time for campaigns, when compared to the cost of media campaigns in the United States, has much to recommend it. Yet, the restrictive nature of the Election Law, under which the October 1996 elections using the new system were conducted, is part of the corruption problem because it makes open contact between candidates and voters so difficult. Part of the Kaifu government's recommendations for political reform in 1990 included raising the ban on house-to-house canvassing, a measure that would go a long way toward shortening the distance between the public and the officials it elects.

The distance served the LDP's interests because it helped prevent the op-position parties from waging successful campaigns against incumbents (Hre-benar, 1986:49). The stalemate after 1955 between the LDP and a seemingly permanent opposition engendered the brokerage role the LDP played between business and the state bureaucracy in exchange for political funds. A significant reform has been the emergence of two moderate political parties: the New Frontier Party (Shin Shinto, 1994) and the Democratic Party (1996). The result of this realignment, it is hoped, will be meaningful competition between parties for control of the government.

How would this address the corruption problem? Recent scandals in Western Europe suggest that corruption can survive even in political systems in which parties rotate in power; it does not need the dominance of one politi-cal party to exist. In the Japanese case, however, the issue is not corruption per se but its structural nature. In such a case, therefore, it is possible that rotation in power would curb corruption by reducing the incentives to businesses to bribe politicians in exchange for access to preferential political goods. If parties periodically replace one another as legislative majorities, then policies, and their impact on the bureaucracy and society, differ over time. The cozy relationship between corporate interests and the LDP that characterized the 1955 system would be harder to maintain. Indeed, business would no longer be beholden to the LDP as the only party capable of maintaining a favorable economic and social environment.

Most of the reforms outlined above suggest ways that political corruption in Japan can be controlled by changing the rules by which the electoral system works. I do not expect that they will eliminate corruption. Indeed, the New Frontier Party was barely two months old when one of its members was implicated in a scandal involving illegal loans from a recently failed credit union (*New York Times*, 16 February 1995). Former Prime Minister Hosokawa's troubles in 1997 suggest that new rules engender new ways to get around them.

The institutional features outlined earlier, moreover, suggest some of the more enduring obstacles to the control of corruption. The limited role of law and the weak nature of legal restraints on corruption remain. In Japan the wheels of justice continue to grind slowly and imperfectly. No better example of this fact can be seen than in the recent Supreme Court ruling on the 1974 Lockheed Scandal case. In February 1995 the Supreme Court upheld the lower court guilty verdicts against the two remaining defendants in that case. In doing so, the Court also indirectly confirmed the Tokyo High Court's 1983 guilty verdict against Tanaka Kakuei — 18 years after the scandal and 14 months after the former Prime Minister's death (*Asahi Shinbun*, 23 February 1995). As long as the law does not provide vigorous sanction against crime by state actors, those crimes will continue.

It remains to be seen whether public attitudes toward politicians change to correspond to the new reforms. In particular, if the electoral reforms induce a cleaner style of politics, will citizens perceive the changes or will they continue to view their elected officials as corrupt, aloof and out of touch with broad popular sentiment? Will citizens take it upon themselves actually to remove corrupt representatives? Here we again must acknowledge that corruption is a valence issue lacking a durable base in public consciousness. Recent polls suggest that citizens are about equally concerned with economic recovery and political reform. As the new electoral system is installed we should expect to see a waning of popular concern about corruption as the media and government move on to other issues.

Even if citizens remain aware of and concerned about corruption the new system does not guarantee that they can translate that concern into effective action. Single-member districts still create a potential buffer between corrupt politicians disliked by the general public but who have assiduously cultivated constituents with particularistic benefits. Certainly, single-member districts in the United States have existed side by side with personalized candidacies largely independent of party control. The new reforms, therefore, build in a safety net for the kinds of behavior they are intended to change.

NOTES

1. The tale is based on an actual incident in the early eighteenth century in which 46 samurai avenged the unjust execution of their slighted lord.

2. About $250 at recent exchange rates.

3. Rae does not address corruption as a consequence of electoral rules. Indeed, he argues that corruption "is probably very rare in general elections" (p.68n.) He does not include Japan in his study.

4. In practice, the Communist Party policy of fielding candidates in every district amounted to a protest since it won very few seats.

5. The author experienced a version of this in 1990 when he was invited to the Komoto faction's summer training session. It was a training session in name only. The faction arranged for key constituents from each member's *koenkai* to attend a two-day meeting at an expensive resort hotel south of Tokyo. For a nominal fee, constituents were treated to two days in the hotel, meals, after-hours drinks with their Diet member, and presentations by the faction leader, a former ambassador to the United States, and several news commentators.

6. The Sagawa Kyubin scandal was especially troubling because it made clear the links between key leaders in the LDP, the *yakuza* (organized crime) and ultranationalist groups clamoring for a return to the undemocratic prewar social and political system.

7. A high suicide rate among personal secretaries is a striking feature of this arrangement.

8. House of Councillors districts remain unchanged.

NINE.
WHAT HAVE WE LEARNED AND WHAT IS THE NEXT STEP?[1]

by

Jeffrey Ian Ross

NOW THAT THE case studies of controls on state crimes in particular advanced capitalist countries have been reviewed, it appears logical to comment on what we have learned from this exercise, and what is the next step in research and policy development. The following discussion will answer: what are the controls that have been implemented in the countries reviewed?; how theoretical and policy work must develop; and argues that state crimes in nondemocratic countries should be examined in a systematic fashion.

WHAT ARE THE CONTROLS THAT HAVE BEEN FOUND?

The most socially relevant outcome is control (Gibbs, 1989). These processes may operate independently or in concert with other mechanisms such as public relations and internal resistance (Ross, 2000, 1995c), and may be ordered along a continuum of "tangible" (e.g., firing a police officer/s) versus "symbolic" actions (e.g., press conferences) (e.g., Edelman, 1971, 1964; Gusfield, 1963). However, the distinction between tangible and symbolic actions is problematic because tangible actions carry with them symbolic benefits as well (e.g., Wilson, 1973).

In general, there are two potentially complementary principal outcomes: external control and internal control initiatives. In the long run external control initiatives that demand, impose, or legislate more control in and of state agencies are met with three possible responses from state agents: resistance, public relations and internal controls. Too often, attempts by the government or outsiders to control state crime results in coverups and obstruction of justice. Controls that are initiated from inside state agencies will carry more weight than will those implemented from outside. And those controls directed against individuals will be more effective than those involving the entire organization (Ross, 1995b, 1995c). Changing an entire organization is much more difficult than targeting a singular person.

Thankfully, citizens are not powerless against state crime. To begin with, several sources can be consulted to get a picture of the nature and extent of state crimes, including but not limited to judicial documents, the reports of government and nongovernmental inquiries, judicial actions against Members of Parliament, mass media reporting and books like this.

Most democracies are bound by constitutions, the rule of law and, usually, a separation of powers and systems of checks and balances among the executive, legislative and judicial branches of government. These notions were outlined by the framers of the U.S. Constitution, which was developed in part through a careful reading and interpretation of political theory and the British and French Constitutions as they existed at that time. It is believed that these legal mechanisms will provide a large measure of control over state crimes. A number of other methods have been instituted in democracies, including political competition (in the form of political parties, interest groups and social movements) that minimizes and, in some cases, helps control state crimes. In other states, as is reviewed in this book, controls include the reform of public administration, ensuring that the bureaucracy is paid enough and imposing temporal limits on the time public officials can be in power.

THEORETICAL WORK

So far, the majority of writing on the causes and control of state crime has been in the structural theoretical tradition. Clearly, the psychological and public administration/policy theories have to be examined. Applying psychological and public administration/policy theories that examine individual level processes at the individual and group level can shed more light on the problems and opportunities inherent in controlling state crime. For example, organizational behavior theory and social psychological theory can provide insights into why collectivities and, by extension, states, engage in crimes.

RESEARCH WORK

The effort to develop theoretically informed case studies for other advanced industrialized countries should continue. A number of important advanced industrialized democracies were not covered in this book such as Australia, Austria, Germany, The Netherlands, New Zealand, the Scandinavian countries, Portugal and Spain. Case studies of these countries should provide additional insights on how to proceed with theoretical and policy development, implementation and evaluation.

POLICY WORK

Perhaps, more important than theory and research should be the area of policy development, particularly the implementation and evaluation of programs and methods to control state crime. Evaluation is a "powerful tool for planning, developing and managing... [governmental] programs. As an objective means of documenting success, identifying problems and guiding refinements, program evaluation is important to a variety of stakeholders" (Przybylski, 1995:4).

POLICY IMPLEMENTATION/PRAXIS

By far the greatest efforts should be concentrated in policy implementation/praxis. The activities of organizations such as domestic civil liberties associations or unions, Human Rights Watch, Amnesty International, and the National Lawyers Guild are important steps in the battle against state crime. The introduction of whistleblower legislation and work by progressive law reform organizations are also necessary in the battle against state crime.

MOVING THE DISCUSSION TOWARDS LESSER DEVELOPED AND NON-ADVANCED INDUSTRIALIZED DEMOCRACIES

The next step in the emerging research agenda of state criminality will be to address these issues in lesser developed countries, many of which were or are client states of the larger advanced industrialized countries. Although many excellent studies of coercive regimes and countries have been conducted, they need to be consolidated and approached in the same theoretically oriented manner as has been done in this book.

CONCLUSION

Research in this area is a herculean task. Assembling case studies that rigorously analyze the controls in various countries is difficult at best. Having analysts sing from the same sheet or music is hard given vagaries in disciplines, training and languages. The information presented in this book, however, should be perceived not as an end in itself, but a continuation in the battle to combat state crimes and preserve democracy.

Acknowledgments: Special thanks to William McDonald and Stephen Richards for comments on an earlier version of this chapter.

NOTES

1. This chapter builds on Ross (1999, 1998b).

ABOUT THE AUTHORS

Michael J. Avey is an Assistant Professor of Political Science at Lander University. He was a COINTELPRO target during the 1970s and has sued a municipality for state crime activity. He wrote on the impact of state crime on the electoral system in the U.S. in the *Demobilization of the American Voter* (1989). Among the current courses he teaches are Constitutional Law, Political Organization and Campaign Management. His current research interest is on voter mobilization.

Gregg Barak is a Professor of Criminology and Criminal Justice at Eastern Michigan University. He is the author and/or editor of several books, including the award-winning *Gimme Shelter: A Social History of Homelessness in Contemporary America* (1991), *Integrating Criminologies* (1998), *Media, Criminal Justice and Mass Culture, 2nd edition* (2000) and *Crime and Crime Control: A Global View* (2000).

Raymond R. Corrado is a Professor in the School of Criminology at Simon Fraser University. He has co-edited three books, *Current Issues in Juvenile Justice, Evaluation and Criminal Justice Policy* (1981) and *Juvenile Justice in Canada* (1992), as well as having published various articles and book chapters on terrorism, political crime and juvenile justice.

Donatella della Porta is a professor of Political Science at the University of Florence. She carried out research in Italy, France, Spain, the Federal Republic of Germany and the United States. Her main fields of research include social movements, political violence, terrorism, political corruption, maladministration, public order and the police. She published extensively in several journals and collective volumes in Italy and abroad. Among her recent books are *Lo scambio occulto* (1992), *Corruzione politica e amministrazione pubblica* (1994), *Democratie et Corruption en Europe* (1995), *Corrupt Exchanges* (1999) and *Social Movements, Political Violence and the State* (1995).

Garth Davies received his Masters degree in Criminology from Simon Fraser University in 1994. His thesis was an empirical evaluation of structural terrorism models. He is currently a Ph.D. candidate in the School of Criminology at Rutgers University, Newark.

R. Reuben Miller received his Ph.D. from the University of Denver. He served as Research Associate at Abbott Associates, Inc. in Springfield, VA. His research, contracted by the Defense Department, produced a number of reports. His work was published in: *The Encyclopedia of Terrorism, Terrorism and Political Violence, Mediterranean Quarterly, Comparative Political Studies, Conflict Quarterly, Intelligence and National Security, Terrorism: An International Journal, Current World Leaders,* other academic journals, professional magazines and newspapers. He is the author of *Confrontational Terrorism: The Dilemma of Response* (forthcoming). Dr. Miller has extensive teaching experience at the graduate and undergraduate levels. He has lectured on: International Relations, International Terrorism, American Foreign and Defense Policy, the Arab-Israeli Conflict and National & International Security. Currently he is an adjunct professor at the University of Colorado at Denver. Dr. Miller is an independent research analyst, and serves as a contract consultant for the U.S. State Department.

David M. Potter is Associate Professor of Japanese Politics and Comparative Politics in the Department of Political Science at Northern Kentucky University. He has published articles in *Pacific Affairs, The Journal of Economic Issues,* and *The International Journal of Comparative and Applied Criminal Justice* and he is the author of *Japan's Foreign Aid to Thailand and Philippines* (1996).

Stephen C. Richards is an Associate Professor of Sociology and Criminology at Northern Kentucky University. He is a former federal prisoner. His published work has been on tattoos, prison conditions, prison release, parole and community punishments. Richards is the author of *The Structure of Prison Release* (1995), and *The Sociological Significance of Tattoos* (1995). He is currently co-editing a book, with Jeffrey Ian Ross, *Convict Criminology.*

Jeffrey Ian Ross is an Assistant Professor with the Division of Criminology, Criminal Justice and Social Policy at the University of Baltimore, and has conducted research, written and lectured on national security, political violence, political crime, violent crime, corrections and policing for over a decade. His work has appeared in many academic journals and books, as well as in popular magazines. Ross is the editor of *Controlling State Crime* (1995), *Violence in Canada: Sociopolitical Perspectives* (1995), *Cutting the Edge: Current Perspectives on Radical/Critical Criminology and Criminal Justice* (1998); and the author of *Making News of Police Violence* (2000), and *The Dynamics of Political Crime* (forthcoming). Ross was a Research Associate for the

Center for Comparative Politics at the University of Colorado, Boulder, and a Research Associate at the International Centre for Comparative Criminology at the University of Montréal. He is also a fellow of the Center for Comparative and International Law at the University of Baltimore.

Alberto Vannucci is a researcher at the Department of Political Sciences of the University of Pisa. He is author and coauthor of several articles on political corruption, mafia and philosophy of social science published by academic journals. In 1996 he worked in the Committee for the Prevention of Corruption instituted by the Italian Chambre of Deputies. Among his books on corruption are *Corruzione politica e amministrazione pubblica* (1994; co-authored with D. della Porta), *Il mercato della corruzione* (1997), *Corrupt Exchanges* (1999) and *Un paese anormale* (1999).

Jim Wolfreys has been a Lecturer in French Politics at King's College, University of London, since 1994. He is coauthor (with Peter Fysh) of *The Politics of Racism in France* (1998). His published work also includes book chapters and articles (for *Parliamentary Affairs*) on the extreme right, the left and class struggles in France.

References

Aberbach, J.D, R.D. Putnam and B.A. Rockman (1981). *Bureaucrats and Politicians in Western Democracies.* Cambridge, MA: Harvard University Press.

APN (1993). "Richiesta di Autorizzazione a Procedere." *La Repubblica* April 15.

Albanese, J.S. (1995). *White Collar Crime in America.* Englewood Cliffs, NJ: Prentice Hall.

Alderson, J.C. (1984). *Law and Disorder.* London, UK: Hamish Hamilton.

Alexander, H. (1992). *Financing Politics: Money, Elections, and Political Reform.* Washington, DC: C.Q. Press.

────── and A. Corrado (1995). *Financing the 1992 Election.* Armonk, NY: M.E. Sharpe.

Almond, G. (1956). "Comparative Political Systems." *Journal of Politics* 18(3):391-409.

────── and G.B. Powell, Jr. (1966). *Comparative Politics: A Developmental Approach.* Boston, MA: Little, Brown.

────── and S. Verba (1963). *The Civic Culture.* Princeton, NJ: Princeton University Press.

Alperovitz, G. and J. Faux (1984). *Rebuilding America: A Blueprint for the New Economy.* New York, NY: Pantheon.

Alpert, G.P. and R.G. Dunham (1992). *Policing Urban America.* Prospect Heights, IL: Waveland Press.

Amato, G. (1980). *Una Repubblica da Riformare.* Bologna, IT: Il Mulino.

American Friends Service Committee (1979). *The Police Threat to Political Liberty.* Philadelphia, PA: author.

Andreas, P. (1997). "The Rise of the American Crimefare State." *World Policy Journal* 14(3):37-45.

Andreoli, M. (1993). *Andavamo in Piazza Duomo.* Milano, IT: Sperling & Kupfer.

Andvig, J.C. (1991). "The Economics of Corruption." *Studi Economici* 46:57-96.

Arabbia, A.G. and V. Giammusso (1994). "Profilo Statistico della Pubblica Amministrazione." In: C. Cassese and C. Franchini (eds.), *L'amministrazione Pubblica Italiana.* Bologna, IT: Il Mulino.

Aronson, G. (1984). *Creating Facts: Israel, Palestinians and the West Bank.* Washington, DC: Institute for Palestine Studies.

Asimov, L. and F. Homer (1988). "Democracies and the Role of Acquiescence in International Terrorism." In: M. Stohl and G.A. Lopez (eds.), *Terrible Beyond Endurance?* Westport, CT: Greenwood Press.

Avey, M.J. (1989). *The Demobilization of American Voters: A Comprehensive Theory of Voter Turnout.* Westport, CT: Greenwood Press.

Bachrach, P. and M.S. Baratz (1962). "Two Faces of Power." *The American Political Science Review* 56:947-952.

Bacon, D. (1997). "Labor Slaps the Smug New Face of Union Busting." *CovertAction Quarterly* (Spring):33-38.

Banfield, E.C. (1975). "Corruption as a Feature of Governmental Organization." *Journal of Law and Economics* 18(3):587-605.

Banton, M. (1975). "A New Approach to Police Authorities." *Police* 7:24-25.

Barak, G. (ed.) (1994). *Varieties of Criminology: Readings from a Dynamic Discipline.* Westport, CT: Praeger.

—— (1991a). "Resisting State Criminality and the Struggle for Justice." In: G. Barak (ed.), *Crimes by the Capitalist State: An Introduction to State Criminality.* Albany, NY: State University of New York Press.

—— (ed.) (1991b). *Crimes by the Capitalist State: An Introduction to State Criminality.* Albany, NY: State University of New York Press.

—— (1990). "Crime, Criminology, and Human Rights: Towards an Understanding of State Criminality." *Journal of Human Justice* 2:11-28.

Bar, M. (1990). *Red Lines in Israel's Deterrence Strategy* (in Hebrew). Tel Aviv, ISR: Ma'arachot - IDF Publishing House.

Bar-On, M. (1985). *Peace Now* (in Hebrew). Tel Aviv, ISR: Hakibutz Hameuchad Publishing House Ltd.

Bartlett, D. and J.B. Steel (1992). *America: What Went Wrong.* Kansas City, MO: McAndrews and McMeel.

Bayley, D. (1994). *Police for the Future.* New York, NY: Oxford University Press.

—— (1985). *Patterns of Policing: A Comparative International Analysis.* New Brunswick, NJ: Rutgers University Press.

—— (1979). "Police Function, Structure, and Control in Western Europe and North America." In: N. Morris and Michael Tonry (eds.), *Crime and Justice: An Annual Review of Research,* vol. 1. Chicago, IL: University of Chicago Press.

—— (1976). *Forces of Order.* Berkeley, CA: University of California Press.

Beck, P.A. (1990). *Party Politics in America.* New York, NY: Longman.

Becker, G. (1968). "Crime and Punishment. An Economic Approach." *Journal of Political Economy* 76(2):169- 217.

Becker, G.S and G.J. Stigler (1974). "Law Enforcement, Malfeasance, and Compensation of Enforcers." *Journal of Legal Studies* 3:1-18.

Benot, Y. (1994). *Massacres Coloniaux.* Paris, FR: La Découverte.

Benson, B.L. and J. Baden (1985). "The Political Economy of Governmental Corruption: The Logic of Underground Government." *Journal of Legal Studies* 14:381-410.

Benson, M.L. (1984). "The Fall from Grace: Loss of Occupational Status as a Consequence of Conviction for a White Collar Crime." *Criminology* 22(4):573-593.

Benvenisti, M. (1992). *Fatal Embrace* (in Hebrew). Jerusalem, ISR: Keter Publishing, Ltd.

Benyon, J. (1984). *Scarman and After: Essays Reflecting on Lord Scarman's Report, The Riots and Their Aftermath*. New York, NY: Pergamon Press.

Berger, P.L. (1990). *A Rumor of Angels: Modern Society and the Rediscovery of the Supernatural*. New York, NY: Doubleday.

Berlet, C. (1992). "Activists Face Increased Harassment." *Utne Reader* (Jan/Feb):85-89.

Bettati, C. (1993). *Responsables et Coupables. Une Affaire de Sang*. Paris, FR: Seuil.

Bettin, G. and A. Magnier (1991). *Chi Governa la Città*. Padova, IT: Cedam.

Bigaud, C. (1994). "*La Réforme Constitutionnelle de Juillet 1993, Regards sur l'actualité.*" 198 (Feb.):3-42.

Birnbaum, P. (1994). *Les Sommets de l'Etat*. Paris, FR: Seuil.

Blackstock, N. (1975). *COINTELPRO: The FBI's Secret War on Political Freedom*. New York, NY: Vintage Books.

Bluestone, B. and B. Harrison (1982). *The Deindustrialization of America*. New York, NY: Basic Books.

Bobbio, N. (1980). "La Democrazia e il Potere Invisobile." *Rivista Italiana di Scienze Politiche* 10:181-203.

Boggio, P. and A. Rollat (1988). *Ce Terrible Monsieur Pasqua*. Paris, FR: Olivier Orban.

Bornstein, S.E. (1988). "The Greenpeace Affair and the Peculiarities of French Politics." In: A.S. Markovits and M. Silverstein (eds.), *The Politics of Scandal*. New York, NY: Holmes and Meier.

Bowles, S.D., M. Gordon and T.E. Weisskopf (1984). *Beyond the Waste Land: A Democratic Alternative to Economic Decline*. Garden City, NY: Doubleday/Anchor.

Braithwaite, J. (1985). "White Collar Crime." *Annual Review of Sociology* 11:1-25.

Bristol Trade Union Council (TUC) (1981). *Slumbering Volcano? Report of an Enquiry into the Origins of the Eruption in St. Paul's Bristol on 2 April 1980*. Bristol, UK: author.

Brogden, M. (1982). *Police: Autonomy and Consent*. Toronto, CAN: Academic Press.

——— (1977). "A Police Authority - the Denial of Conflict." *Sociological Review* 25 (May):325-350.

Brown, L. and C. Brown. (1973). *An Unauthorized History of the RCMP*. Toronto, CAN: James Lorimer.

Bunyan, T. (1976). *The Political Police in Britain*. New York, NY: St. Martin's Press.

Burnham, W.D. (1980). "The Appearance and Disappearance of The American Voter." In: R. Rose (ed.), *Electoral Participation: A Comparative Perspective*. Newbury Park, CA: Sage.

——— (1965). "The Changing Shape of the American Political Universe." *American Political Science Review* 59:7-28.

Buscetta, T. (1992). "Questione di Rispetto." Interview by Enzo Biagi, in *Mafia*, supplement to *Panorama*, October.

Cadot, O. (1987). "Corruption as a Gamble." *Journal of Public Economics* 33:223-244.

Cahm, E. (1996). *The Dreyfus Affair in French Society and Politics.* London, UK: Longman.

Caiden, G.E. and Caiden, N.J. (1977). "Administrative Corruption." *Public Administration Review* 37(3):301-309.

Cameron, S. (1994). *On the Take: Crime, Corruption and Greed in the Mulroney Years.* Toronto, CAN: Macfarlane, Walter & Ross.

Campbell, D. (1997). "NASA's Business Plan: Global Access." *CovertAction Quarterly* (Winter 1996-97):12.

Carignon, A. (1995). *Une Saison dans la Nuit.* Paris, FR: Grasset.

Carnoy, M. and D. Schearer (1980). *Economic Democracy: The Challenge of 1980s.* Armonk, NY: M.E. Sharpe.

Carter, D.L. (1990). "Drug Related Corruption of Police Officers: A Contemporary Typology." *Journal of Criminal Justice* 18:85-98.

——— and D.W. Stephens (1991). "An Overview of Issues Concerning Police Officer Drug Use." In: T. Barker and D.L. Carter (eds.), *Police Deviance.* Cincinnati, OH: Anderson Publishing Company.

Cassese, S. (1994). "Il Sistema Amministrativo Italiano, Ovvero L'arte di Arran-giarsi." In: S. Cassese and C. Franchini. (eds.), *L'amministrazione Pubblica Italiana.* Bologna, IT: Il Mulino.

——— (1992). "Appalti e Tangenti." *La Repubblica* September 9.

——— (1980). *Servitori dello Stato.* Interview by Redento Mori, Bologna, IT: Zanichelli.

Castberg, D. (1990). *Japanese Criminal Justice.* New York, NY: Praeger.

Caulfield, S.L. (1991). "Subcultures as Crime: The Theft of Legitimacy of Dissent in the United States." In: G. Barak (ed.), *Crimes by the Capitalist State: An Introduction to State Criminality.* Albany, NY: State University of New York Press.

Cazzola, F. (1992). *L'Italia del Pizzo.* Torino, IT: Einaudi.

——— (1988). *Della Corruzione. Fisiologia e Patologia di un Sistema Politico.* Bologna, IT: Il Mulino.

Chalier, Y. (1991). *La République Corrompue.* Paris, FR: Robert Laffont.

Chamber of Deputies (1992-1993) *Domanda di autorizzazione a procedere in giudizio, doc. IV.* Rome, IT: Atti Parlamentari.

Chambliss, W.J. (1989). "State Organized Crime." *Criminology* 27:183-208.

——— (1988). *On the Take: From Petty Crooks to Presidents.* Bloomington, IN: Indiana University Press.

Chapman, W. (1991). *Inventing Japan.* New York, NY: Prentice-Hall.

Chomsky, N. (1989). *Necessary Illusions: Thought Control in Democratic Societies.* Boston, MA: South End Press.

—— (1988). *The Culture of Terrorism.* Boston, MA: South End Press.

—— (1985). *Turning the Tide.* Boston, MA: South End Press.

Christie, N. (1993). *Crime Control as Industry.* New York, NY: Routledge.

Chubb J. and M. Vannicelli (1988). "Italy: a Web of Scandals in a Flawed Democracy." In: A.S. Markovits and M. Silverstein (eds.), *The Politics of Scandal.* New York-London: Holmes & Meier.

Churchill, W. (1990). *The Cointelpro Papers.* Boston, MA: South End Press.

—— and J. Vander Wall (1988). *Agents of Repression: The FBI's Secret Wars Against The Black Panther Party and The American Indian Movement.* Boston, MA: South End Press.

Clement, W. (1977). "The Corporate Elite, the Capitalist Class, and the Canadian State." In: L. Panitch (ed.), *The Canadian State: Political Economy and Political Power.* Toronto, CAN: University of Toronto Press.

Cleroux, R. (1990). *Official Secrets: The Story Behind the Canadian Security Intelligence Service.* Toronto, CAN: McGraw-Hill Ryerson.

Clinard, M. and R. Quinney (1978). "Crimes by Government." In: D. Ermann and R. Lundman (eds.), *Corporate and Government Deviance.* New York, NY: Oxford University Press.

—— and P.C. Yeager (1980). *Corporate Crime.* New York, NY: The Free Press.

Cohen, J. and J. Rogers (1983). *On Democracy: Toward a Transformation of American Society.* Baltimore, MD: Penguin.

Cohen, S. (1979). "Guilt, Justice, and Tolerance: Some Old Concepts for a New Criminology." In: D. Downes and P. Rock (eds.), *Deviance Interpretations.* London, UK: Martin Robertson.

Cohen, S.A. (1993). "'Masqueraders' in the Israeli Defense Forces, 1991-1992: The Military Unit and the Public Debate." *Low Intensity Conflict & Law Enforcement* 2(2):282-300.

Coignard, S. and J-F. Lacan (1989). *La République Bananière: De la Démocratie en France.* Paris, FR: Pierre Belfond.

Colby, W. and P. Forbath (1981). *La Mia Vita Nella CIA.* Milano, IT: Mursia.

Coleman, J.W. (1998). *The Criminal Elite: The Sociology of White Collar Crime* (4th ed.). New York, NY: St. Martin's Press.

Colombo, G. (1996). *Il Vizio della Memoria.* Milano, IT: Feltrinelli.

Comitato di Studio Sulla Prevenzione della Corruzione (1996). *Rapporto al Presidente della Camera dei Deputati.* Rome, IT: Unpublished report, October 23.

Cornwell, R. (1983). *God's Banker: An Account of Life and Death of Roberto Calvi*. London, UK: Victor Gollancz.

Corrado, R.R. (1992). "Political Crime in Canada." In: R. Linden (ed.), *Criminology: A Canadian Perspective*. Toronto, CAN: Harcourt, Brace, Jovanovich.

—— (1991). "Contemporary Political Crime: National and International Terrorism." In: C.T. Griffiths and M.A. Jackson (eds.), *Canadian Criminology: Perspectives on Crime and Criminality*. Toronto, CAN: Harcourt, Brace, Jovanovich.

—— A. Oliverio and P. Lauderdale (1992). "Political Deviance." In: V.F. Sacco (ed.), *Deviance: Conformity and Control in Canadian Society*. Scarborough, ONT: Prentice-Hall.

Coulter, J, S. Miller and M. Walker (1984). *State of Siege: Miner's Strike 1984*. London, UK: Canary Press.

Court of Bari (Tribunale di Bari) (1985). *Sentenza* n. 861/85, 29/11/1985.

Cowell, J. and J. Young (1982). *Policing the Riots*. London, UK: Junction Books.

Criley, R. (1990). *The FBI vs. the First Amendment*. Los Angeles, CA: The First Amendment Foundation.

Critchley, T.A. ([1967]1978). *History of Police in England and Wales*. London, UK: Constable.

Crozier, M. (1964). *The Bureaucratic Phenomenon*. Chicago, IL: University of Chicago Press.

Cullen, F.T. and J.P. Wright (1996). "Two Futures for American Corrections." In: B. Maguire and P.F. Radosh (eds.), *The Past, Present and Future of American Criminal Justice*. Dix Hills, NY: General Hall.

Currie, E. (1996). "Missing Pieces: Notes on Crime, Poverty, and Social Policy." *Critical Criminology: An International Journal* 7(1):37-52.

—— (1993). *Reckoning: Drugs, The Cities, and The American Future*. New York, NY: Hill and Wang

—— (1985). *Confronting Crime*. New York, NY: Pantheon Books.

Curtis, G. (1988). *The Japanese Way of Politics*. New York, NY: Columbia University Press.

—— (1983). *Election Campaigning Japanese Style*. Tokyo, Japan, New York, NY and San Francisco, CA: Kodansha International.

Dahl, R. (1961). *Who Governs? Democracy and Power in an American City*. New Haven, CT: Yale University Press.

Dalyell, T. (1987). *Misrule: How Mrs. Thatcher has Misled Parliament from the Sinking of the Belgrano to the Wright Affair*. London, UK: Hamilton.

Darwish, A. and G. Alexander. (1991). *Unholy Babylon: The Secret History of Saddam's War*. New York, NY: St. Martins Press.

D'Auria, G. (1993). "Modelli di Controllo nel Settore Pubblico: Organi, Parametri, Misure, i Controlli della Pubblica Amministrazione." In: S. Cassese (ed.), *I Controlli della Pubblica Amministrazione*. Bologna, IT: Il Mulino.

Davis, A.Y. (1998). "Masked Racism: Reflections on the Prison Industrial Complex." *Colorlines*. Oakland, CA: Applied Research Center and Center for Third World Organizer, Fall:11-17.

Davis, M. (1986). *Prisoners of the American Dream*. London, UK: Verso Edition.

Davigo, P. (1993). "Tempo per un Nuovo Inizio." Interview by Claudio Demattè, *Economia & Management*, 2.

Deacon, R. (1990). *The French Secret Service*. London, UK: Grafton.

Del Gaudio, M. (1992). *La Toga Strappata*. Napoli, IT: Tullio Pironti.

della Porta, D. (1995a). *Social Movements, Political Violence, and the State*. Cambridge, UK and New York, NY: Cambridge University Press.

—— (1995b). "Les Cercles Vicieux de la Corruption." In: D. della Porta and Y. Mény (eds.), *Démocratie et Corruption en Europe*. Paris, FR: La Découverte.

—— (1993). "Institutional Responses to Terrorism: The Italian Case." In: A.P. Schmid and R.D. Crelinsten (eds.), *Western Responses to Terrorism*. London, UK: Frank Cass.

—— (1992). *Lo Scambio Occulto*. Bologna, IT: Il Mulino.

—— (1990). *Il Terrorismo di Sinistra*. Bologna, IT: Il Mulino.

—— and A. Vannucci (1999). *Corrupt Exchanges*. New York, NY: Aldine de Gruyter.

—— and A. Vannucci (1997). "Magistrati e Corruzione Politica: La 'Felice Anomalia' del Caso Italiano." In: I. Diamanti and M. Lazar (eds.), *Stanchi di Miracoli. Il Sistema Politico Italiano in Cerca di Normalità*. Milano, IT: Guerini e Associati.

—— and A. Vannucci (1995). "Politics, the Mafia and the Market for Corrupt Exchange." In: C. Mershon and G. Pasquino (eds.), *Italian Politics. Ending of the First Republic*. Boulder/San Francisco/Oxford: Westview Press.

—— and A. Vannucci (1994). *Corruzione Politica e Amministrazione Pubblica, Risorse, Meccanismi, Attori*. Bologna, IT: Il Mulino.

De Lutiis, G. (1996). *Il Lato Oscuro del Potere*. Roma, IT: Editori Riuniti.

—— (1991). *Storia dei Servizi Segreti in Italia*. Roma, IT: Editori Riuniti.

De Leon, P. (1993). *Thinking about Political Corruption*. Armonk, NY: M.E. Sharpe.

DeMont, J. (1997). "Bitter to the End: The Somalia Inquiry Takes its Best Shot — and Ottawa Fires Back." *Maclean's* 110(28) (July 14):12-16.

Dérogy, J. and J-M. Pontaut (1986). *Enquête sur Trois Secrets d'Etat*. Paris, FR: Robert Laffont.

Diamond, L. (1995). *Promoting Democracy in the 1990s*. New York, NY: Report to the Carnegie Commission on Preventing Deadly Conflict.

Dion, R. (1982). *Crimes of the Secret Police*. Montréal, CAN: Black Rose Books.

Di Palma, G. (1978). *Sopravvivere Senza Governare. I Partiti nel Parlamento Italiano*. Bologna, IT: Il Mulino.

Dillon, J. (1997). "Networking with Spooks." *CovertAction Quarterly* (Winter):30-31.

Domhoff, G.W. (1990). *The Power Elite and the State*. New York, NY: Aldine de Gryter.

—— (1983). *Who Rules America Now?* Englewood Cliffs, NJ: Prentice-Hall.

—— (1972). *Fat Cats and Democrats*. Englewood Cliffs, NJ: Prentice-Hall.

—— (1967). *Who Rules America?* Englewood Cliffs, NJ: Prentice-Hall.

Donner, F. (1990). *Protectors of Privilege*. Berkeley, CA: University of California Press.

Donziger, S. (1996). *The Real War on Crime*. New York, NY: Harper Collins.

Doherty, F. (1986). *The Stalker Affair: Including an Account of British Secret Service Operations in Ireland*. Cork and Dublin, IRE: Mercier Press.

Dore, R. (1978). *Shinohata*. New York, NY: Pantheon Books.

Dorril, S. and R. Ramsay (1991). *Smear! Wilson and the Secret State*. London, UK: Fourth Estate.

Draper, H. (1977). *Karl Marx's Theory of Revolution. Volume 1: State and Bureaucracy*. London, UK: Monthly Review Press.

Drew, E. (1983). *Politics and Money: The New Road to Corruption*. New York, NY: Macmillan.

Ducloux, L. (1958). *From Blackmail to Treason: Political Crime and Corruption in France 1920-1940*. London, UK: Deutsch.

Dupuis, J., J-M. Pontaut and J-L Reverier (1995). "100 Élus dans le Collimateur." *Le Point*, June 10.

—— and J-M. Pontaut (1994). *"Affaire Pelat. Le Rapport Secret." Le Point* January 8.

Duus, P. (1968). *Party Rivalry and Political Change in Taisho Japan*. Cambridge, MA: Harvard University Press.

Dyson, J. (1986). *Sink the Rainbow! An Enquiry into the "Greenpeace Affair."* London, UK: Victor Gollancz.

Easton, D. (1975). "A Reassessment of the Concept of Political Support." *British Journal of Political Science* 26:435-457.

Edelman, M. (1971). *Politics as Symbolic Action*. Chicago, IL: Markham Publishing Company.

—— (1964). *The Symbolic Uses of Politics*. Urbana. IL: University of Illinois Press.

Efrat, E. (1994). "Jewish Settlements in the West Bank: Past, Present and Future." In: E. Karsh (ed.), *Peace in the Middle East: The Challenge for Israel*. Essex, UK: Frank Cass & Co., Ltd.

Einaudi, J-L. (1991). *La Bataille de Paris*. Paris, FR: Seuil.

Eisenstadt, S.N. and L. Roniger (1984). *Patrons, Clients and Friends. Interpersonal Relations and Structure of Trust in Society*. Cambridge, UK: Cambridge University Press.

Elster, J. (1989). *Nuts and Bolts for Social Sciences*. Cambridge, UK: Cambridge University Press.

Ericson, R.V., P.M. Baranek and J.B.L. Chan (1987). *Visualizing Deviance: A Study of News Organization*. Toronto, CAN: University of Toronto Press.

Ermann, D.M. and R.J. Lundman (1996). *Corporate and Governmental Deviance: Problems of Organizational Behavior in Contemporary Society*. New York, NY: Oxford University Press.

Etzioni-Halevy, E. (1989). "Exchanging Material Benefits for Political Support: A Comparative Analysis." In: A.J. Heidenheimer, M. Johnston and V. LeVine (eds.), *Political Corruption. A Handbook*. New Brunswick, NJ: Transaction.

Evans, T.D., R.L. LaGrange and C.L. Willis (1996). "Theoretical Development of Comparative Criminology: Rekindling an Interest." *International Journal of Comparative and Applied Criminal Justice* 20(1):15-29.

Faligot, R. and P. Krop (1985). *La Piscine: Les Services Secrets Français 1944-84*. Paris, FR: Seuil.

Farley, M. (1996). "Japan's Press and the Politics of Scandal." In: E. Krauss and S. Pharr (eds.), *Media and Politics in Japan*. Honolulu, HI: University of Hawaii Press.

Farson, A.S. (1991). "Old Wine, New Bottles, and Fancy Labels: The Rediscovery of Organizational Culture in the Control of Intelligence." In: G. Barak (ed.), *Crimes by the Capitalist State: An Introduction to State Criminality*. New York, NY: State University of New York Press.

Federal Election Commission (1996). "Presidential Campaign Disbursements." Washington, DC: author.

Ferguson, T. and J. Rogers (1986). *Right Turn*. New York, NY: Hill and Wang.

Ferrell, J. (1994). "Confronting the Agenda of Authority: Critical Criminology, Anarchism, and Urban Graffiti." In: G. Barak (ed.)., *Varieties of Criminology: Readings from a Dynamic Discipline*. Westport, CT: Praeger.

Ferrand, S. and G. Lecavalier (1982). *Aux ordres du SAC*. Paris, FR: Albin Michel.

Fife, R. and J. Warren (1991). *A Capital Scandal*. Toronto, CAN: Key Porter Books.

Fine, R and R. Millar (eds.) (1985). *Policing the Miner's Strike*. London, UK: Cobden Trust.

FIPE (Federazione italiana pubblici esercizi) (1992). "Malati di tangenti." Rome, IT: Unpublished dossier.

Flamigni, S. (1988). *La Tela del Ragno*. Roma, IT: Edizioni Associate.

Flanagan, S. (1991). "The Changing Japanese Voter and the 1989 and 1990 Elections." In: S. Flanagan, S. Kohei, I. Miyake, B. Richardson and J. Watanuki (eds.), *The Japanese Voter*. New Haven, CT: Yale University Press.

Folster, D. (1977). "Fredericton: Somebody's Got to Go." *Maclean's* 90(12)(March 21):23-24.

Fosdick, R.B. ([1915]1975). *European Police Systems* New York, NY: Century Co.

Foucault, M. (1977). *Discipline and Punish: The Birth of the Prison.* New York, NY: Pantheon Books.

Fowler, N. (1979). *After the Riots.* London, UK: Davis-Paynter.

Frears, J. (1988). "Not Sex, the Abuse of Power: Political Scandal in France." *Corruption and Reform* 3:307-322.

Freddi, G. (1992). "La Pubblica Amministrazione: Perché Funziona in Modo Così Deludente." In: G. Urbani. (ed.), *Dentro la Politica..* Torino, IT: Fondazione Agnelli.

French, R.D. and A. Beliveau (1979). *The RCMP and the Management of National Security.* Montréal, CAN: Butterworths.

Friedrichs, D.O. (ed.) (1998a). *State Crime,* vol. I. Aldershot, UK: Ashgate Publishing Ltd.

—— (ed.) (1998b). *State Crime,* vol. II. Aldershot, UK: Ashgate Publishing Ltd.

—— (1996). *Trusted Criminals: White Collar Crime in American Society.* Belmont, CA: Wadsworth.

—— (1995). "State Crime or Governmental Crime: Making Sense of the Conceptual Confusion." In: J.I. Ross (ed.), *Controlling State Crime.* New York, NY: Garland Publishing.

Frost, M. (1997). "Inside the US-Canada Spyworld." *CovertAction Quarterly* (Winter 1996-97):18-23.

Fukui, H. (1970). *Party in Power.* Berkeley and Los Angeles: University of California Press.

—— and S. Fukai. (1992). "Diet Elections and Election Campaigns in Japan: Case Studies." Prepared for the Workshop on the Pacific Rim, University of California Irvine, February 23.

Furlong, P. (1981). "Political Terrorism in Italy: Responses, Reactions, and Immobilism." In: J. Lodge (ed.), *Terrorism: A Challenge to the State.* Oxford, UK: Martin Robinson.

Fyfe, J. (1988). "Police Use of Deadly Force." *Justice Quarterly* 5(2):165-205.

Gaetner, G. (1992). *L'argent Facile. Dictionnaire de la Corruption en France.* Paris, FR: Stock.

Galli, G. (1991). *Affari di Stato.* Milano, IT: Kaos Edizioni.

—— (1986). *Storia del Partito Armato.* Milano, IT: Rizzoli.

—— (1983). *L'Italia Sotterranea. Storia, Politica e Scandali.* Roma-Bari, IT: Laterza.

Gal-Or, N. (1990). *The Jewish Underground: Our Terrorism.* Tel Aviv, ISR: Hakibutz Hameuchad Publishing House, Ltd.

Gardiner, J.A. and D.J. Olson (eds.) (1974). *Theft of the City*. Bloomington, IN: Indiana University Press.

Garrigou, A. (1989). "Strategic Analysis of a Scandal: 'Carrefour du Développement.'" *Corruption and Reform* 4:159-179.

Gaudino, A. (1990). *L'enquête Impossible*. Paris, FR: Albin Michel.

Geary, R. (1985). *Policing Industrial Disputes: 1893 to 1985*. Cambridge, UK: Cambridge University Press.

Geis, G. (1988). "From Deuteronomy to Deniability: A Historical Perlustration of White-Collar Crime." *Justice Quarterly* 1:1-32.

—— and E. Stotland (eds.) (1980). *White Collar Crime: Theory and Research*. Newbury Park, CA: Sage.

—— and R.F. Meier (eds.) (1977). *White Collar Crime: Offenses in Business, Politics, and the Professions*. New York, NY: Free Press.

Gerlach, L.P. (1976). *People, Power, Change*. Indianapolis, IN: Bobbs-Merrill.

Gibbons, K.M. (1976). "The Political Culture of Corruption in Canada." In: K.M. Gibbons and D.C. Rowat (eds.), *Political Corruption in Canada: Cases, Causes and Cure*. Carleton, CAN: McClelland and Stewart.

Gibbs, J. (1989). *Control: Sociology's Central Notion*. Urbana, IL: University of Illinois Press.

Gidley, I. and R. Shears (1986). *The Rainbow Affair*. London, UK: Unwin.

Giglioli, P.P. (1996). "Political Corruption and the Media: The Tangentopoli Affair." *International Social Science Journal* 149:381-394.

Gill, P. (1995). "Controlling State Crimes by National Security Agencies." In: J.I. Ross (ed.), *Controlling State Crime*. New York, NY: Garland Publishing.

Glick, B. (1989). *The War at Home*. Boston, MA: South End Press.

Goodman, P. (1967). *Like a Conquered Province: The Moral Ambiguity of America*. New York, NY: Random House.

Gordon, D.R. (1991). *The Justice Juggernaut: Fighting Street Crime, Controlling Citizens*. New Brunswick, NJ: Rutgers University Press.

Graziano, L. (1980). *Clientelismo e Sistema Politico. Il Caso Dell'italia*. Milano, IT: Angeli.

Greider, W. (1992). *Who Will Tell the People: The Betrayal of American Democracy*. New York, NY: Simon & Schuster.

Guarnieri, C. (1991). "Magistratura e Politica: Il Caso Italiano." *Rivista Italiana di Scienza Politica* 21:3-32.

Guccione, V. (1993). "Controlli Ex-Ante e Controlli Ex-Post Nella Normativa Pubblica." In: S. Cassese (ed.), *I Controlli della Pubblica Amministrazione*. Bologna, IT: Il Mulino.

Guérin, D. (1991). *Ben Barka, Ses Assassins*. Paris, FR: Syllepse et Périscope.

Gurr, T.R. (1988). "War, Revolution and the Growth of the Coercive State." *Comparative Political Studies* 21(1):45-65.

—— (1977). "Contemporary Crime in Historical Perspective: A Comparative Study of London, Stockholm, and Sydney." *Annals of the American Academy of Political and Social Science* 434:114-136.

Gusfield, J. (1963). *Symbolic Crusade: Status Politics and the American Temperance Movement.* Urbana, IL: University of Illinois Press.

Habermas, J. (1975). *Legitimation Crisis.* Boston, MA: Beacon.

Hager, N. (1997a). "Exposing the Global Surveillance System." *CovertAction Quarterly* (Winter 1996-97):11-17.

—— (1997b). "Greenpeace Warrior." *CovertAction Quarterly* (Winter 1996-97):13.

Haley, J.O. (1991). *Authority Without Power.* New York and Oxford: Oxford University Press.

Halperin, M., J.J. Berman, R.L. Borosage and C.M. Marwick (1977). *The Lawless State: The Crimes of the U.S. Intelligence Agencies.* New York, NY: Penguin Books.

Hamm, M.S. (1995). *The Abandoned Ones: The Imprisonment and Uprising of the Mariel Boat People.* Boston, MA: Northeastern University Press.

—— (1991). "The Abandoned Ones: A History of the Oakdale and Atlanta Prison Riots." In: G. Barak (ed.), *Crimes by the Capitalist State: An Introduction to State Criminality.* Albany, NY: State University of New York Press.

Harrington, M. (1984). *The New American Poverty.* New York, NY: Holt, Rinehart, and Winston.

Harsagor, M. and M. Stroun (1992). *All Of It Is Mine? Towards the End of the Israeli-Palestinian Conflict* (in Hebrew). Kineret, ISR: Kineret Publishing House.

Harstrich, J. and F. Calvi (1991). *R.G. 20 Ans de Police Politique.* Paris, FR: Calmann-Lévy.

Hayden, T. (1980). *The American Future: New Visions Beyond Old Frontiers.* Boston, MA: South End Press.

Henry, S. (1991). "The Informal Economy: A Crime of Omission by the State." In: G. Barak (ed.), *Crimes by the Capitalist State: An Introduction to State Criminality.* Albany, NY: State University of New York Press.

Herzog, P. (1993). *Japan's Pseudo-Democracy.* New York, NY: New York University Press.

Hightower, J. (1993). "NAFTA – We Don't Hafta." *Utne Reader* (July/Aug.):97-100.

Hiley, N. (1993). "An Open Secret: Political Accountability and the Changing Role of MI5." *Queen's Quarterly* 100(2):371-382.

Hirose, M. (1989). *Seiji to Kane* (Politics and Money). Tokyo, Japan: Iwanami Shoten.

Hirsch, M. (1993). "L'affaire du Sang Contaminé." *Politiques* 5:55-63.

Hirschi, T. and M. Gottfredson (1987). "Causes of White Collar Crime." *Criminology* 25:949-974.

Hochstedler, E. (1984). *Corporations as Criminals.* Newbury Park, CA: Sage.

Home Affairs Committee (1980). "Deaths in Custody." London, UK: Her Majesty's Stationery Office.

Howorth, J. and P. Cerny (eds.) (1981). *Elites in France: Origins, Reproduction and Power.* London, UK: Pinter.

Hrebenar, R. (1986). *The Japanese Party System: From One-party Rule to Coalition Government.* Boulder, CO: Westview Press.

Human Rights Watch/Asia Watch (1995). *Prison Conditions in Japan.* New York, NY: author.

Hunter, R.F. (1993). *The Palestinian Uprising* (2nd ed.). Los Angeles, CA: University of California Press.

Hurwitz, L. (1995). "International State-Sponsored Organizations to Control State Crime: The European Convention on Human Rights." In: J.I. Ross (ed.), *Controlling State Crime.* New York, NY: Garland Publishing.

Independent Advisory Team (1987). *People and Process in Transition.* Ottawa, CAN: Solicitor General of Canada.

Ingelhart, R. (1990). *Culture Shift in Advanced Industrial Society.* Princeton, NJ: Princeton University Press.

—— (1977). *Silent Revolution: Changing Values and Political Styles among Western Publics.* Princeton, NJ: Princeton University Press.

International Monetary Fund (1993). *International Statistics Yearbook.* New York: author.

Irwin, J. (1985). *The Jail.* Berkeley. CA: University of California Press.

—— and J. Austin (1997). *It's About Time: America's Imprisonment Binge.* Belmont, CA: Wadsworth.

Istat (1997). *Annuario di Statistiche Giudiziarie.* Roma, IT: author.

Japan Ministry of Home Affairs (1995). *Sangiin Senkyo no Tebiki (Manual for House of Councilors Elections.)* Tokyo, Japan: Jijisho Senkyobu.

Jeanneney, J-N (1984). *L'argent Cacheé: Milieux D'affaires et Pouvoirs Politiques dans la France du XXe Siècle.* Paris, FR: Fayard.

Jefferson, T. and R. Grimshaw (1984). *Controlling the Constable: Police Accountability in England and Wales.* London, UK: Cobden Trust.

—— (1982). "Law, Democracy and Justice: The Question of Police Accountability." In: D. Cowell, T. Jones and J. Young (eds.), *Policing the Riots.* London, UK: Junction Books.

Jeffery, K. (1988). "Review of 'Peter Taylor, Stalker: The Search for Truth" and Frank Doherty, 'The Stalker Affair: Including an Account of British Secret Service Operations in Ireland.'" *Intelligence and National Security* 3(2):344-345.

—— and K. Hidetoshi (1993). "Senkyo ni Okeru Seiji Fuhai to Hoseido no Genjitsu." (Political Corruption in Elections and the Reality of the Legal System.) Hogaku Seijigaku Ronkyu, 17, Summer:281-300.

Johns, C.J. and J.M. Borrero (1991). "The War on Drugs: Nothing Succeeds Like Failure." In: G. Barak (ed.), *Crimes by the Capitalist State: An Introduction to State Criminality.* Albany, NY: State University of New York Press.

Johnson, C. (1986). "Tanaka Kakuei (Structural Corruption and the Advent of Machine Politics in Japan)." *Journal of Japanese Studies* 12(1):1-28.

Joshua, H., T. Wallace and H. Booth (1983). *To Ride the Storm: The 1980 Bristol 'Riot' and the State.* London, UK: Heinemann.

Kahn, R.S. (1996). *Other People's Blood: U. S. Immigration Prison in the Reagan Decade.* Boulder, CO: Westview Press.

Kahoku Shimpo (1998). "Seiji Shikin: Chihobun, 15 Paasento-Sho no 1495-oku En." ("Political Funds; Regional Share Decreases 15% to 14.95 Trillion Yen.") (December 25):2.

Kappeler, V.E. R.D. Sluder and G.P. Alpert (1994). *Forces of Deviance: Understanding the Dark Side of Policing.* Prospect Heights, IL: Waveland Press.

Kaufman, E. (1993). "War, Occupation, and the Effects on Israeli Society." In: E. Kaufman, S.B. Abed and R.L. Rothstein (eds.), *Democracy, Peace, and the Israeli-Palestinian Conflict.* Boulder, CO: Lynne Rienner Publishers.

Kauzlarich, D. and R.C. Kramer (1998). *Crimes of the American Nuclear State: At Home and Abroad.* Boston, MA: Northeastern University Press.

Kayden, X. and E. Mahe, Jr. (1985). *The Party Goes On.* New York, NY: Basic Books.

Keisatsuch, (1992). *Hanzai Hakusho no Pointo (Summary of the White Paper on Crime).* Tokyo, Japan: Homusho.

Kelley, K.J. (1996). "Good NAFTA." *Utne Reader* (Jan/Feb):20-22.

Kernaghan, K. (1994). "Rules are Not Enough: Ethics, Politics, and Public Service in Ontario." In: J. W. Langford. and A. Tupper (eds.), *Corruption, Character and Conduct: Essays on Canadian Government Ethics.* Toronto, CAN: Oxford University Press.

Kesselman, M., J. Kriefer, C.S. Allen, J. Debardeleben, S. Hellman and J. Pontusson (1997). *European Politics in Transition* (3rd ed.). Boston, MA: Houghton Mifflin.

Kettle, M. and L. Hodges. (1982). *Uprising! The Police, The People and the Riots in Britain's Cities.* London, UK: Pan Books.

Key, V.O. (1967). *Politics, Parties, and Pressure Groups.* New York, NY: Thomas Y. Cromwell.

Kishima T. (1992). *Political Life in Japan*. Princeton, NJ: Princeton University Press.

Kleppner, P. (1982). *Who Voted*. New York, NY: Praeger.

—— and S.C. Baker (1980). "The Impact of Voter Turnout Registration Requirements on Electoral Turnout 1900-1916." *Journal of Political and Military Sociology* 8:205-26.

Krauss, E. (1984). "Conflict in the Diet: Toward Conflict Management in Parliamentary Politics." In: E. Krauss and P. Steinhoff (eds.), *Conflict in Japan*. Honolulu: University of Hawaii Press.

—— and P. Steinhoff (eds.) (1984). *Conflict in Japan*. Honolulu, HI: University of Hawaii Press.

Kornberg, A., W. Mishler and H.D. Clarke (1982). *Representative Democracy in the Canadian Provinces*. Scarborough, ONT: Prentice-Hall.

Kornbluh, P. and M. Byrne (1993). *The Iran-Contra Scandal: The Declassified History*. New York, NY: The New Press.

Kovel, J. (1994). *Red Hunting in the Promised Land: Anti-Communism and the Making of America*. New York, NY: Basic Books.

Kozol, J. (1991). *Savage Inequalities: Children in America's Schools*. New York, NY: Crown.

Kraska, P.B. and V.E. Kappeler (1988). "Police On-Duty Drug Use: A Theoretical and Descriptive Examination." *American Journal of Police* 7(1): 1-28.

Krisberg, B. (1975). *Crime and Privilege: Toward a New Criminology*. Englewood Cliffs, NJ: Prentice-Hall.

Kubo H. (1986). *Nihon no Kensatsu (Prosecution in Japan)*. Tokyo, Japan: Kodansha.

Kyogoku J. (1986). *Nihonjin to Seji (The Japanese and Politics)*. Tokyo, Japan: Tokyo Daigaku Shuppankyoku.

Lacoste, P. (1997). *Un Amiral au Secret*. Paris, FR: Flammarion.

Lange, P. and H. Meadwell. (1985). "Typologies of Democratic Systems: From Political Inputs to Political Economy." In: H.J. Wiarda (ed.), *New Directions in Comparative Politics*. Boulder, CO: Westview Press.

Langford, J.W. (1994). "Quasi-Crimes and Eager Beavers: Public Sector Ethics in British Columbia." In: J.W. Langford and A. Tupper (eds.), *Corruption, Character and Conduct: Essays on Canadian Government Ethics*. Toronto, CAN: Oxford University Press.

—— and A. Tupper (1994). "The Good, the Bad, and the Ugly: Thinking About the Conduct of Public Officials." In: J.W. Langford and A. Tupper (eds.), *Corruption, Character and Conduct: Essays on Canadian Government Ethics*. Toronto, CAN: Oxford University Press.

La Palombara, J. and G. Poggi (1975). "Clientela e Parentela nella Burocrazia." In: F. Ferraresi and A. Spreafico (eds.), *La Burocrazia*. Bologna, IT: Il Mulino.

Laqueur, W. (1985). *A World of Secrets*. New York, NY: The Twentieth Century Fund.

Laschingtr, J. and G. Stevens (1992). *Leaders and Lesser Mortals: Backroom Politics in Canada*. Toronto, CAN: Key Porter Books.

Lasswell, H.D. (1941). "The Garrison State." *American Journal of Sociology* 46:455-467.

Laughland, J. (1994). *The Death of Politics. France under Mitterrand*. London, UK: Michael Joseph.

Lecomte, C. (1985). *Coulez le Rainbow Warrior!* Paris, FR: Messidor

Legorjus, P. (1990). *La Morale et l'Action*. Paris, FR: Fixot.

Leigh, D. (1986). *The Wilson Plot: The Intelligence Services and the Discrediting of a Prime Minister*. London, UK: Heinemann.

Levine, M. (1985). *Les Ratonnades d'Octobre: Un Meurtre Collectif à Paris en 1961*. Paris, FR: Ramsay.

Levite, A. (1988). *Offense and Defense in Israeli Military Doctrine*. (in Hebrew). Tel Aviv, ISR: Hakibbutz Hameuchad Publishing House, Ltd.

Lévy, J. (1992). *Le Dossier Georges Albertini: Une Intelligence avec L'ennemi*. Paris, FR: L'Harmattan.

Licandro, A. and A. Varano (1993). *La Città Dolente. Confessioni di un Sindaco Corrotto*. Torino, IT: Einaudi.

Lilly, J.R. and P. Knepper (1993). "The Corrections-Commercial Complex." *Crime & Delinquency* 39(2):150-166.

Lijphart, A. (1984). *Democracies*. New Haven, CT: Yale University Press.

—— (1975). "The Comparative-Cases Strategy in Comparative Research." *Comparative Political Studies* 8(2):158-175.

—— (1971). "Comparative Politics and the Comparative Model." *American Political Science Review* 65(3):682-693.

Lodge, J. (ed.) (1981). *Terrorism: A Challenge to the State*. New York, NY: St. Martins Press.

Lorenzi, P-A. (1995). *Corruption et Imposture*. Paris, FR: Balland.

Lumley, B. and P. Schlesinger (1982). "The Press, the State, and its Enemies: The Italian Case." *Sociological Review* 30(4):603-26.

Lustgarten, L. (1986). *The Governance of Police*. London, UK: Sweet and Maxwell.

Lynch, M.J. (1996). "Assessing the State of Radical Criminology." In: P. Cordella and L. Siegel (eds.), *Readings in Contemporary Criminological Theory*. Boston, MA: Northeastern University Press.

—— and W.B. Groves (1989). *A Primer in Radical Criminology*. New York, NY: Harrow and Heston.

MacDougall, T. (1986). "The Lockheed Scandal and the High Cost of Politics in Japan." In: A.S. Markovits and M. Silverstein (eds.), *The Politics of Scandal*. New York and London: Holmes and Meier.

Madsen, W. (1997). "The Battle for Cyberspace." *CovertAction Quarterly* (Winter 1996-97):24-29.

Magnolfi, L. (1996). *Networks di Potere e Mercati Illeciti. Il Caso della Loggia Massonica P2.* Messina, IT: Rubbetti.

Malarek, V. (1985). "95% of CSIS Staff Veterans of the RCMP." *Globe and Mail* July 11:M1, M5.

Mann, E. and J.A. Lee (1979). *The RCMP vs. the People: Inside Canada's Security Service.* Don Mills, ONT: General Publishing.

Manning, P.K. and L.J. Redlinger (1978). "Working Bases For Corruption: Organizational Ambiguities and Narcotics Law Enforcement." In: A.S. Trebach (ed.), *Drugs, Crime, and Politics.* New York, NY: Praeger.

—— (1977). "Invitational Edges of Corruption: Some Consequences of Narcotic Law Enforcement." In: J.D. Douglas and J.M. Johnson (eds.), *Readings in Malfeasance, and other Forms of Corruption.* Philadelphia, PA: J.B. Lippincott.

Marion, G. and E. Plenel (1989). "*Les Clairs-Obsurs de L'affaire Pechiney.*" *Le Monde* 25 May 1989.

Markovitz, A.S. and M. Silverstein (eds.) (1988a). *The Politics of Scandal.* New York, NY: Holmes and Meire.

—— (1988b). "Introduction: Power and Process in Liberal Democracies." In: A. Markovits and M. Silverstein (eds.), *The Politics of Scandal.* New York, NY: Holmes and Meier.

Marrus, M.R. and R.O. Paxton (1981). *Vichy France and the Jews.* New York, NY: Basic Books.

Marshall, G. (1965). *Police and Government.* London, UK: Methuen.

Martin, C. and B. Stronach (1992). *Politics East and West.* Armonk, NY: M.E. Sharpe.

Marx, B. (1992). "*Le Non Profit Contaminé.*" *Economie et Politique* (April):56-58.

Marx, G.T. (1988). *Undercover: Police Surveillance in America.* Berkeley, CA: University of California Press.

Marx, K. (1976). "Critique of the Gotha Programme." In: K. Marx and F. Engels, *Collected Works,* Vol. 5. London, UK: Lawrence and Wishart.

—— (1968). "The Eighteenth Brumaire of Louis Bonaparte." In: K. Marx and F. Engels, *Selected Works in One Volume.* London, UK: Lawrence and Wishart.

—— and F. Engels (1976). "The German Ideology." In: K. Marx and F. Engels, *Collected Works* Vol. 5. London, UK: Lawrence and Wishart.

Mastropaolo, A. (1987). "Scambio Politico e Ceto Politico." *Democrazia e Diritto* 27-62.

McMillan, J. (1991). *Dango: Japan's Price-Fixing Conspiracies.* Pacific Economic Papers #194. Canberra, AUS: Australia-Japan Research Centre.

Meier, R.F. and G. Geis (1997). *Victimless Crime?: Prostitution, Drugs, Homosexuality, Abortion.* Los Angeles, CA: Roxbury.

Menuchin I. and D. Menuchin (eds.) (1989). *The Limits of Obedience* (3rd ed.). (in Hebrew) Tel Aviv, ISR: Siman Kri'a Books.

Mény, Y. (1992). *La Corruption de la République.* Paris, FR: Fayard.

Mershon, C. and G. Paquino (eds.) (1995). *Italian Politics. Ending of the First Republic.* Boulder, CO: Westview Press.

Michalowski, R.J. (1985). *Order, Law, and Crime: An Introduction to Criminology.* New York, NY: Random House.

Migdal, J. (1988). *Strong Societies and Weak States.* Princeton, NJ: Princeton University Press.

—— A. Kohli and V. Shue (eds.) (1994). *State Power and Social Forces.* Cambridge, MA: Cambridge University Press.

Migliorno, L. (1992). "Sur la Déclaration d'illicéite Comme Forme de Satisfaction: À Propos de la Sentence Arbitrale du 30 Avril 1990 dans L'affaire du Rainbow Warrior." *Revue Générale de Droit International Public* 96(1):61-74.

Mill, J.S. (1951). *Utilitarianism, Liberty, and Representative Government.* New York, NY: Dutton.

Miller, A. (1991). "Terrorism and the Media in the United Kingdom: Government Policy as Symbolic Ritual." In: D. Charters (ed.), *Democratic Responses to International Terrorism.* Ardsley, NY: Transnational Publishers, Inc.

Miller, J.C. (1996). *Search and Destroy: African-American Males in the Criminal Justice System.* Cambridge, UK: Cambridge University Press.

Miller, R. (1985). "Richard Hatfield Under Fire." *Maclean's* 98(7) (Feb.18):12-15.

Mills, C.W. (1956). *The Power Elite.* New York, NY: Oxford University Press.

Minc, A. (1990). *L'Argent Fou.* Paris, FR: Grasset.

Mitchell, J.D.B. (1962). "The Constitutional Position of the Police in Scotland." *Juridical Review* 7(1):1-20.

Mitchell, R. (1996). *Political Bribery in Japan.* Honolulu, HI: University of Hawaii Press.

Mitterrand, F. (1964). *Le Coup d'Etat Permanent.* Paris, FR: Plon.

Miyazawa, S. (1992). *Policing in Japan: A Study on Making Crime.* Tr. Frank Bennett. Albany, NY: State University of New York.

Mizuguchi, Hiroshi (1993). "Political Reform: Much Ado about Nothing?" *Japan Quarterly* (July-Sept):246- 57.

Mokhiber, R. (1988). *Corporate Crime and Violence: Big Business Power and the Abuse of the Public Trust.* San Francisco, CA: Sierra Club Books.

Mola, A. (1992). *Storia della Massoneria Italiana dalle Origini ai Giorni Nostri.* Milano, IT: Bompiani.

Molina, L.F. (1995). "Can States Commit Crimes? The Limits of Formal International Law." In: J.I. Ross (ed.), *Controlling State Crime*. New York, NY: Garland Publishing.

Mongini, R. (1992). *Gli Impuniti*. Milano, IT: Sperling & Kupfer.

Morlino, L. and J.M. Montero (1994). "Legittimità, Consolidamento e Crisi Nell'europa Meridionale." *Rivista italiana di scienza politica* 24:27-66.

Morris, D. (1993). "How About a Fair Trade Agreement?" *Utne Reader* (July/Aug):101-103.

—— (1991). "Trading our Way to Devastation." *Utne Reader* (March/April):25-31.

Murai Y., Y. Fujibayashi, H. Kanda, Y. Satake and Y. Okura (1989). *Musekinin Enjo Taikoku Nippon Japan (The Irresponsible Aid Power)*. Tokyo, Japan: JICC Shuppanbu.

Muratet, R. (1967). *On a Tué Ben Barka*. Paris, FR: Plon.

Murobushi T. (1981). *Oshoku no Kozo* (The Structure of Corruption). Tokyo, Japan: Iwanami Shoten.

Nadelmann, E. (1993). *Cops Across Borders*. University Park, PA: Pennsylvania State University Press.

Nascimbeni, E. and A. Pamparana (1992). *Le Mani Pulite*. Milano, IT: Mondadori.

National Institute of Justice (1997). *Criminal Justice Research Under the Crime Act-1995 to 1996*. Research Report. Washington, DC: author.

Navarro, V. (1991). "The Class Gap." *Utne Reader* (Jan/Aug):113.

Nelken, D. (1996). "A Legal Revolution? The Judges and Tangentopoli." In: S. Gundle and S. Parker (eds.), *The New Italian Republic: From the Fall of the Berlin Wall to Berlusconi*. London, UK: Routledge.

Nester, W. (1990). "Japan's Recruit Scandal: Government and Business for Sale." *Third World Quarterly* 12 (Apr.):91-109.

New York Times (1994). "C.I.A. Spent Millions to Support Japanese Right in 50's and 60's." *New York Times* October 9, A1, 14.

Norton-Taylor, R. (1995). *Truth is a Difficult Concept: Inside the Scott Enquiry*. London, UK: Fourth Estate.

Oakley, R. (1990). "Police Training on Ethnic Relations in Britain." *Police Studies* 13(2):47-56.

O'Brien W.V. (1991). *Law and Morality in Israel's War with the PLO*. New York, NY: Routledge.

O'Conner, J. (1973). *The Fiscal Crisis of the State*. New York, NY: St. Martin's Press.

Olson, M. (1965). *The Logic of Collective Action*. New York, NY: Shocken.

Ozawa, I. (1994). *Blueprint for a New Japan*. Tr. Louisa Rubinfien. Tokyo, Japan: Kodansha International.

Palango, P. (1994). *Above the Law: The Crooks, the Politicians, the Mounties, and Rod Stamler.* Toronto, CAN: McClelland and Stewart.

Papon, M. (1988). *Les Chevaux du Pouvoir.* Paris, FR: Plon.

Parenti, M. (1995). *Democracy for the Few.* New York, NY: St. Martin's Press.

Pareto, V. (1916). *Trattato di sociologia generale.* G. Barbera (ed.), Catania.

Parliamentary Committee of Inquiry on the Mafia (CPMF) (1993). Rapporto finale su mafia e politica.elazione finale su mafia e politica. *La Repubblica (supplement)* April 10, 1993.

Parliamentary Committee of Inquiry on the P2 (1984). *Relazioni finali ed allegati, doc.XXIII,* n.2. Rome, IT: Atti Parlamentari.

Pasquino, G. (1991). *La Repubblica dei Cittadini Ombra.* Milano, IT: Garzanti.

—— (1987). "Per un'analisi del Ceto Politico Italiano: Cause, Problemi, Rimedi." *Democrazia e Diritto* 6:7-25.

—— (1985). "Partiti, Società Civile e Istituzioni." In: G. Pasquino (ed.), *Il Sistema Politico Italiano.* Bari, IT: Laterza.

Paxton, R.O. (1972). *Vichy France: Old Guard and New Order.* New York, NY: Alfred A Knopf.

Pelletier, G. (1971). *The October Crisis.* Toronto, CAN: McClelland and Stewart.

Pelletier, J. (1980). "Impure Grits." *Toronto Sun* May 22:A1, A2.

Pepinsky, H.E. and R. Quinney (1991). *Criminology as Peacemaking.* Bloomington, IN: Indiana University.

Peretz, D. (1990). *Intifada: The Palestinian Uprising.* Boulder, CO: Westview Press.

Phillips, K. (1990). *The Politics of the Rich and Poor.* New York, NY: Random House.

Pinkas, A. (1993). "Garrison Democracy: The Impact of the 1967 Occupation of Territories on Institutional Democracy in Israel." In: E. Kaufman, R.L. Rothstein and S.B. Abed (eds.), *Democracy, Peace, and the Israeli-Palestinian Conflict.* Boulder, CO: Lynne Rienner Publishers.

Pinto, R. (1990). "L'affaire du Rainbow Warrior. A Propos de la Sentence Arbitrale du 30 Avril 1990." *Journal du Droit International* (Winter):841-860.

Pinto-Duschinski, M. (1977). "Corruption in Britain." *Political Studies* 25(2):274-284.

Pippig, G. (1990). "Verwaltungsskandale. Zur Korruption in der Öffentlichen Verwaltung." *Aus Politik und Zeitgeschichte* 7:11-20.

Pitkin, H.F. (1967). *The Concept of Representation.* Berkeley, CA: University of California Press.

Piven, F.F. and R.A. Cloward (1985). *The New Class War.* New York, NY: Pantheon Books.

Pizzorno, A. (1993). *Le Radici della Politica Assoluta.* Milano, IT: Feltrinelli.

—— (1992). "La Corruzione nel Sistema Politico." In: D. della Porta (ed.), *Lo Scambio Occulto*. Bologna, IT: Il Muli.

—— (1980). *I Soggetti del Pluralismo. Classi, Partiti, Sindacati*. Bologna, IT: Il Muli.

—— and D. della Porta (1993). "'Geschäftspolitiker' in Italien: Überlegungen im Anschluß an eine Studie über Politische Korruption." *Kölner Zeitschrift für Soziologie und Sozialpsychologie* 3:439-464.

Plenel, E. (1994). *La Part d'Ombre*. Paris, FR: Gallimard.

—— and A. Rollat (1988). *Mourir à Ouvéa*. Paris, FR: La Découverte.

Pontaut, J-M. and F. Szpiner (1989). *L'Etat hors la Loi*. Paris, FR: Fayard.

Porter, J. (1965). *The Vertical Mosaic*. Toronto, CAN: University of Toronto Press.

Potter, D. (1996). *Japan's Foreign Aid to Thailand and the Philippines*. New York, NY: St. Martin's Press.

Poulantzas, N. (1978). *State, Power, Socialism*. London, UK: New Left Books.

Press, P.N. (1991). *Il Dissesto Programmato. Le Partecipazioni Statali nel Sistema di Potere Democristia*. Bari, IT: Dedalo.

PRP: Procura della Repubblica presso il Tribunale di Palermo, Richiesta per l'applicazione di cautelari, n.2789/90N.C.

Przybylski, R. (1995). "Evaluation as Important Tool in Criminal Justice Planning." *The Compiler* (Summer):4-17.

Public Offices Election Law (1958). Tokyo, Japan: Eibun Horeisha, EHS Law Bulletin Series, 1110.

Public Prosecutor at the Court of Palermo (DAP) (1993*). Domanda di autorizzazione a procedere contro il senatore Giulio Andreotti* March 27, 1993, in *Panorama*, April 11, 1993.

Public Prosecutor at the Court of Palermo, District Anti-Mafia Direction. (1995). *Memoria del Pubblico Ministero nel p. p. n. 3538/94 N.R. contro Giulio Andreotti*. Published as *La vera storia d'Italia*. Napoli, Tullio Pironti, 1995.

Putnam, R.D. (1973). "Atteggiamenti dell'Alta Burocrazia Nell'europa Occidentale." *Rivista Italiana di Scienza Politica* 1:145-186.

Quinney, R. (1997). "Peacemaking." In: B.D. Maclean and D. Milovanovic (eds.), *Thinking Critically About Crime*. Vancouver, CAN: The Collective Press.

—— (1977). *Class, State, and Crime: On the Theory and Practice of Criminal Justice*. New York, NY: Longman.

—— (1970). *Social Reality of Crime*. Boston, MA: Little, Brown Co.

Rachum, I. (1990). *The Israeli General Security Service Affair* (in Hebrew). Jerusalem, ISR: Carmel.

Rae, D. (1971). *The Political Consequences of Electoral Laws*. New Haven, CT: Yale University Press.

Raviv, D. and Y. Melman (1990). *Every Spy a Prince.* Boston, MA: Houghton Mifflin.

Regards sur l'actualité (1995). "Propositions de lutte contre la corruption: les rapports Séguin et Rozès." *Regards sur l'actualité,* January.

Reich, R.B. (1990). "Why the Rich are Getting Richer and the Poor Poorer." *Utne Reader* (Jan./Feb.):42-48.

Reiman, J.H. (1997). *The Rich Get Richer and the Poor Get Prison: Ideology, Crime, and Criminal Justice.* New York, NY: Macmillan.

Reiner, R. (1985). *The Politics of the Police.* New York, NY: St. Martin's Press.

Reiter, H. (1993). *Parties and Elections in Corporate America.* New York, NY: Longman.

Reith, C. (1943). *British Police and the Democratic Ideal.* Oxford, UK: Oxford University Press.

Rhind, J.A. (1981). "The Need for Accountability." In: D.W. Pope and N.L. Wiener (eds.), *Modern Policing.* London, UK: Croom Helm.

Richards, S.C. (1998). "Critical and Radical Perspectives on Community Punishment: Lesson from the Darkness." In: J.I. Ross (ed.), *Cutting the Edge: Current Perspectives in Radical/Critical Criminology and Criminal Justice.* Westport, CT: Praeger.

—— (1990). "Sociological Penetration of the American Gulag." *Wisconsin Sociologist* 27(4):18-28.

—— and R.S. Jones (1997). "Perpetual Incarceration Machine: Structural Impediments to Postprison Success." *Journal of Contemporary Criminal Justice* 13(1):4-22.

Richardson, B. (1974). *The Political Culture of Japan.* Berkeley and Los Angeles, CA: University of California Press.

—— and S. Flanagan (1984). *Politics in Japan.* Boston, MA: Little, Brown and Co.

Roberts, A. (1976). "The British Armed Forces and Politics: A Historical Perspective." In: C. Enloe and U. Semin-Panzer (eds.), *The Military, the Police and Domestic Order.* London, UK: Richardson Institute for Conflict and Peace Research.

Roberts, L. (1963). *The Chief.* Toronto, CAN: Clarke, Irwin.

Rodotà, S. (1984). "La Risposta dello Stato al Terrorismo: Gli Apparati." In: G. Pasquino (ed.), *La Prova delle Armi.* Bologna, IT: Il Muli.

Rognoni, V. (1989). *Intervista sul Terrorismo.* Bari-Roma, IT: Laterza.

Ronen, D. (1990). *The Year of the Shabak* (in Hebrew). Tel Aviv, ISR: Ministry of Defense.

Rose, R. (1988). *L'espansione della Sfera Pubblica.* Bologna, IT: Il Mulino.

Rose-Ackermann, S. (1986). "Reforming Public Bureaucracies through Economic Incentives?" *Journal of Law, Economics and Organization* 2:131-161.

—— (1978). *Corruption: A Study in Political Economy.* New York, NY: Academic Press.

Ross, J.I. (2000). *Making News of Police Violence.* Westport, CT: Praeger.

—— (1999) "State (Organized) Crime, Its Control, Unintended Consequences, and Suggestions for Future Research." In: S. Einstein and M. Amir (eds.), *Organized Crime: Uncertainties and Dilemmas*. Chicago, IL: Office of International Criminal Justice, University of Illinois at Chicago.

—— (1998a). "Radical and Critical Criminology's Treatment of Municipal Policing." In: J.I. Ross (ed.), *Cutting the Edge: Current Perspectives in Radical/Critical Criminology and Criminal Justice*. Westport, CT: Praeger.

—— (1998b). "Situating the Academic Study of Controlling State Crime." *Crime, Law, and Social Change* 29:331-340.

—— (ed.) (1995a). *Controlling State Crime*. New York, NY: Garland Publishing.

—— (1995b). "Controlling State Crime: Toward an Integrated Structural Model." In: J.I. Ross (ed.), *Controlling State Crime*. New York, NY: Garland Publishing.

—— (1995c). "Confronting Community Policing: Minimizing Community Policing as Public Relations." In: P.C. Kratcoski and D. Dukes (eds.), *Issues in Community Policing*. Cincinnati, OH: Anderson Publishing.

—— (1995d). "A Process Model of Public Police Violence in Advanced Industrialized Democracies." *Criminal Justice Policy Review* 17(2):67-90.

—— (1995e). "Violence by Municipal Police in Canada: 1977-1992." In: J.I. Ross (ed.), *Violence in Canada: Sociopolitical Perspectives*. Don Mills, ONT: Oxford University Press.

—— (1994). "The Future of Municipal Violence in Advanced Industrialized Democracies: Towards a Structural Causal Model." *Police Studies* 17(2):1-27.

—— (1992). "The Outcomes of Public Police Violence: A Neglected Research Agenda." *Police Studies* 15:1-12.

—— and R.R. Miller (1997). "The Effects of Oppositional Political Terrorism: Five Actor-Based Models." *Low Intensity Conflict & Law Enforcement* 6(3):76-107.

—— G. Barak, J. Ferrell, D. Kauzlarich, M. Hamm, D. Friedrichs, R. Matthews, S. Pickering, M. Presdee, P. Kraska and V. Kappeler (1999). "The State of State Crime Research: A Commentary." *Humanity and Society* 23(3):273-281.

Rossi, E. (1993). *Capitalismo Inquinato*. Bari-Roma, IT: Laterza.

Royal Commission on Criminal Procedure (1981). *Report*. London, UK: Her Majesty's Stationery Office.

Royal Commission on Newspaper (1981). *Final Report*. Ottawa, CAN: Supply and Services Canada.

Royal Commission on the Police (1962). *Final Report*. London, UK: Her Majesty's Stationery Office.

Rubinstein, D. (1982). *On the Lord's Side: Gush Emunim* (in Hebrew). Tel Aviv, ISR: Hakibbutz Hameuchad.

Ruggiero, V. (1996). *Economie Sporche. L'Impresa Criminale in Europa.* Torino, IT: Bollate Boringhieri.

Rusk, J. (1974). "Comment: The American Political Universe: Speculation and Evidence." *American Political Science Review* 68:28-49.

Sabato, L. (1990). *PAC Power: Inside the World of Political Action Committees.* New York, NY: W.W. Norton.

—— (1988). *The Party's Just Beginning.* Glenwood, IL: Scott, Foreman.

—— (1981). *The Rise of the Political Consultants.* New York, NY: Basic Books.

Sampson, A. (1982). *The Changing Anatomy of Britain.* New York, NY: Vintage Books.

Sapsford, J. and M. Kanabayashi (1994). "Japanese Court Sends Mixed Signals in Light Sentence of Guilty Politician." *Asian Wall Street Journal Weekly* October 31:13.

Sarne, D. (1966). *L'Affaire Ben Barka.* Paris, FR: La Table Ronde.

Sawatsky, J. (1980). *Men in the Shadows: The RCMP Security Service.* Toronto, CAN: Doubleday.

Scalapino, R. (1967). *Democracy and the Party Movement in Prewar Japan.* Berkeley and Los Angeles, CA: University of California Press.

Scarman, Lord (1981). *The Brixton Disorders 10-12 April 1981: Report of an Inquiry by the Rt. Hon the Lord Scarman OBE.* London, UK: Her Majesty's Stationery Office.

Schattschneider, E.E. (1983). *The Semi-Sovereign People.* Chicago, IL: Holt, Rinehart, and Winston.

—— (1969). *Two Hundred Million Americans In Search of a Government.* New York, NY: Holt, Rinehart and Winston.

Schiff, Z. and E. Yaari (1990). *The Palestinian Uprising - Israel's Third Front.* New York, NY: Simon and Schuster.

Schlosser, E. (1998). "The Prison-Industrial Complex." *The Atlantic Monthly* 282(6):51-77.

Scraton, P. (1985). *The State of the Police.* London, UK: Pluto Press.

—— and K. Chadwick (1985). *In the Arms of the Law: Deaths in Custody.* London, UK: Cobden Trust.

Segal, H. (1987). *Dear Brothers* (in Hebrew). Jerusalem, ISR: Keter Publishing House.

Sgubbi, F. (1990). *Il Reato Come Rischio Sociale.* Bologna, IT: Il Mulino.

Shalev, A. (1990). *The Intifada: Causes and Effects* (in Hebrew). Tel Aviv, ISR: Yafe Center for Strategic Studies & Tel Aviv University Press.

Shapiro, S.P. (1990). "Collaring the Crime, Not the Criminal: Reconsidering the Concept of White Collar Crime." *American Sociological Review* 55:346-365.

Sharkansky, I. (1995). "A State Action May Be Nasty but Is Not Likely to Be a Crime." In: J.I. Ross (ed.), *Controlling State Crime.* New York, NY: Garland Publishing.

Sherman, L.W. (1980). "Perspectives on Police and Violence." *Annals of the American Academy of Political and Social Science* 452:1-11.

—— (1978). *Scandal and Reform: Controlling Police Corruption.* Berkeley, CA: University of California Press.

Shikita M. and S. Tsuchiya (1992). *Crime and Criminal Policy in Japan.* New York, NY: Springer-Verlag.

Simey, M. (1988). *Democracy Rediscovered: A Study in Police Accountability.* London, UK: Pluto Press.

Simon, D.R. and D.S. Eitzen (1999). *Elite Deviance* (6th ed.). Boston, MA: Allyn and Bacon.

—— ([1990]1993). *Elite Deviance.* Boston, MA: Allyn and Bacon.

Simpson, J. (1988). *Spoils of Power: The Politics of Patronage.* Toronto, CAN: Collins.

Simpson, S. and C.S. Koper (1992). "Deterring Corporate Crime." *Criminology* 30:347-375.

Skolnick, J.H. (1994). *Justice Without Trial: Law Enforcement in Democratic Society.* New York, NY: Macmillan.

—— and J. Fyfe (1993). *Above the Law: Police and the Excessive Use of Force.* New York, NY: Free Press.

—— and D.H. Bayley (1986). *The New Blue Line: Police Innovation in Six American Cities.* New York, NY: Free Press.

Smith, D.J. (1991). "The Origins of Black Hostility To the Police." *Policing and Society* 2:1-15.

Sprinzak, E. (1991). *The Ascendance of Israel's Radical Right.* Oxford, UK: Oxford University Press.

—— (1987). *Every Man Whatsoever Is Right in His Own Eyes — Illegalism in Israeli Society* (in Hebrew). Tel Aviv, ISR: Sifriat Poalim Publishing House, Ltd.

—— (1986a). *Fundamentalism, Terrorism, and Democracy: The Case of Gush Emunim Underground.* Occasional Paper #4, Washington, DC: Smithsonian Institution, The Wilson Center.

—— (1986b). *Gush Emunim: The Politics of Zionist Fundamentalism in Israel.* New York, NY: American Jewish Committee, Institute of Human Relations.

Stalker, J. (1988). *Stalker.* London, UK: Harra.

Stark, R. (1972). *Police Riots.* Belmont, CA: Wadsworth Publishing.

Stevenson, G. (1979). *Unfilled Union.* Toronto, CAN: Macmillan.

Stigler, J.S. (1970). "The Optimum Enforcement of Laws." *Journal of Political Economy* 78(3):526-536.

Stohl, M. and G.A. Lopez (eds.) (1988). *Terrible Beyond Endurance?* Westport, CT: Greenwood Press.

—— (eds.) (1984). *The State as Terrorist: The Dynamics of Governmental Violence and Repression*. Westport, CT: Greenwood Press.

Straschnov, A. (1994). *Justice Under Fire*. Tel Aviv, ISR: Yedioth Ahronoth.

Streiff, G. (1990). *La Rosenclatrue: L'Etat PS*. Paris, FR: Messidor.

Suleiman, E. (1991). "The Politics of Corruption and the Corruption of Politics." *French Politics and Society* (Winter):57-68.

—— (1980). "Presidential Government in France." In: R. Rose and E. Suleiman (eds.), *Presidents and Prime Ministers*. Washington, DC: American Enterprise Institute for Public Policy Research.

—— (1979). *Les Elites en France, Grands Corps et Grandes Écoles*. Paris, FR: Seuil.

Sutherland, E.H. (1949). *White Collar Crime*. New York, NY: Holt, Rinehart & Winston.

Tangentopoli (1993). "Le carte che scottano." Excerpt from: *Richiesta di autorizzaione a proocedere nei confronti dell'on. Bettino Craxi*. Supplement to *Panorama*, February 1993.

Taylor, P. (1987). *Stalker: The Search for the Truth*. London, UK: Faber and Faber.

Tenon, Y. (1995). *L'Etat Criminel. Les Génocides au XXe Siècle*. Paris, FR: Seuil.

Teodori, M. (1986). *P2: La Controstoria*. Milano, IT: Sugarco.

Thayer, N. (1969). *How the Conservatives Rule Japan*. Princeton, NJ: Princeton University Press.

The Sunday Times Insight Team (1986). *Rainbow Warrior: The French Attempt to Sink Greenpeace*. London, UK: Arrow Books.

Thornburn, H.G. (1979). *Party Politics in Canada*. Scarborough, ONT: Prentice-Hall.

Thurlow, R. (1994). *The Secret State: British Internal Security in the Twentieth Century*. Cambridge, MA: Blackwell.

Tifft, L.L. (1975). "Control Systems, Social Bases of Power Exercise in Police Organizations." *Journal of Police Science and Administration* 3(1):66-76.

Tilly, C. (1985). "War Making and State Making as Organized Crime." In: P.B. Evans, D. Rueschemeyer and T. Skocpol (eds.), *Bringing the State Back In*. Cambridge, UK: Cambridge University Press.

Tranfaglia, N. (ed.) (1994). *Cirillo, Ligato e Lima. Tre Storie di Mafia e Politica*. Bari-Roma, IT: Laterza.

Transparency International-University of Göttingen, 1996. *Corruption Index*. http:www.transparency.de.

Tunnell, K.D. (1995). "Crimes of the Capitalist State against Labor." In: J.I. Ross (ed.), *Controlling State Crime*. New York, NY: Garland Publishing.

—— (ed.) (1993). *Political Crime in Contemporary America*. New York, NY: Garland Publishing.

Turk, A. (1982). *Political Criminality*. Newbury Park, CA: Sage.

Turore, S. (1992). *Politica Ladra. Storia della Corruzione in Italia 1861-1992.* Bari-Roma, IT: Laterza.

Unofficial Committee of Enquiry (1981). *The Death of Blair Peach.* London, UK: National Committee on Civil Liberties.

Unofficial Committee of Enquiry (1980). *Report: Southall 23 April 1979.* London, UK: National Committee on Civil Liberties.

Upham, F. (1987). *Law and Social Change in Postwar Japan.* Cambridge, MA: Harvard University Press.

U.S. Department of Justice (1996). "Uniform Crime Reports for the United States: 1995." Washington, DC: U.S. Government Printing Office.

Vannucci, A. (1997a). *Il Mercato della Corruzione.* Milano, IT: Società Aperta.

—— (1997b). "Come Combattere la Corruzione in Italia?" *Quaderni di Sociologia:*14- 41.

—— (1995). "La Razionalità Occulta della Corruzione Politica." In: A.A. Martino and F. Ruggeri (eds.), *Scelta Razionale e Azione Politica.* Milano, IT: Franco Angeli.

—— (1994). "La Corruzione nei Sistemi Politici Democratici. Alcuni Spunti per un'Analisi Comparata." *Ragione Pratica* 3:74-108.

Veit, J. (1998). "HT Interview with Noam Chomsky: The drug-war industrial complex," *High Times* April:64-68.

Vidal-Naquet, P. (1975). *Les Crimes de l'Armée Française.* Paris, FR: Maspero.

Violante, L. (1984). "Politica della Sicurezza, Relazioni Internazionali e Terrorismo." In: G. Pasquino (ed.), *La Prova delle Armi.* Bologna, IT: Il Muli.

Waltz, M. (1997a). "Policing Activists: Think Global, Act Local." *CovertAction Quarterly* (Summer):21-28.

—— (1997b). "Chicago: The New Multi-Agency Red Squad in Action." *CovertAction Quarterly* (Summer):22.

—— (1997c). "One City's Squad." *CovertAction Quarterly* (Summer):27.

Wardlaw, G. (1984). "Terrorism, Counter-Terrorism, and the Democratic Society." In: M. Stohl and G. Lopez (eds.), *The State as Terrorist.* Westport, CT: Greenwood Press.

Wayne, S.J. (1997). *The Road to the White House 1996.* New York, NY: St. Martin's Press.

Weisburd, D. (1989). *Jewish Settler Violence: Deviance as Social Reaction.* University Park, PA: Pennsylvania State University Press.

—— E. Waring and E. Chayet (1995). "Specific Deterrence in a Sample of Offenders Convicted of White-Collar Crimes." *Criminology* 33(4):587-605.

—— with V. Vered (1984). "Vigilantism as Rational Social Control: The Case of Gush Emunim Settlers." In: M.J. Aronoff (ed.), *Political Anthropology.* New Brunswick, NJ: Transaction.

Welch, M. (1997). "Questioning the Utility and Fairness of INS Detention: Criticisms of Poor Institutional Conditions and Protracted Periods of Confinement for Undocumented Immigrants." *Journal of Contemporary Criminal Justice* 13(1):1-54.

Werner, S.B. (1983). "New Directions in the Study of Administrative Corruption." *Public Administration Review* :116-156.

Widgery, D. (1989). *Preserving Disorder.* London, UK: Pluto Press.

Widgery, J.P. (1972). *Report of the Tribunal Appointed to Inquire into the Events on Sunday 30th January 1972 Which Led to Loss of Life in Connection with the Procession in Londonderry on That Day.* London, UK: Her Majesty's Stationery Office.

Wilkinson, J. (1993). "Lords of Corruption." *AMPO* 24(4):4-6.

Wilkinson, P. (1986). *Terrorism and the Liberal State* (2nd ed.). New York, NY: New York University Press.

Williams, P. (1970). *Wars, Plots and Scandals in Post-War France.* Cambridge, UK: Cambridge University Press.

Wilson, J.Q. (1973). *Political Organizations.* New York, NY: Basic Books.

Wilson, W.J. (1987). *The Truly Disadvantaged: The Inner City, the Underclass, and Public Policy.* Chicago, IL: University of Chicago Press.

Wise, D. (1976). *The American Police State: The Government Against the People.* New York, NY: Random House.

———— and T. Rose (1968). *The Invisible Government.* London, UK: Mayflower.

Wolfe, E. III. (1992). "Japan's LDP Considers Electoral Reform." *Asian Survey* 22(9):773-86.

Wood, C. (1985). "Hatfield's Day in Court." *Maclean's* 98(6) (Feb.11):9-10.

Woodall, B. (1993). "The Logic of Collusive Action: The Political Roots of Japan's Dango System." *Comparative Politics* 25(3):297-312.

Wright, V. (1989). *The Government and Politics of France.* London, UK: Unwin Hyman.

Yanaga, C. (1968). *Big Business in Japanese Politics.* New Haven, CT: Yale University Press.

Yanagawa T. (1994). "Seito e no 'Koho Josei' no Mondaiten o Arau." (Cleaning Up the Problems of 'Public Subsidies' to the Parties). *Gekkan Kankai.* February:70-81.

Young, T.R. (1996). "Beyond Crime and Punishment: Part I-Beginning with Crime and Punishment." *Critical Criminology: An International Journal* 7(1):107-120.

Zeitlin, M. (1978). "Who Owns America? The Same Old Gang." *The Progressive* 42(6):14-19.

Zipp, J.F. (1985). "Perceived Representativeness and Voting: An Assessment of the Impact of 'Choices' Versus 'Echoes.'" *American Political Science Review* 79(March):50-61.

—— R. Landerman and P. Luebke (1983). "Political Parties and Political Participation: Reexamination of the Standard Socioeconomic Model." *Social Forces* 60(4):1140-1153.

—— and J. Smith (1982). "A Structural Analysis of Class Voting." *Social Forces* 60:738-759.